PHOTOGRAPHY AND THE MAKING OF THE NAZI RACIAL COMMUNITY

PHOTOGRAPHY AND THE MAKING OF THE NAZI RACIAL COMMUNITY

JULIE R. KERESZTES

CORNELL UNIVERSITY PRESS
Ithaca and London
Published in Association with the United States Holocaust Memorial Museum

First published 2024 by Cornell University Press

Library of Congress Cataloging-in-Publication Data

Names: Keresztes, Julie R., 1990– author.
Title: Photography and the making of the Nazi racial community / Julie R. Keresztes.
Description: Ithaca : Cornell University Press, 2025. | Includes bibliographical references and index.
Identifiers: LCCN 2024021680 (print) | LCCN 2024021681 (ebook) | ISBN 9781501779299 (hardcover) | ISBN 9781501779749 (paperback) | ISBN 9781501779305 (epub) | ISBN 9781501779312 (pdf)
Subjects: LCSH: Photography—Germany—History—20th century. | Photography—Social aspects—Germany—History—20th century. | Photography—Political aspects—Germany—History—20th century. | Vernacular photography—Germany—History—20th century. | Antisemitism—Social aspects—Germany—History—20th century. | National socialism—Social aspects. | World War, 1939–1945—Photography. | Germany—Social conditions—1933–1945.
Classification: LCC TR73 .K47 2025 (print) | LCC TR73 (ebook) | DDC 779/.943—dc23/eng/20240904
LC record available at https://lccn.loc.gov/2024021680
LC ebook record available at https://lccn.loc.gov/2024021681

CONTENTS

Acknowledgments

Many people made this book possible. First and foremost, I thank Jonathan Zatlin for his constant support and kindness over the years. His precision continues to serve as the model for my own work, and I could not have written this book without him. I also thank Julian Bourg, Charles Dellheim, Devin Pendas, and Alexis Peri for their thoughtful feedback on every chapter. Matt Lavallee was instrumental in helping me transform earlier versions of the text into a book, and it came to fruition only because of his steadfast encouragement. Additional thanks go to the many other colleagues who provided me with so much helpful commentary along the way, especially Cari Babitzke, Andrew Bell, Agnes Burt, Kristen Che, Elizabeth Foster, Eric Grube, Felix Jiménez Botta, Nina Kapuza, Stacie Kent, Shannon Monaghan, Alisha Rankin, and Jon Roberts.

I am thankful for my time as the 2022–2025 American University and Jack, Joseph and Morton Mandel Center for Advanced Holocaust Studies Postdoctoral Fellow, which has allowed me to finish the book. I am also fortunate to have benefited from the expertise and generosity of Michael Brenner and Pamela Nadell in the Department of History at American University, as well as Betsy Anthony, Lisa Leff, Jürgen Matthäus, and many other scholars and research fellows at the Mandel Center for Advanced Holocaust Studies at the United States Holocaust Memorial Museum. I am particularly grateful to Daniel Magilow for giving so much of his time to discuss the book and share source materials with me.

I am indebted to the staff at archives and libraries in the United States and Germany for their guidance. I thank Liviu Carare, Megan Lewis, and Elliott Wrenn at the United States Holocaust Memorial Museum and the archivists at the Harvard University Houghton Library, Library of Congress, Leo Baeck Institute, Center for Creative Photography, Milne Special Collections Library and Archive, Berlin Feldpost-Archiv,

Bundesarchiv Lichterfelde, Bundesarchiv Militärchiv Freiburg, Landesarchiv Berlin, Staatsbibliothek zu Berlin, and Staatsarchiv Hamburg.

I thank the entire production team at Cornell University Press, above all my editors, Bethany Wasik and Susan Specter, for their care and diligence throughout the publication process, as well as Amanda Heller for her skillful copyediting. I also thank the anonymous reviewers of the book for their invaluable suggestions and insights. Tremendous thanks go to Steven Feldman and Laura Foster as well, who guided the book through copublication with the United States Holocaust Memorial Museum. The opinions expressed here, of course, are my own and do not represent and are not endorsed by the museum or the Mandel Center.

Finally, I thank my family for standing by me so lovingly since the day I began writing. My sister Amy has always been a source of inspiration and strength. My parents, Debbie and Will, gave me the courage to see this project through to the end, and it is to them that I dedicate this book.

PHOTOGRAPHY AND THE MAKING
OF THE NAZI RACIAL COMMUNITY

Introduction

On September 12, 1944, US Army private Heinz Landmann wrote to his parents in New York from the newly liberated French village of Visoul. They had not heard from him in over a week, he realized, and he did not want them to worry. Since he saw no German soldiers around, Landmann entered the former headquarters of the Gestapo and sat at the "fine mahogany desk" that stood just inside the entrance. He selected a sheet of the gray stationery left behind, crossed out the Gestapo letterhead, and replaced it with "Under New Management." Then he began to write. He told his parents that the Germans had been putting up "a hell of a fight" but that once their "last bullet was shot," they surrendered en masse. "I sure as hell enjoyed every minute and every thought that I was violating their precious Gestapo headquarters," he told his biographer, Ralph I. López. "For good measure, I sent a few more letters to some friends in the States."[1]

This was no ordinary moment of wartime retribution, for Landmann and his family were German Jews.[2] During the Kristallnacht pogroms of November 9–10, 1938, Gestapo agents arrested the eighteen-year-old Heinz and his father, Josef, and imprisoned them both at Dachau. After their release, the family left Germany. Following a short stay in England, Landmann eventually joined his father, mother, and two sisters in the Washington Heights neighborhood of New York City. In 1943, he joined the US Army and served in North Africa, Italy, and France before returning to Germany in April 1945 to liberate his hometown of Augsburg. The Nazis murdered fifteen of Landmann's closest relatives during the Holocaust.[3]

Serving with the US Army allowed Landmann to confront the armed representatives of the country that had caused his family so much grief and suffering. After capturing German soldiers at Cisterna, Italy, in January 1944, Landmann recalled what it felt like to face them. This time, their fate was in his hands. "The enemy was now at my mercy," he told López. "These superheroes that spat on me, that had forbidden me my rights in my own land, my own streets, my own home, were now sitting on the ground with their hands on their heads. I stared at them full face, eye to eye, the way I had never been allowed to do in Augsburg. This one Jew was staring at the Aryan on the floor. They looked foolish and helpless, and I tried so hard to hate them."[4] His inability to completely hate them owed itself to the compassion that Landmann possessed but had been hard-pressed to find in return in Nazi Germany.

Landmann's military service also allowed him to pursue photography. His biographer described him as "a camera buff, as was his father before him." As his unit captured more and more German troops in 1944, he and his fellow American soldiers helped themselves to their photography equipment, including cameras, photo paper, and film. As Landmann explained in his September 1944 letter to his parents: "The other day, my company captured a fort with over 200 Jerries and their equipment. I have a much better [wristwatch] now. Besides, we get a lot of field glasses, cameras, and pistols all 'made in Germany.'"[5] With these materials as well as the supplies sent to him at the front by his family, Landmann took numerous snapshots from his travels. He sent many of them home to his sister Joan, whom he tasked with compiling a wartime photo album for him.[6]

By taking pictures and compiling this album, Landmann reclaimed his right to participate in a practice the Nazis had denied not just to him but to all Jews in Germany. As this book shows, antisemitism was one of two defining features of the practice of photography during the Third Reich. The Nazis restricted access to photography for Jews like Landmann and his father. With the cooperation of businesspeople and fellow civilians, Nazi officials confiscated equipment from hobbyists and expelled them from photography interest associations. Moreover, they stole from and impoverished the Jewish men and women who worked professionally in the industry. What ultimately made this dispossession and theft possible was the larger purpose for photography that Nazi officials envisioned.[7] To them, photography was a transformative act that could unite non-Jewish Germans as members of the same racially exclusive community (*Volksgemeinschaft*). This second defining feature of photography under Nazism prompted the dictatorship to promote photography for all those who belonged to that community and prohibit anyone who did not from practicing it. The respect for photographic expertise held by the Nazis would ironically create spaces for resistance and revenge among those they deemed unfit to pursue the practice.[8]

Part of what makes Heinz Landmann's album so powerful, then, is that it is framed as a challenge not only to the place he once called home but to the Nazis' configuration of photography as well. His Jewish identity is made a defining feature of that defiance through its very inscription onto the pages of the album. On the second page is a Star of David, probably drawn by Landmann himself following his return to New York in 1945. Subsequent pages show several pictures of the synagogue in Oran, Algeria, where he attended Friday services while in North Africa. Only by leaving Germany in 1939 could Landmann have had the kind of life that allowed him to configure this challenge in the way that he did. Indeed, only by leaving could he have had a life at all.

This book explains how photography became a key practice through which Germans interpreted the sinister promises and hopes of the Nazi *Volksgemeinschaft* concept. The idea of a national community had become popular during World War I, drawing many Germans to the possibility of uniting people across class divides in support of a common purpose. During the Weimar Republic, the concept gained traction within the right wing, and the Nazi Party soon adapted it to their own set of racist and antisemitic goals. The Nazi interpretation of the concept held that German society would be united across class divides by the common "Aryan" racial ancestry of its members. Once the Nazis came to power, the *Volksgemeinschaft* idea directed many of the policies that, on one hand, advanced the social, economic, and political status of non-Jewish Germans and also, on the other, disenfranchised, impoverished, and purged Jews and others targeted as racially undesirable from German public life—and, after 1941, systematically murdered them. Many Germans did see the promise of a united community as a worthwhile aspiration, interpreting and applying it to their everyday lives in unique ways, often to the detriment of their Jewish neighbors and colleagues.[9] Hitler and his inner circle as well as German citizens sought to make the *Volksgemeinschaft* concept a reality. The appeal of the idea among many

Germans meant its daily invocation as Jewish and non-Jewish Germans alike navigated, interpreted, and enacted new Nazi legislation. So powerful was the notion among the public that it helped propel the Nazis to victory in 1932–33, turn Christians against their Jewish neighbors, mobilize them for war, and, even when the war began to favor the Allies after 1942, motivate them to keep fighting. It also underwrote the Nazi regime's enthusiastic promotion of photography for all non-Jewish Germans as they excluded Jews from it.

There was already a receptive audience for this project. Well before the Nazi takeover in 1933, Germans took and gathered photographs to help make sense not only of themselves but of the German nation as well.[10] Between 1871 and 1918, the European-wide frenzy for collecting *carte de visite* photographs of the royal family as well as other cultural and political celebrities permeated German society just as it did in France and England. The Berlin firm L. Haase & Co. discovered that it "could not print their *carte* portraits of the royal family and other Prussian celebrities quickly enough" to meet popular demand.[11] Marketing such pictures also helped promote German imperialism, as many of the photographs on display also represented the country's colonial expansion in Africa and the Pacific.[12] Postcards soon supplanted the *carte de visite*, for they were cheaper to produce, acquire, and circulate, and Germans collected these by the hundreds of thousands. They often placed these images alongside family photographs of birthdays, weddings, and vacations in private albums, which manufacturers began mass-producing in the 1870s to make them more accessible to lower-middle-class families.[13]

These albums would take on new importance for German families during World War I. As the war wreaked havoc on the European continent from 1914 to 1918, many soldiers and their families used photography to commemorate their lives and tell stories about their wartime experiences. The introduction of compact cameras such as the Ur-Leica in 1914 made it easier for many German soldiers, especially high-ranking officers, to send portraits and group snapshots home.[14] In keeping with the broader official use of photography for propaganda purposes, the German military press collected many of these pictures to illustrate their official reports. And despite the fact that during World War I more photographs had been taken and exchanged between war and home fronts than in any prior war, the Nazis would later argue that German officials did not go far enough in mobilizing wartime photography not only for propaganda material but also as a social practice that could boost morale.

The technical innovations that cultivated popular photography during World War I accelerated during the period of Germany's troubled first democracy, the Weimar Republic. Photography became more accessible than ever before to the German public, creating a "photo-consciousness" without parallel in prior decades.[15] Advancements in roll film as well as the introduction of compact, less expensive camera models like the Leica I Model A and Ernemann Ermanox in 1925 facilitated widespread access to photography.[16] The illustrated press for which the Weimar period is well known surrounded Germans with images on a daily basis as it also developed the careers of professional photographers at the same time, many of them women, and many of them Jewish.[17] Within the pages of publications such as *Das Deutsche Lichtbild*, *Photofreund*, and *Berliner Illustrirte Zeitung*, professionals, hobbyists, and observers discussed and thereby strengthened the role of photography in German society and culture. Their considerations ranged from more insidious discussions of how it could be used to decipher *who* counted as German to more nostalgic explorations of *what* Germany was through photographic meditations on political life and the country's landscapes and natural terrain.[18]

Heimat photography—the photography of home and homeland—became a particularly popular genre during the 1920s in Germany before taking root in neighboring Austria.[19] The practice of taking, gathering, and sharing pictures of the German countryside as well as portraits of farmers and other rural inhabitants was promoted in the photographic press for hobbyists and professionals alike as a way to use their cameras to connect themselves and others to a mythic German past that also often tended to reinforce ideas of Germanic racial superiority.[20] During the early 1930s, Austria's authoritarian governments leveraged *Heimat* photography to reinforce traditional Austrian customs and Catholic values while also promoting Austrian tourism.[21] But in Germany, it would take the Nazis to do the same thing toward even more extreme ends.

When it was viewed as more of a vulgar paramilitary formation than a viable political faction during the 1920s, the early Nazi Party used photography to rally the German public around Adolf Hitler and National Socialism more broadly. The Nazi illustrated magazine *Illustrierter Beobachter* repeatedly featured articles and photographs that encouraged Germans to see themselves as members of a racially exclusive *Volksgemeinschaft* that could realize its true potential only under Nazi leadership. Echoing the photographic practices of the imperial period, Heinrich Hoffmann, the Nazi Party's photographer, produced and sold postcard portraits of Hitler and other Nazi personalities to enhance their popularity and give the Nazi Party political legitimacy.[22] By the time Paul von Hindenburg, president of the Weimar Republic, appointed Hitler as chancellor in 1933, the Nazi Party was more than prepared to build on these precedents to more radically mobilize photography as a practice that could bring Germans together as members of a new, Nazified *Volksgemeinschaft*.

More than in other dictatorial states of the twentieth century, this formulation would be put into practice most consistently in Nazi Germany. Only the Nazis were so actively involved in promoting photography for the public. Dictatorships elsewhere valued photography primarily for its representational impact rather than the possibilities for social bonding offered when cameras were placed in the hands of the masses. The Italian and Soviet dictatorships, for instance, valued photography for its visual impact but ultimately considered it an enterprise best left to professional photojournalists.[23] The Nazis, though, saw photography as a social practice that could mobilize and transform the masses, and they would devote considerable resources to promoting photography for this very reason. They persisted in their efforts to increase popular access to photography as a community-building exercise long after 1933. These efforts accelerated as Germany began public rearmament in 1934 and would reach their peak as German troops mobilized for war in eastern and western Europe in 1939.

Understanding the Nazi configuration of photography can therefore help to explain why so many wartime photo albums compiled by German soldiers do not contain images of atrocities. To be sure, photographs in some personal collections do show this violence, and the growing literature on photography during the Nazi era has offered important insights into some of the more shocking pictures produced by German troops as they invaded and occupied Europe.[24] But as the countless photographs and albums that fill archives today indicate, these kinds of images are quite rare. Personal collections are instead overflowing with far more innocuous images of leisure, friendship, and sociability. This book's argument that the dual configuration of photography under Nazism as a unifying practice, on the one hand, for "Aryan" Germans and an exclusionary one, on the other, that kept out Jews explains why. The absence of Jews both in front of and behind the camera was what Nazi officials and many civilians hoped to achieve for popular photography. In this light, it should come as no surprise that German soldiers and their families prioritized themselves and other members of the Nazi

Volksgemeinschaft in their photography rather than Jews or any other victims of the Third Reich.

To show how and why Germans chose photography to interpret and enact the *Volksgemeinschaft* concept, this book brings together a wide range of written and visual sources, especially the vast body of seemingly mundane and therefore greatly understudied photographs Germans made during the Second World War. The reluctance of scholars to engage with these sources stems from the understandable concern that doing so would somehow exonerate the men responsible for these collections and the violence and mass murder they invariably perpetrated. Far from doing so, however, the material examined here only makes the involvement of these men in war crimes and genocide even more disturbing. The men who executed prisoners of war, shot civilians, rounded up Jews and murdered them had wives, children, and parents back home whom they loved and missed, and who were the primary recipients of their photographs. That they were capable of normal human emotions like affection, homesickness, and gratitude while conducting such horrific acts only serves as a chilling reminder that ordinary people helped perpetrate the Holocaust under the cover of total war.[25]

The first part of the book examines the role of photography in Nazi plans for making the idea of *Volksgemeinschaft* a reality and the consequences of those plans for Jewish photographers. Chapter 1 explains how the idea that photography could help build a united national community shaped the practice under Nazism from the very beginning. Nazi leaders believed that photography could mobilize Germans into becoming enthusiastic supporters of the Nazi government. For them, taking pictures was a social practice that fostered active participation and inner transformation rather than passive indoctrination. The Nazis envisioned photography as a tool to help individuals internalize National Socialist values and transform themselves into members of the people's community. By taking photographs, sharing them with family, friends, and neighbors, and reflecting together on the experiences the images depicted, Germans could create that community deliberately and voluntarily.

Exclusion gave the practice even more meaning. Chapter 2 demonstrates how Nazi authorities began closing off the photographic industry to German Jews in 1933, prohibiting them from practicing photography and eagerly stealing Jewish-owned photography supply companies and studios. With accelerating effort after 1935 and decisive impact in 1938, Nazi officials, businesspeople, and colleagues excluded

Jews from organized professional photography as well as amateur interest groups and associations. Photographic supplies were redistributed to non-Jewish Germans, and dispossessed Jewish photographers were replaced by "Aryan" ones. Such measures further reinforced the association between photography and racial and national belonging. But the Nazi officials who enforced the restructuring of the photographic industry also inadvertently created spaces in which photography could be used for resistance and revenge, especially in concentration camps.

With photography defined all along by the Nazis as a social practice reserved for members of the *Volksgemeinschaft*, it was precisely those deemed unfit to participate in the practice who would ultimately use it to cast light on the experiences of the Nazi regime's victims. Chapter 3 shows that in Nazi concentration camps, SS photographers captured executions, beatings, and other acts for camp administrative records. Certain prisoners who had access to those records through their forced labor in the Erkennungsdienst, the camp photographic identification service, used this proximity to gather evidence of what was really taking place there. To them, photography meant opportunities for humiliation but also survival and resistance. Many of the photographs produced in the Erkennungsdienst survived only because of the efforts made by prisoners to save and, in some exceptional cases, create them. It ultimately fell to concentration camp prisoners to expose the horrors of the Nazi project—horrors that ordinary Germans generally did not show in their private photographs and albums.

The second part of the book argues that photography's close relationship to the idea of the *Volksgemeinschaft* under Nazism explains why so many wartime photo collections created by members of Germany's armed forces do not show atrocities. Chapter 4 examines why the bulk of photograph collections curated by Wehrmacht soldiers at the front present scenes of camaraderie and family gatherings instead of the violence, antisemitism, and terror we might expect. The chapter explains how state and Wehrmacht authorities urged Germans to exchange photographs to keep in touch and boost wartime morale. Doing so not only ensured familial harmony but also promoted the ability of photography to remind non-Jewish Germans of their shared membership in the Nazi racial community. With the encouragement of the Nazi regime, German Wehrmacht soldiers and their families understood exchanging photographs and compiling photo albums not as mere acts of personal communication but as their patriotic duty. Photography likewise allowed Germans in the SS to enact and represent the Nazis' project of building a *Volksgemeinschaft*. Chapter 5 demonstrates that like the photograph albums created and compiled by Wehrmacht soldiers at the war front, those serving in Waffen-SS combat units or staffing Nazi concentration camps and killing centers emphasized comradeship, family, and community in their collections. Such emphases testify to the success of Nazi efforts to persuade Germans that photography was never meant to be a documentary tool alone but was rather a social practice designed to strengthen both their personal relationships and their faith in Germany's chances of winning the war.

Ultimately the photography Germans engaged in during the Third Reich helped perpetuate the concept of a racially exclusive national community, an idea that had shaped and validated the practice from the very beginning of Nazi rule. Its resilience lasted long after the dictatorship fell apart and the war ended. For the narratives of comradeship and family contained in the seemingly innocuous photographs examined here framed not only how Germans interpreted the years of Nazi rule and war as they unfolded but how they remembered that same period after 1945 as well. The book's epilogue reinterprets the controversial 1995 "Crimes of the Wehrmacht" exhibition to point out that it was the distance between what former soldiers and their families saw in their personal wartime photo albums and what they were being shown that constitutes part of the reason why it took Germany so long to develop the candid memory culture for which it is now widely known and respected.

Part I

CHAPTER 1

The People's Art

When Adolf Hitler was appointed chancellor of Germany on January 30, 1933, top Nazis recognized that they still needed to persuade many Germans that National Socialism would benefit them. The very phrase "National Socialism," after all, carried with it promises to provide racially desirable Germans with opportunities for social, economic, and cultural advancement. "Now it is a matter of tilling the conquered soil in the National Socialist sense, penetrating the whole people with [its] ideas and winning them over to a higher cause," the Nazi enthusiast and writer G. A. Kanitzberg observed. He further noted that winning over the German people could not happen without putting all that was "useful and good" in "the service of this powerful idea." And one way to do so, Kanitzberg argued, was through photography, which "is also called to help and to cooperate" in the effort.[1]

As Hitler's new regime consolidated power after 1933, officials urged businesspeople and civilians to use photography to transform themselves into devout Nazis. This chapter examines why in 1933–1937 Nazi leaders believed that photography could mobilize Germans into becoming enthusiastic supporters of the Nazi government and devoted members of a united national community. The Nazis saw photography as a public practice that fostered active participation rather than passive indoctrination. Officials in the Reich Propaganda Ministry and the

German Labor Front revered photography as a "people's art" that was accessible to everyone. They also saw it as a way of uniting the members of the German *Volk*. By going out and making photographs, sharing them with family, friends, and neighbors, and reflecting together on the experiences the images depicted, Germans could help one another become devoted *Volksgenossen*—members of the people's community—of their own free will. With the help of camera retailers and Nazi organizations, the regime set about promoting photography for those who belonged to that community, relying on photography classes and public displays like the November 1933 exhibition "Die Kamera" to reinforce this message.

How the Nazis used photography to build National Socialism mirrored their broader attempts to consolidate power after 1933. The new regime relied on a combination of terror and persuasion to align German society with National Socialism.[2] As storm troopers harassed, imprisoned, and murdered suspected "enemies of the state," Nazi authorities hoped to secure popular legitimacy by convincing "true" Germans that the new government would directly benefit them. This was in part a cultural project, because top Nazis saw National Socialism as a cultural revolution as well as a political one. "As with any genuine revolution," Reich propaganda minister Joseph Goebbels declared in 1933, "ours also seeks to initiate a drastic overhaul of our collective cultural capital and intellectual creative production."[3] They planned to create a new German culture that reflected National Socialist values and strengthened their political power but would be sufficiently embraced by the public to "convert the whole German people to their way of thinking."[4] The Nazis envisioned cultural reform as a means to help them realize their utopian project of a united "people's community"—the *Volksgemeinschaft*. Once individually converted to National Socialism, Germans would come together to form a harmonious and racially defined citizenry. Making the *Volksgemeinschaft* idea a reality animated Nazi policy and procedure after 1933. Many Germans, moreover, believed in its validity and interpreted the meaning of the concept in their own ways.[5]

Achieving such a massive social transformation required freeing German culture from the Weimar Republic's supposedly "degenerate" influence. Beginning in the 1920s, right-wing critics blamed the experimentation and modernism that defined Weimar culture—and the democratic system that enabled it—for two key problems. One was what they interpreted as a general decline in moral and artistic standards. The other was class warfare and political division.[6] The Nazis held Jews and communists singularly responsible for allegedly desecrating German culture and art.[7] During the Reichstag elections of the late 1920s and early 1930s, the Nazi Party campaigned on a promise to return cultural life to the masses and restore the more traditional aesthetics of the imperial period, all while purging the arts of racially and politically undesirable practitioners as well. Once the Nazis came to power, both goals framed their cultural policy.

The visual arts were central to these plans for cultural restoration, and not just for personal enrichment or creating propaganda.[8] Only through mass involvement could the arts acquire any real significance. Hitler himself believed that access to art would unite the German people: "That is decisive: art which cannot count on the readiest and most intimate agreement of the great mass of the people, an art which must rely upon the support of small cliques, is intolerable."[9] The Nazis used the arts to secure genuine approval from the public as engaged participants, not passive spectators. Doing so successfully required providing Germans with regular opportunities for cultural and artistic activity. By visiting art galleries and exhibitions, Germans would eventually "recognize the beauty and greatness of life in harmony with those who share their convictions."[10] In doing so, they would come together of their own volition to forge both a united racial community and a new visual culture informed by National Socialist tastes.

Cultural restoration through the visual arts also depended on making those opportunities affordable for all Germans, especially workers and their families.[11] The regime's cultural authorities made cheap tickets available to visit art exhibitions and galleries as well as attend concerts and operas and to go on overseas cruises and hikes in the Black Forest.[12] In this way, the Nazis hoped to win over German workers and incorporate them into the people's community. The role of the visual arts in the Nazis' consolidation of power and transformation of Germany's cultural and social life has been the subject of much historical inquiry. And yet photography is strangely absent from these discussions. While the more traditional visual arts of painting and sculpture typically capture the attention of most historians working on these programs, it was photography that the Nazis themselves considered uniquely well suited to achieving this project.[13]

At first glance, photography's alignment with the familiar contours of Nazi cultural politics seems to explain why. Having rapidly expanded its presence in Germany since the imperial period, photography was yet another area of the visual arts that Nazi authorities hoped to control.[14]

As was the case for painting, sculpture, music, and architecture, the coordination (*Gleichschaltung*) of the photographic industry allowed the regime to dictate what content was acceptable to show German citizens in exhibitions, official publications, and the press.[15] It also allowed the regime to determine who could legitimately practice photography, restricting professional photography to only those whom the Nazi officials considered racially desirable members of the German *Volk*.[16]

Intervention in the photographic industry would allow the Nazi state to "grease the palm" of the public, too, an objective that shaped much of Nazi economic planning after 1933. After Hitler came to power that year, the Nazi regime promised Germans that the new government would end unemployment and restore prosperity and abundance in the aftermath of the Great Depression. In addition to creating jobs, the regime would stimulate mass consumption. Making consumer goods more accessible would help raise living standards for German citizens and shore up support for the new government.[17] Though these ambitions would often fall far short of popular expectations during the years of Nazi rule, such efforts nevertheless gave industries producing leisure goods, such as radios, harmonicas, and cigarettes, opportunities for significant growth. Photography was yet another area the regime targeted for increased production in pursuit of these aims.[18]

Photography also suited Nazi aesthetics. Influenced by the "New Objectivity" (Neue Sachlichkeit) art movement of the 1920s, Hitler himself preferred artworks that showed the world "as it was."[19] Abstraction and embellishment confused rather than enlightened the German people, Hitler argued, while photographic realism objectively and truthfully depicted people and places in ways most Germans generally found more appealing. "To be German is to be clear," he declared in a speech on culture at the 1934 Nazi Party Congress.[20] It was no coincidence that as he wandered the halls of the "Große Deutsche Kunstausstellung" exhibition three years later, Hitler would proudly note that the paintings he had selected after many months of indecision and dissatisfaction looked "just like photographs!"[21]

Photographs helped reinforce Nazi racism as well.[22] To persuade Germans of their own superior "Aryan" status, propagandists routinely generated images that embodied the decades-old nationalist fantasy of uniting a racially defined national body of Germans (*Blut*) on German soil (*Boden*).[23] Pictures of racially valued individuals and their families set amidst the German countryside filled the Nazi press as well as art exhibitions and film reels, often juxtaposed with images of racially inferior

Jews, Slavs, and others in "un-German" surroundings.[24] Photography was the ideal tool to illustrate this fantasy of a united racial community because to many, the medium itself already seemed to give the impression of documentary fact and objectivity.[25]

But state use of photography to strengthen national culture and consumerism, promote political ideology, and illustrate racist thought was hardly unique to the Nazis. During the first half of the twentieth century, state officials throughout Europe, North America, and Asia similarly harnessed photography for its consumer potential and representational impact.[26] What made photography truly different under Nazism and so well suited to the regime's larger project of building a united racial community was how the Nazis themselves defined it: as a social practice rather than just a collection of usable images. Photography's mass accessibility meant that it could mobilize the population in ways that other visual arts could not. As a tool to help individuals internalize National Socialist values, taking pictures could build the people's community rather than just illustrate the idea of one. By going out and creating photographs, sharing them with family, friends, and neighbors, and reflecting together on the experiences the images depicted, Germans voluntarily and collaboratively helped one another become devoted *Volksgenossen*.

In comparison to other dictatorial states of the twentieth century, this formulation was put into practice most consistently in Nazi Germany. Dictatorships elsewhere valued photography primarily for its representational impact rather than the possibilities for social bonding it offered when cameras were placed in the hands of the masses. Italian and Soviet leaders, for instance, ultimately considered photography an enterprise best left to the professionals. In Italy, the ability to practice photography was generally restricted to photojournalists who were willing to create images glorifying Mussolini and his Fascist government's cultural and diplomatic triumphs.[27] In the Soviet Union, early ambitions to supplant "bourgeois" culture with the help of a "proletarian" photography were quickly thwarted by supply shortages and the state's prioritization of professional photojournalists over amateur photographers.[28] By 1937, professional photography had entirely eclipsed the amateur photography movement, something Soviet leaders themselves openly acknowledged as one of their principal failures.[29] In contrast, Nazi officials would persist in their efforts to increase popular access to photography as a community-building exercise long after 1933. These efforts accelerated with fervor once Germany began to militarize and would reach their peak as German troops mobilized for war in eastern and western Europe in 1939.

After the spring of 1933, Nazi cultural authorities directed the photographic industry toward the ambition of forging a people's community. Their intervention was a welcome one for professional photographers, who hoped to stabilize the industry. Members of the Central Verband Deutscher Photographen (Central Committee of German Photographers, CVDP) had long advocated for stronger state intervention.[30] Like everyone else, photographers had been hit hard by the economic crisis years of 1928–1936.[31] CVDP representatives saw the Nazi takeover as a potential solution to their problems. "The photographic profession has only arisen in the last hundred years," association representatives wrote in their monthly newsletter. "From its humble beginnings, photography has developed into a significant factor in all the workings of our life. No circle of popular economics, politics, science, or art can survive without photography." Because the craft was so vital in everyday life, the CVDP argued, the industry should benefit from the new state. "It is well known that the craft of photography has been one of the most distressed occupations in the German fatherland for many years. Our association is obliged to point out the damages that affect photographers particularly hard and which must be eliminated."[32] In a direct appeal to the Reich Ministry of Economics, CVDP representatives declared that they spoke on behalf of colleagues throughout Germany when they called for state involvement: "From many letters we are constantly being told that our colleagues expect their government to improve their economic situation through quick and radical injunctions in the interest of our profession." The association concluded by calling on "the Reich Ministry of Economics . . . to exert a more or less gentle pressure on the photographic industry" to alleviate the problems reported by the CVDP. If the authorities protected the field from further setbacks, CVDP leaders promised, the Reich could count on their total cooperation: "The Reich Ministry of Public Enlightenment and Propaganda will also have the guarantee, through our association and with it, [of] an undisturbed influence on the education of our professionals as press photographers in the National Socialist sense."[33] In exchange for their protection, CVDP representatives were willing to Nazify an organization and a field whose very existence was once devoted to the protection of professional photographers from excessive state influence.[34]

But if professional photographers saw state intervention as a path to prosperity, they considered the regime's promotion of amateur photography the road to ruin. In fact, professional photographers hoped that the new regime would exert more control over Germany's "army" of amateur photographers.[35] By 1934 an estimated 5 million Germans owned cameras and practiced some form of amateur photography, 1 million more than the figure recorded for 1930.[36] Professional photographers complained that amateurs took away potential clients. Moreover, because they lacked proper training in photography, they produced poor-quality photographs. "It is precisely through amateur photography that the evils have developed in our craft," CVDP representatives wrote to the Reich Ministry of Economics. "Many who carry out the photographic profession have not learned the craft and therefore can only perform the exercise in an amateurish manner. This lay work . . . must disappear if our craft is to be healthy again and the reputation of our profession is to come back to the level to which it is entitled because of the great importance of photography for the world economy."[37] The CVDP was effectively asking the Nazi regime to restrict amateur photography on its behalf for the sake of stabilizing the profession.

Other professional photographers blamed their challenges on technological developments in the industry. The automatic photo booths that sprang up in European cities in the late 1920s and early 1930s were a particular source of frustration. Photo booths churned out portraits that could be used for identification papers, certificates, and other documents at an even lower cost than amateur photographers requested.[38] The manager of one photography studio in Dortmund was so dismayed by this that he wrote directly to Hitler himself. "In the name of all colleagues in our German homeland, I address this request to you, my Führer, out of great ire and desperation," he pleaded. "On account of the ever-increasing arrangement of machines in all cities, the professional photographers struggle very hard for their existence. Because of the catastrophic economic conditions of the last decades, our occupation was demonstrably hit most sensitively, and now, when everyone in Germany is beginning to hope again, we are constantly being held down by these *partly foreign* machines."[39] It was not lost on the writer, apparently, that appealing to the regime's antisemitism would be a useful strategy to achieve beneficial results. Anatol Josepho, the inventor of the photo booth, was himself a Russian Jew.[40] The CVDP agreed that the machines had to go, declaring that "only the radical prohibition of machines in any form can bring about a recovery of economic conditions in the photographic trade." The CVDP concluded with the observation that "it is irresponsible to have such a mass deception carried out within the population. Through the technical production of photographs, the good taste of the population is constantly undermined and the professional photographer, who endeavors to deliver quality work, can of course not compete in pricing with automatic picture factories."[41] The CVDP demanded that the ministry act on these matters.[42]

Nazi officials needed the support of professional photographers if they were to be successful in their aim of building a united community of camera-carrying Germans. And so the regime restructured the photographic industry to give the impression that the new government could restore unity and prosperity to the field. Efforts to control all areas of cultural life had already begun with the March 14, 1933, founding of the Reich Ministry for Public Enlightenment and Propaganda, which centralized Nazi influence over all areas of cultural and intellectual life.[43] Those efforts reached new heights when, on September 22, 1933, the Nazis created the Chamber of Culture (Reichskulturkammer) with separate chambers devoted to regulating fields including film, literature, sculpture, painting, music, theater, architecture, the press, and radio. Professional photography was administered through the press chamber under the supervision of Max Amann, head of the Nazi Party publishing house Franz Eher Nachfolger.[44]

Nazi cultural authorities had no intention of making amateur photography disappear, as the CVDP would have it. On the contrary, turning as many Germans as possible into photographers lay at the very core of their vision for the industry. The act of taking and sharing pictures could help transform ordinary men, women, and youth into members of the *Volksgemeinschaft*. But the Nazis also subjected amateur photography associations to new regulations and restrictions to show professional photographers that they were just as interested in control as they were in promotion. This was most evident in the case of the Verband deutscher Amateurphotographen-Verein (Association of German Amateur Photographers' Societies), which had been founded in Berlin in 1907 and encompassed 211 local clubs with around twelve thousand members. The association was promptly replaced by the Reichsverband Deutscher Amateurphotographen (Reich Association of German Amateur Photographers), which had been founded in early 1933.[45] The professed aim of the new association was "to provide a uniform summary of all German people who work as amateur photographers." Membership in the Reichsverband provided amateur photographers with opportunities to develop themselves artistically and find new meaning in their art under National Socialism. "The result," as Heiner Kurzbein put it shortly after the organization was founded, "is an extraordinary and extensive field of work for grateful amateur photographers."[46]

There was no more tireless advocate for using photography to bring Germans together than Heiner Kurzbein. Born in Berlin in 1910, Kurzbein joined the Nazi Party in 1929 and was appointed head of the press photography department in the Propaganda Ministry in early 1933. He held that position until he began his war service as SS-Untersturmführer in 1942.[47] Kurzbein promised that the new Nazi government would recognize photography for its value in everyday life. "The National Socialist revolution seized the German people in the spring of 1933 with fundamental force," he wrote in the popular photography magazine *Photofreund*. "No state, no profession, no aspect of private life was passed over by it. After a decade-long struggle for recognition, a government agency for the first time recognizes the purpose and necessity of amateur photography as well as press photography for culture and business."[48] Unlike their contemporaries abroad, Kurzbein argued, Nazi officials understood the value of both popular and professional photography and were determined to guide the field toward its true potential.

For Kurzbein, turning Germans into members of the *Volk* was photography's central purpose. For this to happen, however, people had to go beyond "merely snapping" pictures of everything in sight. Instead, he argued, they should focus on more meaningful content. Kurzbein suggested that Germans document the achievements of National Socialism and see for themselves how the new state positively impacted their lives. For the fall and winter months of 1933, for example, he urged photographers to take pictures documenting the state's efforts to fight hunger, improve workplace conditions, and prepare for the cold. Kurzbein further encouraged Germans to reinterpret their otherwise ordinary photos from special occasions and vacations as opportunities to reflect on what made Germany and Germans extraordinary in a national and racial sense.[49]

Whether Germans really created these kinds of photos mattered less to Kurzbein, however, than the prospect of uniting "hundreds of thousands of people" through photography.[50] Regardless of their content, Kurzbein believed that pictures mattered only when they were shared. "All German amateur photographers are asked for the first time to think about things in their photography that are currently in the interests of all Germans," he advised in the amateur photography journal *Photographie für Alle*.[51] Looking at photographs was no longer a strictly personal matter. Showing pictures to one another and reflecting on the experiences behind them strengthened their ties to one another and to Germany itself. "The photographer will get to know his homeland even more, but he will also be able to draw other people's attention to the beautiful and particularly valuable character of his homeland," Kurzbein contended in a November 1933 lecture on the future of amateur photography under National Socialism. When Germans of all ages shared their photographs with friends and family, they were building a people's community. Photographers could expand this community by inspiring others to take up photography, helping to increase "the photographic activity of hundreds of thousands of other people."[52] According to Kurzbein, then, Germans had to embrace a dual role as both consumers and creators of photography in order to successfully build a united community under National Socialism.

Kurzbein constantly referred to photography as a public service to bolster its appeal for beginners. "Not every citizen can be an SA, SS, or Stahlhelm member or be actively involved in building up the new state in another Nazi organization," he maintained in *Photographie für Alle.* "All people who have a camera, however, have the opportunity to promote the government's will to build." But Kurzbein's configuration of photography as service to "the general public and the new state" was not an invitation to submit photographs for use in state propaganda.[53] Nazi authorities had more than enough official propaganda photographers at their disposal for that purpose, and Joseph Goebbels himself was reluctant to offer such opportunities to amateurs at the expense of professionals.[54] The "service" Kurzbein envisioned instead placed community formation above the pictures themselves. Snapshots of vacations, special occasions, and loved ones provided far more important opportunities for Germans to gather for collective contemplation, reflection, and, ultimately, transformation into Nazi enthusiasts.

Kurzbein saw maintaining good relations with professional photographers as integral to the strength of the community. If photography was to take on new meaning and significance under National Socialism, any hostilities between worker and artist or professional and amateur had to be resolved. To Kurzbein, such tensions were superficial anyway, because the idea of the *Volksgemeinschaft* united Germans around race rather than class or position. "It must also be emphasized that this work of amateur photography does not disturb the interests of professional and press photography," Kurzbein continued in *Photographie für Alle.* Working with "otherwise more professionally structured" groups, he argued, only fostered "the idea of a community" even more.[55] Kurzbein called for harmonious cooperation between amateur and professional photographers in the hopes of preventing the obstacles that could hinder the ability of Germans to come together.

In November 1933 Kurzbein's conviction that photography could unite Germans of all backgrounds would reach an even broader audience.[56] Hosted by the Reich Propaganda Ministry, German Labor Front, and Berlin Exhibition, Trade Fair, and Tourism Cooperation between November 4 and 19, the exhibition "Die Kamera: Ausstellung für Fotografie, Druck und Reproduktion" (The Camera: Exhibition for Photography, Printing, and Reproduction) had two main goals. One was to increase the appeal of photography for beginners. The second was to reassure those who already considered themselves professional or hobby photographers that their work had new meaning and significance in the Third Reich.

In an apparent departure from the political jostling that characterized other areas of cultural bureaucracy after the Nazi takeover, state and industry officials appeared to be in agreement about the importance and meaning of photography.[57] Echoing Kurzbein's formulation of photography as "service" to the nation, propaganda minister Joseph Goebbels declared in his opening day speech that "the purpose of this exhibition is to recognize the value of photography not only for artistic life but also for a practical existence in service of the German nation."[58] Alfred Wischek, director of the Berlin Exhibition Cooperation, echoed Goebbels's sentiments, insisting: "Our lives today are unthinkable without photography. It would be inconceivable for us to do without these tools, which have acquired a fundamental significance for all progress, for every human being, for every people, and for humanity as a whole."[59] As chairman of the exhibition, Kurzbein himself declared: "We are only at the beginning of a great and rich development. It seems all the more important to capture the national currents of the German photographic art, which is a true *Volk* art, and to strengthen them with a careful hand."[60]

The exhibit declared photography to be both an art and a craft to unite the artists and workers who made up the field.[61] Photography was a "people's art," an endorsement of the camera's mass accessibility that was also racially defined, as the exhibition implied that only "Aryan" Germans had the right to take pictures. "True art rises from the depths of the people's soul," Kurzbein proclaimed, "and is closely connected with blood and soil. . . . [S]o too a *Volk* art like photography must receive its strength from race, culture, and *Heimat*."[62] The aim of the exhibition was to incorporate workers from photography's technical, chemical, and industrial branches into this racial community. "Hundreds of thousands of German national comrades are engaged in photography and printing-related enterprises. . . . [A]nyone who wishes to form an accurate assessment of photography's importance for our culture must not consider the accomplishments of photographers alone; he must also turn his attention to the industry whose products actually permit the scientists, professionals and amateurs to pursue their activities."[63] Not only were workers integral to the German racial community, but also they were crucial to the very practice of photography itself. In belaboring this point, the exhibition aimed to dissolve traditional boundaries between artist and craftsman, a gesture that symbolized "the spirit of the new era" supposedly ushered in by Nazism more generally.[64]

The exhibition further emphasized photography's economic advantages for the German people. Hans Biallas, head of the German Labor Front press office, promised to promote professional photography to boost employment. "The graphic arts industry in Germany is in a serious crisis," he warned. "A noticeable revival is now felt in all German industries. The government of Adolf Hitler succeeded in reducing unemployment by a million in a few months. The German Labor Front therefore regards it as its most important task to help the graphic arts as well."[65] Promoting amateur photography, moreover, would stimulate mass consumption. Karl Weiß, editor of the trade journal *Photographische Industrie,* compared the camera's consumer potential to that of the radio.[66] "Despite the enormous spread of photography in Germany, its popularization is still far from over," he advised. "The recent efforts to bring radio listeners to double the number are also fully applied to photography."[67] Nazi leaders oversaw the increased production of "people's radios" (*Volksempfänger*) at a cheaper cost to make radio addresses by Hitler and other top Nazis more accessible to regular Germans. That same method also applied to photography, making it more affordable and accessible to the public.

Exhibition organizers hoped that professional and amateur photographers would acknowledge their shared importance for cultural and economic life. The photographer Wilhelm Niemann, who had joined the Nazi Party in 1933, noted, "If the professional contemptuously looks down on the amateur, it is just as wrong if the amateur rises above the expert." Niemann admonished professional photographers who failed to recognize the contributions amateur photographers made to the field, arguing, "The great importance of the amateur is that he awakens in the breadth of the people with his work understanding of the special photographic values, just as amateur music has led to a deeper and finer understanding of the music performed by professional musicians."[68] Niemann saw professional photographers' obstinacy as a major obstacle to the regime's efforts to make photography an art "of the people."

The organizers of "Die Kamera" made an official commitment to promote amateur photography and protect professional photography. "The promotion of amateur photography," Kurzbein proclaimed, "which is a significant plus for industry, should in no way imply the impairment of professional photography. On the contrary, professional photography, as the representation of a high German *Volk,* is to be given a new impetus, and can expect a promotion from the government which would not have been possible in formerly divided political conditions."[69] Protecting professional photographers, Nazi leaders hoped, would unite the photographic community for the greater good of the *Volk.* A particularly effective display of this support would occur the following year, when the regime restricted the production of identification photos to professional photographers only. If the submitted photograph did not bear the stamp of a commercially registered photographer, it would not be accepted.[70] The Prussian state police notably opposed the order, arguing that enforcing it would make identification photos more expensive and therefore limit the number of people able to secure photo identification.[71] Ultimately the restriction was inconsistently enforced, but it nevertheless signaled to professional photographers that the regime supported them.

Industry and state representatives designed "Die Kamera" to remind Germans of the key sectors involved in the photographing community.[72] The exhibition's five halls were devoted to those areas of photography that Nazi cultural authorities hoped to bring together: professional photography and photojournalism, the technical and chemical branches of the photographic industry, and amateur photography. The regime envisioned all "Aryan" Germans, whether professional or amateur, worker or artist, as essential and capable contributors to the "people's art." The exhibition drove this point home in the official catalog by naming the businesses that supplied labor and equipment to the photographic industry. These included major companies like IG Farben's Agfa, Voigtländer, Zeiss Ikon, and Siemens as well as smaller Berlin firms such as those operated by Karl Glückauf, who sold photograph albums, and

Paul Joachim, who sold cameras. In addition to naming companies, the catalog also listed the names of each individual photographer whose work appeared in the exhibition halls.

Non-Jewish German women had the right to participate in the "people's art" as well.[73] The list of professional photographers who presented their work in "Die Kamera" included Bertha Zillessen and Liselotte Strelow.[74] The list of amateur photographers, too, included Johanna Hahn and Marianne Sudhoff. Since all those listed were members of the Reichsverband Deutscher Amateurphotographen, this was a convenient ploy to show that amateur photographers who belonged to an official Nazi organization enjoyed access to more exhibition opportunities.[75] But it also demonstrated to those who may have been skeptical about the consequences of Nazism for women that there were opportunities for them in photography.[76] Moreover, the promotion of popular photography for women was not necessarily incompatible with Nazis ideas. After all, women could still practice photography in a domestic setting. "The housewife very often develops her own artistic ideas in her apartment," as one correspondent put it. Putting "beautiful cameras" in "delicate women's hands," he continued, gave them unique and precious opportunities to take portraits of their children.[77]

The exhibition even included in the program businesses the regime attacked as Jewish-owned. In one particularly conspicuous example, the official catalog for "Die Kamera" featured a full-page advertisement endorsing the Ullstein publishing house, one of Germany's largest and oldest, which Nazi authorities would later "Aryanize" in 1934 and rename Deutscher Verlag in 1937. Ullstein was already a favored target of Nazi zealots by the time "Die Kamera" opened to the public. The Nazi press had condemned the company and the five brothers who owned it as Jewish early on in May 1933.[78] But the advertisement printed in the exhibition catalog simply described Ullstein as "Europe's biggest and most modern printing company with the most perfect recording and reproduction facilities."[79] The list naming professional photographers who presented their work in the exhibition also included Jewish photographers alongside "true" German ones. The renowned Jewish German portrait photographers Suse Byk and Emil Bieber, for example, whose businesses would be stolen from them four years later by Nazi authorities and former colleagues, were both featured in the exhibition display on professional photography.[80]

The timing of "Die Kamera" offers the best explanation for the appearance of Ullstein, Byk, and Bieber in the exhibition program. The year 1933 was still a period of transition for the Nazi regime. The lack of clear objectives in Jewish policy as the regime consolidated power prompted varying interpretations of "the Jewish question" by Nazi officials, ranging from outright violence to more tacit compliance.[81] Official attempts to rally the masses around National Socialism while maintaining favorable popular opinion thus publicly addressed antisemitism in often contradictory and inconsistent ways.[82] "Die Kamera" was emblematic of this tendency, evident in the inclusion of Ullstein, Byk, and Bieber in the program even as SS and SA thugs were beating and arresting Jews elsewhere in Berlin.[83] It was evident further still when Kurzbein maintained during the exhibition that photography received "its strength from race" but did not elaborate on the topic. Instead, the exhibition's organizers placed a much more concerted emphasis overall on encouraging Germans to take up photography.

Making that pursuit available to them at a lower cost was a central component of that encouragement. The organizers of "Die Kamera" kept admission costs low to make the exhibition as accessible as possible. Unlimited visits while it was in Berlin cost three Reichsmarks (RM).[84] A single visit for adults cost RM 1. Students with photo identification, youths up to eighteen years old, military personnel, police offers, and uniformed members of the SS and SA could visit the exhibition for a reduced price of RM 0.50.[85] The exhibition charged the unemployed an even lower price of RM 0.30, which was roughly the cost of a loaf of bread at the time.[86] Prospective visitors eagerly anticipated the exhibition, prompting some to note months before it even opened its doors that "the interest of all circles in professional and amateur photography is extraordinarily strong."[87]

Amateur photographers were eager for opening day because they interpreted the event as a sign that the new regime took them seriously. Just weeks before their incorporation into the Reichsverband, representatives from the Verband deutscher Amateurphotographen-Verein praised Nazi leaders for acknowledging the meaning and importance of amateur photography: "It is the first time that amateur photography is called to actively participate in the reconstruction work of German *Volk* culture. It is therefore the duty of our clubs and members to do everything in our power to prove that we can fully carry out the tasks we have to fulfill. Then we will also find the support we always strive for and is so necessary for our work. The 1933 exhibition must be the beginning of an even greater expansion work." For members of the association, the "greater work" to be done involved aligning themselves with Nazi ideological goals, particularly those aspirations to connect Germans more closely to *Volk* and *Heimat*, since they considered "*Heimat* always the living source of all our photographic work."[88]

Visitors praised the regime for liberating photography from past economic and social crises. *Photographie für Alle* commented: "The exhibition 'Die Kamera' has a special significance because it is the first exhibition in the area of photography to be sponsored by the Reich. . . . [T]he fact that a ministry has taken over the patronage of a photographic exhibition shows that photography is regarded as an essential factor in the German economy [and] German cultural life." Others were grateful to the exhibition for having shown the public the craft side of the enterprise, most notably in lens and paper production. Critics praised the lens manufacturing display put together by the camera company Voigtländer as "certainly one of the most interesting, because as an amateur you finally had the opportunity to see something that you would otherwise not be able to see."[89] Weeks after the exhibition ended, journalists were still commenting on its influence. "The exhibition 'Die Kamera' is now over, but not its impact on photo enthusiasts," the Berlin-based photographer and journalist Herbert Starke wrote.[90]

The press declared the exhibition's professed goal of bringing Germans of all backgrounds together over a shared interest in photography a success. One reporter noted, "The exhibition 'Die Kamera' is now over, and everyone who visited it will be of the opinion that an extraordinarily instructive and worth-seeing show for the photographer was put together here."[91] Even the left-wing *Revue des Monats*, which had been quick to criticize the Nazis during Hitler's first months in power, covered the exhibition favorably. The journalist Hubert Mikeffa conceded that "the major photographic exhibition at the Funkturm is one of the most interesting exhibitions offered in Berlin in recent years."[92] Personal pictures chronicling visits to the exhibition likewise made a point of showing men, women, and youth of all classes crowding around the entrance outside or mingling together inside the exhibition's five halls. That these images were taken at all only confirms the importance and meaning found by many in what the exhibition offered to aspiring and seasoned camera enthusiasts.[93]

The exhibition also seems to have had the desired effect of mobilizing amateur photographers as co-creators of the *Volksgemeinschaft* with the help of their cameras. A commentator identified as F. Martin pointed out a few weeks later that "shaping the activities of amateurs in such a way that they are in the interest and for the benefit of the *Volksgemeinschaft*" was a gratifying goal. There was still room, Martin argued, for individual expression as long as photographers were guided by National Socialist principles that could strengthen their relationships with loved ones and neighbors when they circulated their pictures. "Let the individual be preserved according to his style, but in general let us keep in mind," Martin added, that "we are supposed to serve the general unity with our work. The entire community is now under the supervision of the new government. We must comply, but we want to and will also be happy to do so for the good cause."[94] For individuals like Martin, helping to bring Germans together as a united community was ultimately a "good cause" that made taking pictures a worthwhile pastime.

The turnout at "Die Kamera" as well as the interest in photography displayed by the regime's corporate and political partners prompted the creation of state-sponsored programs designed to persuade Germans to engage in amateur photography. The leisure management organization Strength through Joy (Kraft durch Freude, KdF) led the charge. Founded in November 1933 as a subsidiary of the German Labor Front, Strength through Joy aimed to dissolve class divisions and garner widespread support by providing workers with opportunities to participate in what the Nazis considered "middle-class" leisure activities, effectively "organizing workers' leisure time rather than allowing them to organize it for themselves," as Shelley Baranowski has argued.[95] KdF organizers hoped to involve Germans in tennis, sailing, theater, opera, tourism, and photography.[96] The survey distributed by KdF officials to the 42,000 workers at the Siemens AG electrical company revealed that KdF organizers had only to harness existing interest in these activities. The survey aimed to demonstrate "how small is the circle of those who carry forward the cultural and physical existence of a nation." It indicated that while only 6,500 of those surveyed went to the theater more than twice a year, 7,500 went to the cinema more than twice a month, and 8,000 bought more than three books a year, 14,000 already considered themselves amateur photographers.[97]

In January 1936 Strength through Joy began offering photography classes to all *Volksgenossen* so that they could learn how to use the estimated "2.5 million devices in their hands."[98] The photography supply company Agfa, whose growth during the Nazi era would continue well into World War II, was particularly involved in providing the materials for KdF courses. That was largely due to the initiative of Bruno Uhl, the director of Agfa's photography division, who had also helped plan "Die Kamera." In 1934, Uhl wrote to Robert Ley, head of the German

Labor Front, to recommend that he integrate photography into KdF course programming for its "educational, cultural and propagandistic benefits."[99] Not only did Ley agree, but also Agfa products took center stage in the courses themselves. All participants received complimentary Agfa cameras and film. "These cameras should be funneled off production and delivered immediately when they are finished," Uhl wrote to his staff, "as it is extraordinarily valuable to us that 'Strength through Joy' offer lessons in 35 millimeter photography with the help of Agfa Karat cameras."[100] Uhl hoped that if Germans were introduced early on to Agfa materials, they would continue to purchase the company's products as they became avid photographers. Those hopes applied in particular to film, which was Agfa's most profitable sector. Efforts to bolster Agfa's consumer base were all the more important given that the sales records for Agfa cameras lagged behind those of the more popular Kodak, Leitz, and Zeiss Ikon brands.[101]

Like "Die Kamera," the KdF courses presented photography as a craft as well as an art to attract participants. The courses were organized and supervised by Alexander de la Croix, a Berliner who had joined the Nazi Party in 1932 and was appointed head of the Office for Adult Education in the German Labor Front shortly after its creation the following year.[102] On the one hand, he urged Germans to learn the craft side of photography so that they could take higher-quality pictures. "What do you know about the wonder of your camera," he asked interested amateurs, "or the laws of optics, the chemical processes on negative and positive. Most cannot make a film, let alone understand how to develop it. Can one demand artistic work from them if they do not understand anything about craftsmanship?" On the other hand, he cautioned, "whoever does not master the craft of photography will never be able to deal with its artistic application."[103] Getting the most out of their cameras, de la Croix argued, required being properly educated about the craft side of photography, and the KdF stood ready to help.

KdF leaders saw photography as a social practice that could persuade Germans to participate in other community-building opportunities they offered in travel, sports, and art. They hoped that Germans would take their cameras with them as they engaged in these and other leisure activities sponsored by the organization and show their friends and family the pictures they had taken. Sharing pictures from KdF-sponsored hikes, cruises, and museum visits would inspire others to participate in these activities as well and create photographs of their own adventures. Carl Seitz, a board member of the Reichsverband Deutscher Amateurphotographen, commented:

> It is possible, through photo classes, that those people who are lucky enough to be able to take part in KdF travel can show others the beautiful things that await them and bring home nice pictures as well. For this reason, the serious amateur who takes part in such a trip has an unconditional duty to provide advice and assistance to other camera students who are not so experienced. After returning from a trip, he should then recruit new friends for these trips and show the pictures in a newspaper, exhibition, or slide show. An infinite amount can be done for *Heimat* and *Volk* by attending lecture courses, hikes, and visits to historical sites. The best helper is amateur photography.[104]

Like Kurzbein and other ideologues, Seitz valued photography for its social function and envisioned the camera as an indispensable tool for persuading Germans that National Socialism benefited them. The act of taking and sharing pictures, moreover, was an effective community-building strategy because it was initiated by fellow German citizens rather than imposed from above by state representatives.

Despite the organization's overtly political plans for amateur photography, KdF depoliticized its photo courses. KdF leaders worried that Germans would not want to participate if the classes were too ideologically overbearing. The organization insisted that it was simply trying to teach Germans how to take better pictures, not convert them to National Socialism. Such a conversion was, of course, precisely what it was trying to accomplish. The official German Labor Front newspaper *Arbeitertum*, for example, maintained that the courses would benefit "working comrades" so that they could "familiarize themselves with the technical aspects of photography, but also to learn how to 'see' correctly." KdF opened the courses "to every member of the *Volk*, even if he is not yet a member of the 'Strength through Joy' National Socialist Association."[105] KdF organizers also promised that the courses would not benefit the regime's corporate partners. A reporter covering the first KdF photography courses noted Alexander de la Croix's guarantee that "all these courses would be kept absolutely neutral and that in no way and under any circumstances should they be associated with any propaganda for photographic companies."[106] Bruno Uhl's determination to establish Agfa as an essential player in the courses, however, casts doubt on the sincerity of that claim.

The strategy of depoliticizing photography courses to gain participants was consistent with KdF efforts to get Germans involved in other recreational opportunities. Organizers also maintained strict political neutrality during swimming classes in order to attract more people. According to one participant who compiled his observations about the experience for a 1936 SOPADE report (reports of the exiled German Social Democratic Party) on working-class support for the new regime: "I attended a KdF swimming course in which over fifty took part, and I have to admit there was very little Party atmosphere. The participants were all ordinary people. There were scarcely any 'Heil Hitlers.' Coming from the old workers' sports clubs as we did, we felt at home, so to speak. I was doubtful about taking part in a KdF function at first, but there is really no alternative. I was all the more pleasantly surprised to find that there was absolutely nothing National Socialist about the way the course was organized and run."[107] Paired with the lack of non-Nazi options available, the organization's neutrality also encouraged long-term participation in the opportunities offered by the KdF, however superficially construed that neutrality had been.

Low entry costs drew participants to the courses as well. KdF officials insisted that, apart from teaching Germans how to use their cameras properly, they promised to keep costs at a minimum to guarantee access "for all racial comrades [*Volksgenossen*]." The courses consisted of eight two-part lessons. KdF charged members of the German Labor Front and their children RM 3.2 to participate. Those who did not belong to the German Labor Front had to pay RM 4.8, but Alexander de la Croix still saw this as a generous offer. According to him, "Since cameras and materials are made available to the participants for the duration of a course, the expenses are considered to be very low."[108] A person working in the textile industry with children at home, however, might have considered spending an entire day's wages on the courses an extravagance.[109] Outside of the courses, Reich Ministry of Economics representatives urged Agfa to continue keeping its film prices low, noting in September 1936 that the company should "make the sales price for roll film as cheap as possible, so that the largest possible circles of the public can get involved in photography."[110] With the help of camera companies and Nazi institutions, Strength through Joy was thus putting into practice one of the core principles espoused by the exhibition "Die Kamera": wealth would not be a requirement in building a new visual culture. Under National Socialism it would be possible for all non-Jewish Germans, whether rich or poor, to participate in photography, an important component of the *Volksgemeinschaft* fantasy more generally.

The approach taken by KdF organizers appears to have paid off. Like the other programs offered by the organization, photography courses were popular.[111] One observer noted that turnout for the first meeting was so massive that KdF hosts began to worry about overcrowding. Public enthusiasm generated high hopes for the future of the courses and the field of amateur photography itself. As *Photofreund* noted, "Anyone who has experienced the onslaught of those who are eager to learn will hope with us that these photo sessions of the KdF will be a blessing to all those who participate and to our good old amateur photography."[112] KdF leaders did not hesitate to declare the courses a triumph, claiming in January 1937 that, thanks to their success, amateur photography was "no longer the prerogative of the wealthy few, having long since become a *Volkssport.*"[113]

Widespread participation, however, did not necessarily mean successful indoctrination. As one Berlin worker put it to a Social Democrat in late 1934, "If you can get it cheaply, it's worth raising your arm every now and then."[114] KdF efforts to turn Germans into National Socialists and unite them as a community were only partially successful. But the opportunities arranged by the leisure organization would be fondly remembered by the men and women who participated in them long after the destruction of the Third Reich.[115] Aided significantly by the general recovery of the German economy that Hitler inherited and took credit for after 1933, Nazi officials were able to put cameras in the hands of more Germans than ever before, if the sales records from Agfa are any indication. In 1937 alone, Agfa sold 201,386 cameras and 15.4 million rolls of film in Germany, tripling the number of cameras and the amount of film the company sold in 1933.[116]

Nowhere else in Europe was the state more actively involved in promoting mass photography than in Nazi Germany after 1933. Nowhere did state representatives devote more resources to framing photography as a social practice rather than a collection of images. That formulation continued to shape official plans for popular photography in the years to come. Prohibiting Jewish Germans from practicing photography became integral to these plans. To demonstrate the extent to which the practice of photography really was a *Volkssport,* the Nazi regime forced German Jews out of professional and popular photography and confiscated their businesses, photographic supplies, and studios. With accelerating effort after 1935 and decisive impact in 1938, Nazi authorities and former colleagues liquidated Jewish-owned photography supply companies and studios and forced the sale of countless others to "Aryan" owners, equipping Gentile Germans for the war to come. Heiner Kurzbein's ambiguous proclamation during the 1933 "Die Kamera" exhibition that photography received its strength from "race and *Heimat*" would soon take concrete and devastating form.

CHAPTER 2

"Taking What Belongs to Us"

"This interests all amateur photographers!" proclaimed the Nazi newspaper *Westdeutscher Beobachter* when it announced that the photographic supply company Photo-Brenner had passed to "Aryan" management in July 1933. Earlier that summer, the Nazis had arrested Rafael Brenner, the Jewish owner of this Cologne-based business, and made his release contingent on his selling the firm to August Schmitt for just 5 percent of its actual value.[1] After the forced sale went through and Brenner was released, he fled Germany with his family for Italy, then the United States. "The company will be continued under the same name," the announcement informed readers, "but under German management and in a German sense. Photo-Brenner is now to be regarded as a 100% purely Aryan company. Germans, take pictures and come to Photo Brenner!"[2]

Several aspects of this announcement stand out. That the forced sale took place as early as it did, for one, as well as the decision to keep the name of the company in recognition of the business's domestic and international success are two particularly unusual features. But the most important part of the announcement is *whom* it addresses: not fellow Nazi Party members, not members of Nazi organizations, but German amateur photographers, as if the "Aryanization" of Photo-Brenner had been carried out on their behalf. In this way the Nazis took one further step toward ensuring that photography itself would be restricted to non-Jewish members of the German *Volksgemeinschaft*.

Rafael Brenner's story is shared by countless men and women who worked in photography and whom the regime persecuted as Jewish after 1933. Photographers are often overlooked in the scholarship on what happened to Jewish artists under Nazism.[3] The stories that are told, moreover, are typically treated as isolated cases rather than part of a broader phenomenon with consequences for all Jews working in the photographic industry.[4] Nazi officials went to considerable lengths to advance the interests of non-Jewish amateur and professional photographers. But they viewed any access Jews had to the photographic industry as not rightfully theirs. Instead, as this chapter will show, Nazi officials, businesspeople, and colleagues excluded Jews from organized professional photography as well as amateur interest groups and associations. They eagerly stole Jewish-owned photography supply companies and studios and transferred them to "Aryan" managers. As Jews desperately tried to flee Germany, the Nazis stole their photography equipment as they left the country and redistributed it among non-Jewish Germans. Such measures further signaled to non-Jewish Germans that practicing photography was synonymous with racial and national belonging.

These efforts took place against the larger backdrop of the dispossession and plunder of German Jewry after 1933. Beginning in that year, Jewish civil servants, businesspeople, doctors, and white-collar employees faced discriminatory legislation that destroyed jobs, careers, and businesses and subjected German Jews to constant harassment. As we saw in chapter 1, Joseph Goebbels founded the Reich Chamber of Culture (Reichskulturkammer, RKK) early in 1933 to control all professional cultural activity, creating seven separate chambers dedicated to the regulation of literature, music, film, writing, visual arts, the press, and radio and to the removal of Jews from those fields.[5] Nazi authorities and ordinary "Aryan" Germans alike busily profited from their plight, taking over Jewish-owned businesses, property, and other confiscated assets.

The April 1933 attack on Jewish-owned businesses targeted photography studios and supply stores just as it did other companies and firms operated by Jews.[6] That had been the case with Photothek Römer & Bernstein, one of the most active photo agencies in Germany during the Weimar Republic, managed by Willy Römer and Walter Bernstein. On the day of the "boycott," a group of SA men stood outside the Phototek and denied Bernstein, who was Jewish, entry to the building. From then on, the company faced threats of bankruptcy and the seizure of assets. In 1937 it finally disappeared from the Berlin commercial register.[7] The Hamburg-based photographer Kurt Schallenberg, too, recalled that on April 1, 1933, vandals scrawled the word "Jew" in paint across the windows of his studio.[8]

To accelerate their social and economic isolation, the Nazi press publicly identified Jews active in photography. In May 1933 the newspaper *Deutsche Nachrichten* published a list identifying "Jews and foreigners" working in German press photography. In fact, the list included only a few full-time photojournalists. Most were studio portrait photographers who occasionally submitted pictures to German periodicals. The distinction was irrelevant for Nazi enthusiasts who hoped to bolster the antisemitic argument that the press in general was "Jewish dominated."[9] The article named fifty-five studios in Berlin and Hamburg believed to be under "Jewish and foreign influence." Among the named Jewish firms were studios run by some of the Weimar era's most prolific photographic artists: Binder, Yva, Emil Bieber, Paul Wolff, Dora Horovitz, Elli Marcus, Dora Kallmus, Erich Salomon, Alfred Eisenstadt, and Walter Süßmann. The names Yva, Dora Kallmus, and Binder are printed in bold, indicating what the Nazis likely perceived as their disproportionate influence. After identifying these "foreign and Jewish" businesses, the *Deutsche Nachrichten* article concluded, "The German press [has] a moral obligation: from now on . . . out of its own impetus and conscience of its Germanness, [to] use only those photographers who belong to the German *Volksgemeinschaft*."[10]

The *Deutsche Nachrichten* list further reveals the extent to which Nazi dispossession policies would disrupt the careers of Jewish women in photography.[11] By 1930, women ran 129 of the 430 photography studios in Berlin, or 30 percent.[12] Men and women alike insisted that the entry of women into the field enhanced the craft. In 1928 the German critic Albert Dresdner wrote: "It is not many years since photography, as an art, seriously devoted itself to the idea of putting its resources at the service of commercial and industrial advertising. . . . [T]he photographer is an artist. He must not only have mastered the whole technique of the art, including all its developments and refinements, but also possess imagination, originality, and aesthetic taste. All these qualities Frau Yva, the accomplished and ambitious photographer of Berlin, unites in herself."[13] Lotte König, who founded the photography studio Atelier König-Rohde in Berlin with two other women, wrote in 1931: "Photography is a wonderful, interesting, and, at the same time, difficult profession for women. . . . [It] is a large, all-encompassing field offering a variety of opportunities."[14] For Jewish women, those opportunities were cut short following the Nazi takeover.

In addition to denouncing the industry's leading men and women as "Jews and foreigners," the *Deutsche Nachrichten* included a list of photographers who belonged to the *Volksgemeinschaft*. The list provided the names and addresses of 112 "pure German" photography studios that readers should patronize instead of their "Jewish and foreign" colleagues. This figure undermined the argument that Jews "dominated" photography, for there were twice as many "Aryan" photographers as "Jewish and foreign" ones named. The photographers listed as "pure German" included Max Gerlach and Hans Retzlaff in Berlin, Walter Winkelmann in Hamburg, and Heinrich Hoffmann, Hitler's personal photographer, who at the time was operating a studio in Munich on Friedrichstraße. Of the "pure German" firms, only two women photographers—Margarethe Stüber and Frau R. Greth, who both operated studios in Berlin—are listed even though there were many more women working as professional photographers at the time. That only Stüber and Greth were included suggests that the Nazis intended to masculinize the profession as they "Aryanized" it and, in the process, stifle the major contributions made to the photographic profession by both Jewish and non-Jewish women alike.

Nazi officials tasked with determining which photographers were Jewish usually did so by examining the surnames that appeared in magazines and picture archives at major publishing houses.[15] The *Deutsche Nachrichten* used that same methodology to craft its list, reporting, "By fleeting comparisons, we have been able to spot some pictures which originate from Jewish and foreign hands."[16] The Nazi newspaper *Deutsche Kultur-Wacht,* too, gathered and identified "Jewish names" from the printed photographs published by the regime's favorite target, Ullstein Verlag. The *Deutsche Kultur-Wacht* announced that "the regular photographers of the Ullstein publishing house are called: Salomon, Munkasci, Balassa, d'Ora, Yva, Binder, and Marcus. There is not one Aryan among them. *Die Dame* of April 2 contains two pictures by German photographers, twenty-one by Jews, and eight which are dubious, the *Dame* of June 1 five pictures by Aryans, twenty-five by Jews, and nine which are dubious. And then 'resident' Jews appear with entire series in one issue, constantly earning sums which a German photographer doesn't earn in one year at Ullstein."[17] That the article declared seventeen names to be "dubious" indicated a certain awareness that depending on names was hardly a foolproof method. It was also one that could invite criticism from photographers whom the newspaper mistakenly identified as Jewish. The *Deutsche Nachrichten* had identified the photographer Hans Koch as Jewish in a list of "Jews and foreigners" that appeared in a previous issue. Koch must have requested a correction, for the *Nachrichten* printed an apology for the mistake in its May 1, 1933, article, announcing that Koch "is today included in the right place, in the German list."[18]

The regime made its antisemitic policies for the photographic industry clear to those who did not subscribe to Nazi newspapers. The November 1933 exhibition "Die Kamera" examined in chapter 1, for example, had introduced the Nazis' plans for photography to a public audience and addressed the antisemitic foundation of those plans. Speakers at the exhibition pointed to racial identity rather than technical skill or artistic accomplishment as the most important quality defining a professional photographer. "True art rises from the depths of the people's soul," Heiner Kurzbein declared during the exhibition's opening ceremony, "and is closely connected with blood and soil. . . . [S]o too a *Volk* art like photography must receive its strength from race, culture and *Heimat*." Not only should the content of Germans' photographs reflect the superior racial qualities of true "Aryan" Germans, Kurzbein argued, but also those behind the camera had to match these characteristics as well. When addressing how these ideas were to be put into practice, Kurzbein added in a seemingly perfunctory aside that "in addition, the professional photographers are particularly keen to promote the photographic profession in the racial sense," implying that this restructuring would happen from within the industry and with the explicit approval of presumably "Aryan" colleagues.[19]

Many professional photographers did indeed support the antisemitic restructuring of their industry. The regime offered "true German" photographers important publicity and gave them opportunities to denounce Jewish colleagues in order to pursue their own professional interests. One example is the case brought against the camera manufacturer and distributor Benno B. Thorsch by Alexander Schwarz in the winter of 1933. Born in 1898 in Austria, Thorsch had established the prominent photographic equipment company Kamera-Werkstätten Guthe & Thorsch GmbH in 1919 with his business partner Paul Guthe near Dresden. Schwarz was a photographer in Stuttgart who worked at the Photo-Kuckuck studio. In December 1933 he wrote to the Reich Ministry of Economics to complain about Thorsch, whom Schwarz accused of charging him unreasonably high tax rates on his products. Schwarz complained that the contract was so "usurious" and "scandalous" that it could force him into bankruptcy. He added for good measure that Thorsch was *a foreign Jew.*[20]

At first the ministry rejected the possibility of any intervention and recommended that Schwarz file a complaint with a public prosecutor.[21] A month later Schwarz resubmitted his request. This time the ministry repeated the suggestion that he contact a public prosecutor or, "if necessary, the State Secret Police [Gestapo]."[22] Schwarz's tip that Thorsch was a "foreign Jew" resulted in Thorsch's business being targeted from then on by the authorities. Finally, in 1937 Thorsch decided to trade the business to the German American entrepreneur Charles A. Noble in exchange for Noble's photo company in Detroit.[23] Thorsch knew Noble through the industry, and they were on friendly terms. In the spring of 1938, Thorsch left Germany with his family and settled in Detroit until the family departed once more for Los Angeles.[24] Noble brought his family to Dresden at the same time, and the factory, which he renamed Kamera-Werkstätten AG, Dresden-Niedersedlitz, manufactured cameras well into the World War II years. The company would prosper because of the war and in 1939 launched the 25 mm SLR Praktiflex camera, which proved to be one of its most popular camera models for decades to come.[25]

Other non-Jewish German managers of photo studios and supply shops seized the opportunity provided by the new regime to uphold their own antisemitism. Many declared that they would no longer serve Jewish customers. One photography shop in Mannheim, for example, emblazoned antisemitic caricatures and warnings that "Jews will not be served here" across its display windows.[26] Amateur photographers, too, drew on the regime's antisemitism. As the regime formalized anti-Jewish policy, amateur photography associations in major cities like Berlin and Hamburg began to deny Jewish men and women admission. Many associations even denounced their Jewish members to the authorities. The Amateur Photographers' Association in the Berlin neighborhood of Kreuzberg (Amateurphotographen Verein Berlin-Kreuzberg), to take one example, was founded on February 9, 1928, on the initial promise of remaining open to all "friends of amateur photography." The association, which had its headquarters in Berlin Mitte, offered daytime and night courses in photography as well as public lectures and exhibitions. The association promoted photography documenting "scientific, artistic, technical and local history." By December 1934, however, the once welcoming association had amended its open membership clause, now prohibiting "non-Aryans" from joining the organization. "Any member of the association can be a lover of photography as long as he is of Aryan descent," the association's new guidelines announced.[27] Racism and antisemitism ultimately replaced love of photography as the club's central membership criteria. This did not necessarily prevent Jewish Germans from taking pictures or compiling photograph albums altogether. Many continued to do so under increasingly difficult circumstances to testify to Nazi antisemitism, document the new restrictions, and defiantly insist on their belonging in German society.[28] But such efforts firmly conveyed to non-Jewish German photography hobbyists that the practice of photography was a racially exclusive one.

The situation grew more serious in 1935 as the Nazi regime strengthened its power and coordinated its institutions. In light of the 1935 Nuremberg Laws stripping Jews of civil and legal rights, Goebbels undertook a number of initiatives to restructure the Reichskulturkammer to ensure that personnel would carry out the organization's increasingly radical policies. The restructuring process transformed the RKK "from a fairly loose confederation of Nazified associations into a more highly centralized organ of the state."[29] In the winter of 1935, Joseph Goebbels told Hans Hinkel, the general manager of the Chamber of Culture, to step up the purges of Jews (*Entjudung*) from all seven chambers, especially the press chamber, where the regime regulated photography.[30] By 1936 the Reich Culture Chamber would become a much more formidable institution than it had been at its founding.

Such extreme conditions granted photography associations and societies an even more active role in helping the regime purge Jewish photographers from economic and social life. In 1935 the Gesellschaft Deutscher Lichtbildner (Society of German Photographers) started barring its Jewish members from the organization and reporting them to the authorities.[31] Kurt Schallenberg, who had helped found the society sixteen years prior with Hugo Erfurth and Franz Grainer, had his once permanent membership revoked that year along with the rest of the society's Jewish members. Like other similar groups, the Gesellschaft quickly granted admission to other, less experienced "Aryan" photographers to provide them with the credentials and status that these prestigious memberships offered.[32]

The centralization process ushered in more radical directives against Jews. The regime relied on business records and compulsory professional memberships to accelerate anti-Jewish actions.[33] Using these records, Nazi officials tracked all existing commercial activity and determined whether company owners complied with the regime's racial laws. They could also use these records to trace business name changes, a sign they typically regarded as evidence of "Jewish" ownership trying to disguise itself as "Aryan."[34] As of 1933, moreover, photographers were required to obtain membership in the Reich Press Chamber. Membership in the Chamber of Crafts (Handwerkskammer) was also mandatory for photographers operating their own studios.[35] The official regulation of photography's technical and artistic dimensions was a promise the regime had made to professional photographers early on in response to the demands of the Central Verband Deutscher Photographen (Central Committee of German Photographers), discussed in chapter 1. In 1933 the CVDP proposed that photographers should carry official documentation in the form of "craftsman's licenses" (*Handwerkskarten*) to legally conduct both the artistic and the technical sides of the business on the same premises. When the CVDP compiled this proposal, it had been amateur photographers, not Jews, who were their primary cause for concern and reform. Amateur photographers, they argued, took business away from professionally trained craftsmen by conducting this work themselves without proper education. The CVDP recommended that "the taking over of photographic work for the amateurs should be permitted only to those who are in possession of a craft card."[36] The Chamber of Crafts finalized legislation on this matter in 1934 through the Decree for the Provisional Reconstruction of German Crafts.[37] The decree clearly distinguished photographers from the photo technicians who handled chemicals when developing, printing, and editing the finished product. As the CVDP had proposed, it required photographers to carry a *Handwerkskarte* to conduct all aspects of the business in their studios.

The mandate seems to have been largely enforced, as personal archives begin to contain government-issued craft cards after the summer of 1934. Lotte Jacobi, to take one example, certified on her October 1, 1934, craft card that she owned a photographic business.[38] Margaret Rosenberg, whose husband was the Berlin-based jurist and writer Kurt Rosenberg, also worked part time as a photographer in addition to practicing medicine in Berlin. She declared herself the owner of a photographic business on her April 4, 1935, craft card, correcting the masculine "Inhaber" (owner) printed on the form to the feminine "Inhaberin" in her own handwriting.[39] Rosenberg had also amassed a rather substantial collection of photography equipment, which the couple declared in addition to lists of all furniture, possessions, and clothing as they prepared to leave Germany for America. Included in the list was a 1933 Rolleiflex camera and assorted lenses, a Zeiss microscope, and a Leica projector, enlarger, and printer.[40]

The regime used existing and pending memberships in the Handwerkskammer and Reichspressekammer to facilitate the dispossession process. Once again the Nazi press proved a willing partner in speeding up the momentum. The Reich Press Chamber used these memberships to routinely publish updated lists identifying "Jewish and foreign" photographers working in the German press. The Hamburg Press Chamber, for instance, noted in August 1935: "In the near future a list of the Jewish picture press agencies will be published. These agencies will not be allowed to continue taking pictures in the future."[41] These memberships allowed both chambers to target Jewish-owned photographic businesses for removal from city commercial registers and economic life.

Expulsion from either chamber made it impossible to continue working. The case of the prominent portrait photographer Lotte Jacobi is an early example of this.[42] In the summer of 1935, a representative from the Press Chamber wrote to Jacobi to inform her that he was revoking her membership in the Reich Culture Chamber altogether, explaining: "One cannot expect from a non-Aryan the strong conviction which must be the condition for a successful collaboration in the foregoing direction. . . . A non-Aryan is to be considered unsuitable and unreliable for working in the field of the Reich Press Chamber."[43] The letter cited as the legal basis for Jacobi's expulsion paragraph 10 of the l933 law establishing the Reich Chamber of Culture, which maintained that "admission into a chamber may be refused, or a member may be expelled, when there exist facts from which it is evident that the person in question does not possess the necessary reliability and aptitude for the practice of his activity." The letter concluded: "The *non-Aryan influence* upon the press will have to be *eliminated* as speedily as possible. . . . Therefore we shall ask for the elimination of your picture service from the Reichspressekammer in view of the management of your enterprise."[44] The Press Chamber also voided the membership of Jacobi's colleague Alexander Bender, the secretary of a close friend of the Jacobi family. Bender had decided a few years prior that he wanted to learn photography from Jacobi and entered into a sort of apprenticeship with her. After the Nazi takeover, Bender agreed to include his more "Aryan" name in the company listing to stave off antisemitic persecution. These efforts ultimately proved futile, however. The letter explained that expulsion from the chamber "applies also to cases where a person is married to a non-Aryan, as such marriage furnishes proof of the fact that there exists an intellectual association with the non-Aryan conception of life."[45] Bender and Jacobi were not married. But they undoubtedly had a "business marriage" of sorts that was founded on precisely the kind of intellectual association the Reich Press Chamber wanted to eliminate.

At first the Reich Press Chamber left Jewish business owners to pick suitable new management for their companies on their own, a process typically referred to as "voluntary Aryanization."[46] The letter to Bender and Jacobi went on to advise them that they had to find new "Aryan" management for the studio: "We wish to inform you now of these facts in order to offer you the opportunity to make a change in the ownership of your enterprise." The letter urged them to see this "change in ownership" as nothing more than a charade, assuring them that they would still retain control of the enterprise behind the scenes: "According to legal regulations it would not mean change of ownership or management if you would appoint a trustee or bring about a situation which would mean only a change of ownership on the outside, but maintain your influence upon the internal business management."[47] In other words, Press Chamber officials more or less suggested that Jacobi arrange a fictive takeover of her studio. According to this proposal, the new "Aryan" manager would be the company's public face but without significant control over internal company operations.

Jacobi and Bender seem to have had a difficult time finding a sufficiently "Aryan" manager to take over, because Bender tried to negotiate a deadline extension for securing a replacement. The fact that he felt able to do so was due to the suggestion that both he and Jacobi could retain internal influence in the company and that the letter had not indicated any time constraints on the appointment process. The restructuring taking place at the Reich Chamber of Culture, however, ultimately had its desired effect. The flexibility once displayed by the individual who oversaw the case quickly hardened. The response to Bender's appeal a week later was a flat "no." "The provision of a grace period is completely impossible," the Chamber official replied. "If Ms. Jacobi does not make the necessary provisions, she will have to face the consequences."[48] As a result, both Bender and Jacobi left Berlin. Jacobi arrived in New York on September 29, 1935, and opened a new studio in Manhattan with her sister Ruth on October 30.[49] Bender moved to London and set up his own studio.[50] Their Berlin studio and everything in it was handed over shortly afterwards to the German photographers Hein Gorny and Karl

Theodor Gremmler, with Gorny's wife, Ruth, assisting with archival and laboratory operations. In 1936 Gorny was admitted to the Gesellschaft Deutscher Lichtbildner, but his membership was revoked two years later when an article in the SS newspaper *Das Schwarze Korps* accused his wife of being Jewish. Even so, Gorny continued to run the studio until a 1943 Allied air strike destroyed the business and its photographic archive.[51]

Hanni Schwarz, too, was prohibited from practicing photography after she had been identified as Jewish on the basis of her membership in the Handwerkskammer. Schwarz was the owner of a portrait photography studio in Berlin-Schöneberg which she had established in the early 1900s.[52] Schwarz had initially started out as a teacher in her father's school in Basel until 1904, when she and a friend, Anna Walter, took over the photographer Johannes Hülsen's studio in Berlin.[53] From the summer of 1919, Schwarz ran the studio with co-owner Marie Luise Schmidt during the Weimar years. Frieda Igogeit was helping Schwarz run the business by the time of the Nazi takeover. In a questionnaire that first summer, Igogeit described the studio as "located in a 7-room apartment with a rental value of 2,945, consisting of 2 large workrooms, 2 studio rooms, 1 laboratory, 1 darkroom, and 1 reception room. 6–8 people are specified as employees, 10–12 suppliers are listed and 800–900 customers."[54] In March 1936 the Handelskammer wrote to the Berlin District Court notifying them that the business had been closed as a result of their investigations and asked that it be removed from the commercial register. "The company Atelier Hanni Schwarz, owner Frieda Igogeit, Berlin Hohenstaufenstrasse 44, registered under No. 50560 in the commercial register Abt A, has closed down the business after our investigations," the notification announced. "On the basis of Section 126 of the Law on Voluntary Jurisdiction of May 17, 1898, we request that the company be deleted from the Commercial Register in accordance with section 31 of the Commercial Code."[55]

What the Nazis themselves called the "fateful year" of 1938, however, was the decisive turning point in the ability of Jewish photographers to remain in Germany.[56] By then the regime would complete the "Aryanization" or liquidation of all remaining studios. For one thing, a flurry of new decrees worsened the situation. Among them was the April 26, 1938, Decree for the Reporting of Jewish-Owned Property, which facilitated the regime's ability to target any Jewish-owned businesses that still turned a profit. The November 12 Decree on the Exclusion of Jews from German Economic Life closed all remaining Jewish-owned businesses. To make matters worse, Nazi storm troopers and Hitler Youth members stole cameras from the Jews they terrorized during the home invasions that accompanied spontaneous antisemitic riots, including during Kristallnacht on November 9–10, 1938.[57]

Nazi authorities carried out compulsory Aryanization of photography studios in response to these decrees. In December 1938 the Hamburg Crafts Chamber informed Kurt Schallenberg that "on the basis of the decree of the elimination of Jews from German business life of November 12, 1938, Jewish owners of craft enterprises are to be deleted from the craft register on December 31, 1938. The craft card is to be confiscated. Since, according to our findings, you are a Jew, you have to close your business on December 31, 1938, and return the craft card to the Chamber of Crafts by no later than this date."[58] As a result, Schallenberg sold his business and left for England, then Sydney, Australia, with his son in May 1939, where he remained until his death in September 1954.

Atelier Yva was yet another photography studio targeted in 1938. Else Neulander was born in 1900. After her father died, her mother managed to support Neulander and her eight siblings single-handedly through her hat-making business. After completing her education in photography at the Lette-Verein in Berlin during the early years of the Weimar Republic, Neulander opened her own photography studio in 1925 under a pseudonym, Yva. She quickly established herself as one of the premier photographers in Berlin and became widely known domestically and abroad for her fashion, commercial, and multiple exposure photography. After the Nazi press named her in articles condemning Jews in photography, Yva chose a friend, the art historian Charlotte Wiedler, to take over the public operation of the studio when it was "Aryanized" in 1936. By 1938, however, anti-Jewish decrees forced the studio to shut down completely. Yva wrote to a former employee that "the business had to close because of the order to eliminate Jews from the German economy of November 12, 1938."[59] She found work in the radiography department of the Jewish Hospital in Berlin. Shortly afterward, she prepared to leave Germany for New York by shipping thirty-four crates containing the contents of the studio to the port of Hamburg. But these plans were unsuccessful. In 1942 the Gestapo arrested Yva and her husband, Alfred Simon, and deported them to the Sobibor killing center, where they were murdered on arrival.[60] Thirteen of the couple's crates were auctioned off in Hamburg, but the identity of the buyers and the whereabouts of Yva's possessions today are unknown.

Foto-Atelier Binder faced the same situation in 1938. Alexander Binder was born in 1888 in Egypt to Swiss parents. He turned to photography after briefly studying then abandoning engineering between 1908 and 1910. In 1913 Binder opened his own photography studio in Berlin, and it became one of the largest and most prominent portrait photography studios in Europe. After his death in 1929, the studio continued to function using the Binder name under the management of Elisabeth von Stengel, though the Nazi press routinely mistook the name of the studio for that of the photographer running it.[61] Because von Stengel was Jewish, the Nazis stole the studio from her in 1938. Hubertus Flöter, who had worked as an assistant to von Stengel in 1935, became the studio's new "Aryan" manager and ran it until he was drafted into military service in 1940. His wife, Ilse Reyer, who had also worked as an apprentice for von Stengel in 1934, took over studio operations while Flöter served as a propaganda photographer on the eastern front.[62] Voh Stengel was deported to the Theresienstadt concentration camp on September 10, 1942.[63] Another apprentice, Inge Schlesinger, was also forced to leave the Binder studio because she was Jewish. Schlesinger performed forced labor at the Zeiss Ikon Filmwerk factory in Berlin manufacturing 35 mm film with nine other Jewish women until she was deported to Auschwitz with her parents in May 1943.[64] A few weeks after she arrived, she was chosen for work as a photographer for Joachim Caesar's Pflanzenzucht Kommando at the Rajsko satellite camp.[65] Both Schlesinger and von Stengel survived the Holocaust.[66]

The year 1938 dealt blows to Suse Byk's studio as well. Born in 1890 in Berlin, Byk opened her own portrait photography studio in 1913 on the Kurfurstendamm after completing her training at the Lette-Verein.[67] She quickly rose to prominence as a portrait photographer and mentored many other photographers during the Weimar years at her studio, including Martha Maas and Lore Feininger. After the Nazi takeover, Byk tried to navigate increasingly hostile working conditions. In 1935 she withdrew the advertisements for her studio that she normally featured in the monthly newsletter published by the Jewish Cultural Association in Berlin.[68] In response to the Decree for the Reporting of Jewish-Owned Property of April 26, 1938, Byk was forced to report her business earnings.[69] After she did so, the studio faced additional threats. That summer, Byk approached a former apprentice, Liselotte Strelow, and asked her to take over the studio but retain the Byk name. Strelow, who had left Byk's studio after her 1932 apprentice year to work at the nearby Kodak company, bought the studio for the woefully undervalued sum of RM 5,000 with a loan she received from the German Labor Front.[70] Byk and her husband left Berlin for London and then New York City shortly afterwards. Strelow renamed the studio Foto-Atelier Strelow and ran it until the studio and its archive were destroyed during the bombing of Berlin in the winter of 1944.[71]

The first "Aryan" managers who took over photography studios owned by Jewish men and women were not necessarily the last. What happened to Emil Bieber's studio is a good example. In 1933 Bieber estimated his annual profits at RM 25,000. By 1937 that amount had fallen to RM 8,500 as a result of escalating attacks on his studio in the press and pressure from the Hamburg Photographers Guild, which called for the deletion of the studio from the commercial register. In March 1938 Bieber and his family left for London before moving on to Cape Town, South Africa. He handed over the business to his youngest employee, Hans Schönborn, who bought it for just RM 4,500.[72] Bieber chose Schönborn to take over because he had always regarded him as "a man of decent disposition and lifestyle" while they worked together. After the transaction Bieber wrote to Schönborn, assuring him: "After I made the decision I was satisfied that I could entrust you with the continuation of my business. I am sure that, in keeping with the high reputation of my firm, you will continue to run the business in the spirit of this tradition."[73]

Shortly afterward, however, Schönborn found that he could not successfully manage the studio. He blamed his difficulties on the fact that the studio still carried Bieber's name. "The summer months have been unfavorable," he reported to the Foreign Exchange Office. "The business is difficult to sustain because it is non-Aryan, and many orders have been canceled or not given."[74] To make matters worse, Schönborn did not possess a Hamburg *Handwerkskarte,* and so was practicing the business illegitimately in the first place. Schönborn decided that "in the interest of the creditors," he should quietly hand over the business to another photographer without informing Bieber or his wife.[75] Arthur C. Boos promptly took over. He stole Emil Bieber's logo and motto ("In constant pursuit of the highest performance") and enjoyed full access to the photographic equipment, eight thousand client contact cards, and fifty thousand photographic plates Bieber left behind. Boos even wrote to Bieber's former clients announcing: "Please take note that the record archive of the former photographer E. Bieber, Hamburg 36, Neuerwall 36 is now in my possession. I inform you now that in my photo workshop at Neuerwall 36 the prestigious portrait is my specialty. Only first-rate, old established employees stand by my side. . . . With German greetings! Arthur C. Boos."[76]

The individuals who helped steal Jewish-owned businesses were often former or current employees and occupied lower-level positions in the photographic industry. Their readiness to take over was no doubt driven by opportunism. Liselotte Strelow, Arthur C. Boos, Hubertus Flöter, Ilse Reyer, and countless others who had been working in low-level positions in the photographic industry and had been in dire financial straits since the depression of the early 1930s leaped at the chance to operate their own studio. Their enthusiasm was also motivated by personal grudges and antisemitism. Strelow, for one, went on to enjoy a remarkably successful career as a studio photographer.[77] Until her death in 1981 she continued to describe Byk resentfully as "an arrogant Jewish woman who degraded me in my apprenticeship."[78] Her hostility is hardly surprising in light of a 1934 article she wrote about how grateful photographers should be to "those who are concerned with racial studies and race care. A sympathetic government of the Reich is emphatically committed to this area, which is extremely important for all German comrades."[79]

The violent attacks on Jewish-owned businesses and homes that began in 1933 worsened in 1938. These tactics peaked during Kristallnacht, November 9–10. In the course of this nationwide pogrom, SS and Hitler Youth members plundered and destroyed photo studios. This was the case for Cornelia and Stefanie Hess, two sisters who ran a prominent portrait photography studio in Frankfurt under their nicknames, Carry and Nini. Carry was not there, for she had already left for Paris in 1933 and would survive the war in hiding in southern France. Nini, however, stayed behind with their mother, Lina, to run the studio on her own. On November 10, 1938, SS men ransacked the studio and destroyed everything in it that they could not easily take with them, including the studio's technical equipment and archive of negatives and prints. Nini and Lina would be deported to Auschwitz and murdered there on arrival in 1942.[80]

Other testimonies show that Nazi thugs plundered but did not destroy Jewish-owned photography studios and shops, probably in anticipation of maintaining the businesses for new "Aryan" management. A particularly vivid description comes from the family of Norbert Wallner, who ran a small photo shop in Vienna, which had recently been incorporated within Germany's borders during the German annexation of Austria (Anschluss) in March 1938.[81] Norbert's son Heinz was only ten years old when he watched two Hitler Youth members force his father from their home. "I will never forget the evening of November 9, 1938," Heinz later recalled. "There was a loud rapping on the door. Two young men in brown Nazi uniforms stood at the threshold. They asked Father to put on his coat and accompany them. They were going to his photo store. . . . I wasn't relieved until Father finally turned up after eleven o'clock. He looked very shaken. He told us that the pair of Hitler Youth had made him unlock the store, then they had pulled down the shutters. It occurred to him that they might kill him without any witnesses." But instead of killing him, Norbert told his son, their only aim was to take the photographic supplies in his shop with them, supplies that, as *Volksgenossen,* they argued, rightfully belonged to them anyway. "Gradually it dawned on him that they were merely bent on plundering as much as they could," Heinz continued. "Cameras, accessories, photo albums . . . were jammed into the sidecars of motorcycles they had parked at the curb. 'We're only taking what belongs to us,' they said. To stall for time, he showed them how these gadgets worked: the flash units, light meters, the newest imported equipment."[82] Norbert told Heinz that he was able to return home unscathed only because an upper-ranking SS officer appeared and scolded the two Hitler Youth members for emptying the shop of its contents for their own personal use.[83] Such episodes reveal how decisive terror could be in compelling Jewish business owners to sell their companies for vastly undervalued amounts. But they also indicate the enthusiasm for photography the Nazi regime had been promoting all along for all *Volksgenossen.* That these two Hitler Youth flouted disciplinary standards to pocket these materials for themselves was no arbitrary act of theft.

It was not only valuable cameras and photo supplies that Nazi agents sought. There is some evidence to suggest that, as they carried out the larger project of the dispossession of the Jews, Nazi officials intended to confiscate photographs archived in photo studios or publishing houses for unrestricted use in Nazi-controlled illustrated magazines and newspapers.[84] In 1934 Heiner Kurzbein had filed a complaint about how long it took to acquire images for use in the press:

> The addition of pictures greatly facilitates the launching of articles to the foreign press. The process previously practiced in-house for the procurement of such images is inadequate: the costs are disproportionately high. There are never enough pictures available to hand over to the technical departments and it takes a few days to complete the work. Thus, the specialist referee has to obtain the approval of the department after detailed presentation of the purpose, then my department has to make the professional selection

of the pictures, order these pictures from the companies, in turn send them to the specialist department, ask for the selected pictures, verify inventory, etc.[85]

Unrestricted access to the photograph archives Jewish photographers had been forced to leave behind allowed the Nazi press to avoid the expensive and slow copyright process Kurzbein described. This meant that Nazi-controlled publications would have had open access to the pictures produced by Germany's Jewish photographers to illustrate their advertisements and articles, though more research is needed in this area. One example, however, can be found in a January 1934 issue of the travel magazine *Atlantis*. The issue credited around a dozen pictures taken by Lotte Jacobi during her trip to the Soviet Union in the late 1920s to Heinz Neustadt, a photographer for the magazine *Volk und Welt*. He was likely one of many to receive credit and compensation for work that was not his.[86]

That the Nazis oversaw the theft of these pictures indicates a certain reverence even for a photograph produced by a Jewish photographer. In the age of visual journalism, photographs held considerable commercial value. Indeed, for the Nazis all artworks were commodities. But they also believed that what made photographs aesthetically valuable was their unique and seemingly impartial ability to show the world "as it really was," a central tenet in the Nazi conception of art. And while the regime's cultural authorities demonstrated through countless exhibitions, burnings, and auctions that paintings retained the "Jewishness" of their creators and therefore had to be destroyed, sold, or hidden, photographs did not. They continued to appear in newspapers and magazines all the same. By 1938 those photographs began to reflect the reality the regime had wanted to create all along: an endless supply of pictures entrusted to photographers who were considered genuine members of the *Volk* and who had helped eliminate their Jewish colleagues from the industry and taken over their businesses.

Nazi officials also capitalized on the opportunities presented by the forced emigration of Jews to seize photographic equipment for redistribution to "Aryan" photographers. Whether or not the equipment would be confiscated by Nazi authorities depended on the collection's value. Consider the case of the Hamburg-based portrait photographer Max Hirsch. According to his 1933 Hamburg Immigration Department file, Hirsch had "operated his company as a photographer since 1919 in Hamburg, and now has to give up his business. Since he does not find further progress in Germany, he wants to settle in the United States as a photographer in order to create a new livelihood."[87] Hirsch and his wife, Luise, began emigration proceedings in February 1939. He was allowed to take his photographic equipment with him—including tripods, bags, and four cameras—because it did not have sufficient value to be detained in Germany. Most of the items in Hirsch's possession were older camera models. The office noted that "the photographic equipment listed is mainly bought before 1933 with the exception of small additions." Had the department deemed his collection valuable, Hirsch would have been required to pay an export fee (*Dego-Abgade*) of three times the original purchase price to the German Central Bank. Officials concluded that in the course of the investigation, Hirsch did not have to pay the *Dego* tax because "the acquisition value of the items is not over RM 50."[88]

The situation was different for those who had purchased photographic equipment after 1933. The case of Alwin Henle, for example, indicates what happened to Jews when Nazi officials considered the photographic equipment they tried to take with them as they left Germany valuable. Henle was an amateur photographer who had amassed a sizable collection of professional-grade photographic equipment. When Henle arranged to leave Germany in November 1938, however, he was denied permission to take his equipment with him. Officials justified this by arguing that since Henle was not a photographer by trade, he had no persuasive cause to bring his equipment with him overseas: "Mr. Henle is to be refused permission to export the Leica entries in the list and the other newly purchased photographic articles totaling RM 209,681, since he is a food agent by profession and has not previously worked in the photographic profession." Henle's collection—which included the latest Leica and Josper cameras, Elmar lenses, and other materials—was clearly considered valuable enough to be confiscated from him. Indeed, shortly after these proceedings, immigration representatives furnished a written confirmation that Henle had surrendered his equipment for resale on December 15, 1938.[89]

Nazi officials claimed that Henle "didn't need" his equipment since he had no plans to make a living as a photographer abroad. At the core of this explanation, however, lay the belief that as a Jew, Henle had no right to own property that would allow him to practice photography. What became of his equipment is unclear. But Hamburg officials seem to have at least planned on reallocating it to help another person set up a photography business, because they solicited the input of the Hamburg School of Photography (Hamburger Foto-Schule) to evaluate whether the collection was substantial enough to "establish an existence as a commercial photographer." The school confirmed that it was, saying that Henle's collection represented the "lower limit" of the material necessary to establish a commercial photographic business.[90] Thus even amateur photographers who tried to leave Germany were prohibited from bringing their equipment with them if they were Jews. If the collection was valuable enough, it would be confiscated and slated for redistribution to an "Aryan" instead. Moreover, even if they managed to leave Germany with their photographic equipment, Jewish photographers often faced an uphill climb in reestablishing themselves elsewhere.[91]

The dispossession of German Jews in the photographic industry made the practice of photography even more exclusive to non-Jewish German members of the *Volksgemeinschaft*. Such measures further reinforced the association between photography and racial and national belonging. But the Nazi officials and civilians who helped enforce that configuration also inadvertently created new spaces for those who had been purged from German society to use photography in acts of resistance and revenge. In the unlikely setting of the Nazi concentration camp, some prisoners did precisely that.

CHAPTER 3

Gathering Evidence

Once he reached the safety of Washington, D.C., Rafael Brenner told an interviewer that the "heyday of German photography is over. The Nazis sent a great many talented men and women out of the country or put them in concentration camps."[1] That was certainly the case for many men and women working in the photographic industry whom the Nazis persecuted as Jewish. But for some the Nazis considered unfit to practice photography, the concentration camp was not the end of the story.

Photography allowed non-Jewish Germans to participate in the Nazi vision of a *Volksgemeinschaft*. But for some of those persecuted during the Third Reich, photography presented an opportunity to gather evidence testifying to the violence, cruelty, and suffering on which that project fundamentally depended.[2] Administrative photography rather than personal collections proved essential to this effort. That was especially true in Nazi concentration camps, where SS officers used photography to keep meticulous records of daily camp operations, executions, beatings, and other scenes testifying to the horrors of the camps.[3] Certain prisoners who had access to camp records in their capacity as photographers or darkroom workers used that position to gather evidence of what was really taking place there. To them, photography meant opportunities for resistance and revenge.

It also meant the possibility for postwar justice, since pictures taken in the camps would provide much of the evidence for the prosecution during war crimes trials in Germany. Surviving prisoner-photographers, moreover, testified as witnesses for the prosecution at those same trials. During the Nuremberg trials of 1946, for example, Francisco Boix would provide witness testimony in the case regarding atrocities committed in the occupied countries of western Europe. Boix, who had been a prisoner-photographer in the photo department at Mauthausen, handed over to the prosecution a number of photographs he had smuggled out of the camp as evidence showing the cruelty and abuses administered against Jewish and non-Jewish prisoners there. He also presented photographs identifying Ernst Kaltenbrunner, one of the defendants standing trial for crimes against humanity in his capacity as chief of the Reich Security Main Office after having replaced Reinhard Heydrich following his assassination in June 1942.[4] During the Auschwitz trials in Frankfurt between 1963 and 1965, another former prisoner, Alfred Wóycicki, testified as a witness against Robert Mulka, the former adjutant to commandant Rudolf Höss. In his testimony Wóycicki, who had worked in the photography lab at Auschwitz, recounted seeing SS men take photographs documenting the arrival process at the camp through his position in the political department.[5]

Despite the significance of the photographic records and workers that made administering the camps possible, as well as bringing camp staff to justice, the subject of concentration camp photography tends to be associated with the photographs Allied soldiers took as they liberated the camps in 1944 and 1945. Marianne Hirsch, for example, traced her "first encounter with the photographic inventory of ultimate horror" to seeing a collection of photographs taken by an American soldier during liberation at Bergen-Belsen and Dachau.[6] Susan Sontag was also speaking of Allied liberation photographs when she wrote, "Nothing I have seen—in photographs or in real life—ever cut me as sharply, deeply, instantaneously."[7] Yet ever since their inception, many of the camps relied on keeping photographic records of their own. When histories of Nazi concentration camps invoke these records, they often use them for little more than their illustrative power, primarily engaging with photographs to identify known perpetrators or victims in the camp system.[8] Why the photographs exist in the first place and who produced them is rarely addressed. Identifying their provenance is less straightforward than it appears, since in the camps it was SS men who typically took the pictures, but it was prisoners who developed, retouched, and copied them.[9] While photographs are valuable traces of who and what they depict, they also testify to a behind-the-camera process that, after 1939, involved concentration camp prisoner labor. Those prisoners would ultimately use their position to preserve and circulate photographic records after German forces surrendered in April 1945.[10]

Understanding the photographic records prisoners created and preserved requires a closer examination of how photography functioned in the camps more generally, for it was the unique presence of official photography in concentration camps in the first place that ultimately facilitated prisoners' proximity to official SS photographic records. Photography had become a part of camp administration during the centralization phase of the *Konzentrationslager* (KL) between 1934 and 1937. Officials saw it as a reputable way to help the SS administer the "modern" camp system they were building.[11] The value of photography for daily recordkeeping prompted SS officers to set up an official photographic identification service (Erkennungsdienst) in concentration camps in the KL system that reported directly to the Gestapo in the Political Department (Politische Abteilung). The SS used the photo service to keep detailed visual records on all prisoners, staff members, and deaths, much in the same way photography had been used in police precincts throughout Europe and North America since the end of the nineteenth century.[12]

The Erkennungsdienst was not a Nazi invention, nor was it unique to the concentration camp system. The service had played a crucial role in German criminal policing ever since the early 1900s, when it was originally set up as a special office for gathering criminological and forensic evidence. The data gathered by Erkennungsdienst officers included fingerprints, biographical records, and, increasingly throughout the 1920s, photographs, which would then be released to state criminal police precincts to help them track down all suspected or convicted criminals.[13] Photography was already central to modern policing throughout the Western world. By 1921, one observer in Germany was noting that "photography . . . has in fact become an indispensable aid in the identification and capture of criminals. Nowadays it is unthinkable that the police force of any developed nation could function successfully without photography."[14] Regional Erkennungsdienst offices increasingly relied on photography to carry out their work. In Düsseldorf, for example, police officers began requesting funds to acquire the latest camera equipment to take photographs for police records rather than depending on their own outdated devices. Higher-quality photographs of evidence would be more effective not only for police forces but also for the courts evaluating the evidence during criminal trials. "For the successful expansion of the identification service and for the better representation of the investigation result in court, the procurement of a practical photo device can no longer be avoided," the department noted.[15] Upon the Nazi takeover, Heinrich Himmler and Reinhard Heydrich swiftly Nazified Germany's police branches, culminating in the official 1936 merger of the German criminal police (Kriminalpolizei) and the state secret police (Gestapo) under the broader purview of the Sicherheitspolizei.[16] Gestapo and criminal police agents maintained the methods of the Erkennungsdienst to weed out political enemies, making ample use of photographic records to do so. At one point, the Gestapo even ordered one hundred of the matchbox sized secret cameras invented by the Berlin-based engineer Hans Curt Peters in the fall of 1933 to assist them in photographing documents, events, and people unnoticed. Hidden cameras could also help the Gestapo invent evidence against individuals and prosecute them as criminals, since "photographic images can be extremely important if the criminal act can be confirmed later."[17] And in their prolonged fight against crime as well as socially undesirable persons, the security police forces made ample use of photography in the rogue's galleries (*Verbrecheralben*) used since the early 1900s to identify and capture those accused of a wide range of criminal offenses, including homosexuality, which had been outlawed under Paragraph 175 of the German Criminal Code as of 1871.[18]

Having firmly established the traditions of the Erkennungsdienst in the newly Nazified domestic criminal police forces, the Gestapo promptly turned their attention to setting up similar offices in concentration camps throughout German-occupied Europe to keep track of all inmates. The photo departments set up at Dachau and Sachsenhausen, two of the earliest camps established for political prisoners, served as the models for the departments established later on in camps including Neuengamme, Auschwitz, Buchenwald, and Mauthausen.[19] Ten miles north of Munich, Dachau opened in March 1933 initially to detain all "communist and—as far as necessary—*Reichsbanner* [prodemocratic paramilitaries] and Marxist functionaries who threaten the security of the state."[20] Sachsenhausen, roughly twenty miles north of Berlin, had opened in the summer of 1936 to detain male political prisoners.[21] SS photographers who helped found the photography services at Dachau and Sachsenhausen often used their expertise in the process to help build services in other camps, bringing some of the equipment from both camps with them. SS-Hauptscharführer Bernhard Walter, for example, had worked as a photographer in the identification service at Sachsenhausen before his arrival at Auschwitz, where he headed the photo department with Ernst Hans Hoffmann.[22] Auschwitz prisoner-photographer Wilhelm Brasse later remembered that the photographic equipment used in the Erkennungsdienst "came from KL Sachsenhausen," though Walter claimed to have personally contributed equipment for the service after Rudolf Höss commanded him to set up the office from scratch.[23]

The primary purpose of the Erkennungsdienst in the camps was to create photographs of all registered prisoners upon their arrival. Prisoners were generally supposed to be photographed after they received a number and uniform and had been shaved. Being summoned to the department could take anywhere from an hour to a few days after arrival depending on how many prisoners the camp had to process. The registration photo showed each prisoner in at least two poses: one taken from the side and another facing front. These poses were consistent with the norms established in police precincts for photographing prisoners for their mug shots, a practice that was thought to increase the likelihood of facial recognition and capture should the prisoner in question escape.[24] The registration photo would supplement additional information on the prisoner's police record, including the racial or political crimes the inmate had allegedly committed as well as other documents like birth and marriage certificates or interrogation transcripts.

At Auschwitz beginning in the second half of 1941, SS staff photographed only those they selected as registered prisoners. Beginning in 1942, all Jews and Poles who were not photographed on arrival were sent to the gas chambers instead. As the SS photographer Ernst Hoffmann put it to Wilhelm Brasse, photographing them "doesn't make sense, they're just going to die," and there was "no sense wasting photographic supplies on such shit."[25] That was why a photographic service did not exist in killing centers like Treblinka and Sobibor. Among the many euphemisms for murder, then, was the phrase "not photographed" (*nicht fotografiert),* which appears in lists documenting the arrivals of new transports to Auschwitz.[26]

Apart from their primary task of photographing prisoners, SS personnel staffing the Erkennungsdienst took pictures documenting the construction and layout of the camps.[27] The purpose of these records was to show high-ranking authorities how the camps worked and that camp personnel were carrying out their orders properly.[28] "When Himmler came to visit the camps," a former Buchenwald prisoner recalled, "they had to be able to show how they operated," and so these photographs constituted "evidence that what he had ordered had been done with zeal."[29] Thus one of the main types of concentration camp photography was explicitly created by the SS to prove to their superiors that they were doing as they were told.

SS photographers also documented all camp deaths, including alleged suicides and deaths during escape attempts. SS-Unterscharführer Pery Broad, whom Claude Lanzmann clandestinely interviewed about his experiences as a guard at Auschwitz between 1942 and 1945 for the film *Shoah*, remembered that Erkennungsdienst personnel were the first to arrive at such scenes with their cameras. "Some [of the dead] were found in the morning strung up with their belts on the planks of their bunks," Broad recalled. "The cases of suicide were then laconically reported at rollcall by the block-senior to the camp leader. The officers of the Erkennungsdienst hurried to the place and photographed the body from all angles, witnesses were lengthily interrogated, to make sure that the victim had not been killed by other prisoners."[30]

Authentic cases of suicide and escape attempts aside, the camp SS also relied on Erkennungsdienst staff to disguise outright murders in camp records as suicides by placing rope, belts, or sharp instruments near the victim's body before it was photographed. Especially during the early phases of the camp system, the SS practiced "suiciding" to preserve their image at home and abroad.[31] The Nazis had, after all, packaged the camps to the public as institutions "where politically misguided men are being trained to become good citizens. They are seen drilling and working in a way that suggests a healthy and a disciplined but not overstrenuous life."[32] Details revealing the extent to which prisoners were being openly murdered would shatter this image and potentially jeopardize popular support for the Nazi regime. Moreover, the camp administration hoped to avoid an official investigation by the Reich Ministry of Justice, which had competed for jurisdiction over the camps during the early years of the dictatorship in a struggle for power that characterized much of Nazi bureaucracy.[33]

The photo identification service hosted a wide range of personalities. SS men were answerable to the Gestapo, but they were not necessarily themselves Gestapo agents. As with the concentration camp system itself, constant change was endemic to the service's management structure and often resulted in adjustments to department leadership.[34] Moreover, SS photographers frequently maintained their position in multiple camps during their careers. The Mauthausen photo department, for example, was headed by SS-Oberscharführer Fritz Kornacz and the nineteen-year-old "Nazi fanatic" SS-Untersturmführer Hermann Schinlauer. Kornacz, who was described by survivors of Mauthausen as a "brute," was sent to the eastern front in June 1941 and was killed there four years later by American troops. Fifty-five-year-old former art professor and SS-Oberscharführer Paul Ricken, who joined the Nazi Party in 1932 and the SS in 1935, arrived to replace Kornacz in August 1939. Ricken appears to have practiced photography in some serious capacity prior to the Nazi takeover, since an entry names him as one of the participants in the 1930 photography exhibition "Das Lichtbild" in Munich.[35] Ricken was described by former Mauthausen prisoners as the only SS man to have been professionally trained in photography, and as a committed Nazi but a relatively decent man who allegedly "turned his eyes away and even wept" when he witnessed executions at the Mauthausen "death wall." The former Mauthausen prisoner Antonio Garcia remembered, "He would give his fellow SS the *Heil Hitler* salute but he never struck any one of us, and I believe we owe our lives to him."[36] Clearly, Kornacz and Schinlauer had set the bar quite low, for "decency" meant little more than refraining from physical abuse. At Auschwitz, Bernhard Walter was likewise described by survivors as a committed Nazi but someone who "quaked with fear" when higher-ranking SS officers were photographed in Erkennungsdienst quarters. The man who oversaw Dachau's photo department, Heinrich Himmler's personal photographer Friedrich Franz Bauer, is best known for his portraits of Himmler and Heydrich and for having created the pictures in the now well-known propaganda essay "The Truth about Dachau," in which prisoners are shown to be well dressed, well fed, and properly treated.[37] "The Truth about Dachau" functioned as a response to articles and brochures about the "Dachau Murder Camp" that had been published abroad.[38] The report portrays the concentration camp as a "normal" education camp, primarily for unruly communists. The Nazi propaganda made use of Bauer's pictures to show neatly dressed prisoners at early morning roll calls or eating meals. Bauer also took some of the first prisoner mug shots at Dachau, emulating the two-frame or three-frame identification photos customary in police photography but photographing all prisoners outdoors, a practice likely discontinued because sunlight made prisoners squint and therefore rendered them less recognizable.[39] He photographed Dachau grounds as well, especially the camp herb garden, and camp guards. At Neuengamme, SS-Oberscharführer Albert Ernst headed the photography department with the assistance of SS-Unterscharführer Josef Schmitt. Born in 1910 in Elbart/Oberpfalz, Germany, Ernst worked as a plumber until he became unemployed in 1929 and joined the Nazi Party and the SS in 1933. Described by survivors as "easily excitable," Ernst was a guard at Dachau before he was relocated to the political department at Mauthausen in 1939. He arrived at Neuengamme in June 1940 and worked as a scribe until November, when he took over the photography department. Three years later he volunteered to go to the front and took part in the suppression of the 1943 Warsaw ghetto uprising.[40]

Depending on the personality of the SS officer present, photographing prisoners proved to be ripe with opportunities to abuse them.[41] A former Neuengamme prisoner remembered that Albert Ernst, for instance, beat prisoners, sometimes to death, when they sat to have their pictures taken. Ernst even installed a protruding nail in the chair prisoners had to sit on in order to cause them to jump up suddenly in pain.[42] As Ernst testified during his postwar trial for excessive violence against prisoners, "I beat inmates in my room, [but] never had a truncheon or a whip or any other weapon, only the flat of my hand, and I do not know that prisoners died as a result of my beatings." He also claimed that the nail in the seat was a practical method established in the Dachau photo service to ensure that prisoners got up faster. In the end, Ernst blamed prisoners themselves for his violent behavior. "If I am guilty of abusing detainees," he insisted, "it was only if they lied to me or otherwise irritated me."[43] Ernst was found guilty and sentenced to death in Hamburg by a British military court. He was hanged on January 23, 1947.[44]

Survivors reported similar abuses while being photographed on arrival in other Nazi camps. Auschwitz survivors, for example, remembered the process of having their picture taken as one that was as much about humiliating them as it was about documenting what they looked like. Numerous survivor accounts testify about the lengths to which SS men went to torment the prisoners they photographed. One survivor recalled: "They sat me in a chair and then took photos of me in three poses. A spring was installed underneath that chair that—if the subject did not stand up fast enough—dumped him on the floor. The subject fell over, of course, which was an occasion for mirth on the part of the SS man in attendance."[45] A second recounted a similar experience, saying, "Sometimes they played a prank on us in which the SS man pushed some kind of button so hard that you flew out of that chair as if from a catapult."[46] A third remembered: "Apparently, prisoners were photographed systematically according to the current enumeration, from 1 upwards, as we were gathered there in such an order. . . . When my number was called out, I was taken to the last door on the right side of the corridor. I was ordered to sit on a rotating seat and a photo was taken in three body positions. You had to leave the rotating seat while it was turned which made the person being photographed fall off."[47] Prisoner-photographer Wilhelm Brasse reinforced all three accounts when he recalled:

> Photographing was not a daily routine in the prisoner's life. Each person was photographed only once. When a prisoner entered the room where the camera was and sat on the seat, he or she planted his or her feet on the round platform. Two pictures were taken en face, but one of them was taken with the head turned slightly. One of them was a profile photograph. When the person being photographed changed his or her body position in relation to the lens, the platform was activated and rotated by pulling a lever. Once all three photos were taken, someone said, "Weg!" [Get lost!], [and] the person being photographed had to stand up lightly and put his or her feet on the ground. The prisoner was leaning a little bit and while he or she was trying to straighten up, Kapo Maltz pulled the lever. The platform movement made the prisoner fall to the floor.[48]

The abuses that prisoners experienced and witnessed when the SS photographed them for camp records only confirmed for those who would be given the chance that the photography department could provide unique opportunities for resistance and revenge when the time came.

That moment arrived when war did in September 1939. As the camps expanded once the war began, between 1939 and 1941 the Erkennungsdienst had to keep up with the steadily rising number of prisoners who arrived and had to be photographed for camp records. Numbers had already swelled when Jews arrived at the camps by the thousands in the aftermath of the Kristallnacht pogrom on November 9–10, 1938. But prisoner arrivals skyrocketed as well as a result of the Nazis' wartime effort to streamline their procedures for rounding up alleged criminals and social outsiders like beggars and homosexuals. New camps like Flossenburg, Mauthausen, and Ravensbrück emerged to accommodate these new prisoners, and the opening of Auschwitz to its first arrivals in the spring of 1940 forced even more people into the camp system. Nazi authorities also rounded up political, military, and racial enemies of the regime from occupied territories in Poland, Ukraine, and the Baltic states and sent them to the camps, making particular use of Auschwitz to do so.[49]

Apart from Paul Ricken, who was the only SS photographer known to have been professionally trained in photography, most SS officers staffing the Erkennungsdienst had at best only basic knowledge of the practice. And so they increasingly relied on prisoner labor to ensure that the Erkennungsdienst functioned properly, recruiting prisoners with professional experience in the photographic industry to work in the photo identification service. As Francisco Boix put it on the witness stand during the Nuremberg trials in 1947: "Like all the SS of the interior services of the camp, they were men who knew nothing. They always needed prisoners to get their work done."[50] SS photographers based their assignments on an initial search of which prisoners reported the profession of photographer for their camp files, followed by questioning about the history of their work in the field.

Prisoners were normally selected during roll call or while waiting in line to be photographed themselves. The French photographer Georges Angéli, for example, was deported to Buchenwald as a political prisoner in the summer of 1943. "We went to the photo service to be photographed for our file," Angéli remembered. "We were [in line] waiting to be photographed. I took a look inside and told my comrades joking that I would not mind being assigned there. When it was my turn, the SS man who had a list with the names, addresses and professions asked me: 'You are a photographer for how long?' I answered him: 'Yes, since the age of fourteen.' The next day I was assigned to the photographic service."[51] Photographer Wilhelm Brasse, too, was sent to Auschwitz in 1940 for refusing to join the Wehrmacht following the invasion of Poland in September 1939. He was working in the potato room at Auschwitz when he was summoned one day by the camp Gestapo. "I was terrified," he recalled, "because a summons to the Political Department often ended at the Death Wall. Aside from me, four other guys were summoned and . . . it turned out that all of us were photographers by occupation. I was the only one of the five prisoners chosen."[52] Upon his arrival at Mauthausen on April 7, 1941, political prisoner Antonio Garcia was assigned to the photography service after indicating that he had trained as a photographer in his parents' photography shop. Similarly, political prisoner Francisco Boix, who arrived at Mauthausen in January 1941 from French exile following the Spanish Civil War, initially worked as an interpreter for the other Spanish prisoners until he entered the photography department. "Owing to my professional knowledge, I was sent to Mauthausen to work in the identification branch of the camp," Boix stated at the Nuremberg trials. "There was a photographic branch, and pictures of everything happening in the camp could be taken and sent to the High Command in Berlin."[53] The same was true for Heinrich Peter Roth. Born in 1907 in St. Ingbert, Germany, Roth was a self-employed photographer sent to Neuengamme following four separate criminal charges of homosexuality between 1934 and 1938.[54] Because Roth had been identified as a photographer in his camp file, he was selected for work in the photo identification service shortly after his arrival at Neuengamme.[55]

Outside of the Erkennungsdienst, prisoners could be recruited as photographers for other camp projects. Inge Schlesinger, to take one particularly extraordinary example, was a Jewish photographer from Berlin. As discussed in chapter 2, she began working as an apprentice in the photography studio Foto-Atelier Binder, which had been founded by Alexander Binder in 1915 and taken over upon his death by the photographer Elisabeth von Stengel, who was also Jewish.[56] After von Stengel was deported to Theresienstadt, Schlesinger performed forced labor at the Berlin-based Zeiss Ikon Filmwerk factory until May 17, 1943, when she was deported to Auschwitz-Birkenau with her parents. A few days after her arrival, Schlesinger remembered, "a call went out for a photographer at roll call. I went forward to give my number, telling them that I was a photographer." Impressed with her record working at Foto-Atelier Binder, which had been one of the best-known photography studios in Berlin, SS-Obersturmbannfuhrer Dr. Hans Joachim Caesar picked Schlesinger to be the main photographer in the plant-breeding Kommando at Auschwitz-Rajsko. The subcamp of Auschwitz-Rajsko had been designed for the production of agricultural labor on an SS farm, including gardening and experimental cultivation of the rubber plant. Assisted by the Polish prisoner and filmmaker Wanda Jakubowska, Schlesinger photographed the stages of rubber plant manufacturing research ordered by Heinrich Himmler and carried out by Caesar on Rajsko grounds. She attributed the presence of photography in the camp to the self-indulgent egotism that characterized many of the men in the SS. "It is hard to believe that a photographer would be needed in a place like Auschwitz," she wrote in her 1992 memoir. "But one has to understand that SS men like Caesar lived like little kings in their kingdom of Auschwitz."[57] For Schlesinger, photography was a luxury that SS men like Caesar used to bolster their own power and prestige. But it was also something they could not do themselves. In Schlesinger's case, officials like Caesar were willing to rely even on Jewish prisoners to carry out photographic work, indicating a certain dependence on those who possessed the photographic knowledge they revered. This would ultimately save Schlesinger's life. Both Inge Schlesinger and Elisabeth von Stengel survived the Holocaust and reconnected in Switzerland after the war.[58]

Back at the Erkennungsdienst, the prisoners chosen for work in the service typically performed darkroom and archival tasks. Inside the photographic identification service was a studio for composing and taking pictures, a darkroom for developing them, and a printing and retouching area for perfecting the finished products. Major photographic supply companies like Agfa, Zeiss Ikon, and Leica stocked Erkennungsdienst shelves with cameras, lenses, tripods, easels, film, and paper.[59] The equipment SS men plundered from prisoners upon their arrival at the camps also proved useful in photo service operations. According to Wilhelm Brasse, at Auschwitz "a precision machinist in the Kommando fixed up the damaged cameras that Jews discarded on the [entrance] ramp. The abandoned cameras often lay in the mud for some time. The machinist cleaned them and fixed them up. Some SS men received those cameras later as a reward. And there were a lot of those repaired cameras left behind in the *Erkennungsdienst.*" Brasse failed to grasp that SS men stole these cameras from Jews who had been misled about where they were going.[60] They were not voluntarily "abandoned" or "discarded." But as Brasse's account shows, stripping Jews of their cameras was as much a feature of the concentration camp system as it had been during the early years of Nazi terror and dispossession between 1933 and 1938. Overall, prisoners working in the Erkennungsdienst were prohibited from taking pictures. Instead, they developed, printed, filed, and copied all official photographs for the camp archive. The case of Brasse, who photographed Auschwitz prisoners as well as SS men for their passport photos, is exceptional in this regard.[61]

The labor and resources to be found in the Erkennungsdienst prompted SS men to use the service to pursue a wide variety of personal photography. The prisoner-photographer Georges Angéli remembered the photo service at Buchenwald becoming an unofficial photo shop that the SS used to their benefit.[62] SS men went to the Erkennungsdienst to sit for portraits, compile personal albums, and develop the photos they wanted to send home. Prisoner-photographer Wilhelm Brasse recalled: "Now with the opportunity of being photographed in [the] camp, the SS men no longer needed to go anywhere because everything was right here. Word must have gone around that I was a good photographer and knew how to make real portraits, because a great many SS men were coming in for photos."[63] Several personal albums created in camps like Mauthausen, Buchenwald, and Auschwitz by high-ranking SS officers testify to the kind of private photography outsourced to the camp photo service and created using prisoner labor. One example is the album made in 1943 for Hermann Pister, then the commandant of Buchenwald, as a comprehensive inventory of the camp and its facilities. Prisoners forced to work in the Erkennungsdienst took the pictures, and the album itself was designed and compiled by forced laborers in the camp's bookbinding department. Upon liberation, a prisoner took the album from the camp and handed it over to the Musée de la Résistance et de la Déportation in Besançon, France.[64] Another example is the photo album created by Karl Koch, commandant of Buchenwald and other camps, and his wife, Ilse, between 1938 and 1941 for their son Artwin. Some of the pictures were taken by the Koch family. Karl Koch forced prisoners in the bookbinding Kommando to produce the album in the warehouse workshops. After the pictures were chosen, a prisoner in the photo department labeled the individual album pages and provided small drawings. The Koch album would be used as evidence by the American prosecution in the Buchenwald trial in Dachau in 1947.[65]

Prisoners' proximity to the volume of official and unofficial photography produced through the Erkennungsdienst troubled camp commandants, who worried that prisoners would circulate these photographs beyond camp walls. In addition to warning SS men about the risks involved in creating and circulating unauthorized photographs, a subject addressed in chapter 4 of this book, SS officers routinely threatened to kill prisoners if any one of them handled or distributed any potentially incriminating photographic material without permission. At Mauthausen, Francisco Boix remembered the SS photographer Karl Schulz warning him not to tell anyone about the pictures; if he did, all prisoners working in the photo service would be "liquidated" in retaliation.[66] At Auschwitz, too, prisoners working in the photography department vividly remembered the day when Gestapo chief Max Grabner ordered the whole group to assemble and announced that if any photograph ever made its way outside the Erkennungsdienst, they would all be shot.[67]

Getting caught copying or distributing any photographs made through the Erkennungsdienst could indeed be fatal. This was the case for Rudolf "Rudi" Opitz, a thirty-one-year-old German political prisoner who had been arrested for treason as a Social Democrat in August 1935 and sentenced to three years at Dachau before his transfer to Buchenwald in 1938. Because of his background in professional photography, the SS assigned Opitz for work in the photo service. During his time there, he managed to collect negatives depicting hangings and executions that had been created to document all "unnatural deaths" taking place in the camp. Opitz gathered these and planned to show them to the public after his release. On the day he was scheduled to leave the camp, however, a guard searched him and discovered the collection of negatives hidden inside a framed photograph Opitz claimed he was bringing back for his wife. Opitz was subsequently locked up and beaten, resulting in his death on August 7, 1939, which SS officers falsely registered in camp records as a suicide by hanging.[68] Since it appeared that Opitz had acted alone, the other prisoner-workers were spared. Georges Angéli would take the role in the photo department once filled by Opitz when he arrived in Buchenwald four years later.

Despite these daily threats, camp survivors acknowledged that working in the photo service was a privileged position. SS officers typically chose non-Jewish prisoners for work in the service precisely because of the improved living conditions to be found there. Working in the photo service also increased prisoners' chances of survival. "Compared to other comrades" at Buchenwald, Angéli reflected, "I was aware of the privilege I had, without having done anything. I benefited from special treatment in the photo service."[69] Other prisoners credited their work in the photo service with access to better living conditions and food. When SS officers were particularly happy with the prints prisoners made for them, they offered "gifts" of bread or sausage and cheese, which the prisoners then shared. As Wilhelm Brasse recalled, "We were lucky because we were able to organize extra food for ourselves and we made something like breakfast." Brasse remembered several instances "when [SS-Unterscharführer Schebeck] picked up [a] picture, he waited for the right moment when my boss was out of sight and earshot and he asked me if I could make him an enlargement of his family portraits."[70] Brasse boldly demanded that Schebeck give him bread and margarine in exchange for the enlargements. At Auschwitz-Rajsko, Inge Schlesinger, too, remembered using her position as a photographer to acquire materials that would make everyday life for the prisoners more bearable: "Since I was able to ask for supplies in the photo lab, I ordered items that would be useful for all of us in other ways [iron, electric heater, retouching easel, wristwatch]. . . . [I]f we were lucky and obtained some newspaper, which was a crime, it was safest to read it in the darkroom. I had told the SS that they had to knock before entering since either the film or the paper would get spoiled. They all complied with my rule."[71] Relying once again on SS men's lack of technical knowledge, Schlesinger seized the opportunity presented by the officers' reverence for photographic expertise to acquire certain resources that would not otherwise have been available to her.

Their proximity to Erkennungsdienst records prompted some prisoner-workers to compile photograph collections of their own. Their efforts mirrored broader attempts by concentration camp inmates to compile as much information as possible about life in the camps. Prisoners created visual and written evidence of their own experiences by making drawings and paintings or composing secret reports, letters, and diaries.[72] When possible, they also gathered official documentation testifying to camp operations. Prisoners who had privileged access to camp records stole or transcribed official SS papers. That had been the case, for instance, for prisoners like the Sachsenhausen inmate Emil Büge, a writer from Stettin, Germany who was sent to Sachsenhausen in 1939 as a political prisoner. Between late 1939 and spring 1943, Büge used his position as a clerk in the political department to copy Gestapo records documenting individual and group prisoner executions on wafer-thin paper, which he hid in his eyeglasses case.[73]

Prisoners secretly printed, copied, and hid as many photographs as they could that identified crimes carried out in the camps as well as key Nazi perpetrators. At Mauthausen, prisoner-photographer Antonio García made extra copies of all the photographs that passed through the service and hid them in the ceiling behind a wooden beam. Stefan Grabowski and Franciso Boix would assist García in these efforts upon their own arrival at Mauthausen. They focused on those photos taken by the SS photographers Paul Ricken and Fritz Kornacz between 1941 and 1943 which showed executions and other atrocities against inmates and Soviet prisoners of war.[74] At Buchenwald, too, Georges Angéli copied and hid the photos of dead prisoners that SS photographers had been taking for camp records on "unnatural" deaths. "When I was doing prints," he remembered, "I saw pictures of executions or deaths that I printed in duplicate and hid. I have some showing the dead in a transport. They had traveled naked and were photographed on arrival, before going to the crematorium, where a number was written on their foreheads to recognize them. I have another of a Russian with a bullet in the neck."[75]

Some Erkennungsdienst prisoner-workers solicited nearby residents to help them preserve the photos. To take one particularly astounding example, the Czech prisoner Karel Kasak relied on a local German photographer to develop and hide the official and personal photographs SS personnel at Dachau instructed him to develop. Born on July 6, 1927, Maria Seidenberger was the second child of Georg and Katharina Seidenberger and grew up in Hebertshausen, where her father was a beekeeper. The family was Catholic and had Social Democratic as well as anti-Nazi sympathies. In 1944 Maria was working for the Soennecken & Company photo lab near Dachau.[76] One day Kasak was assigned to photograph flowers outside the entrance to Dachau, which is where he met her. Kasak believed he could trust Maria when he learned about her family's left-wing political inclinations.[77] He noted in his diary: "The little Seidenberger is a seventeen-year-old photo lab assistant. She works at a large photography company in Munich. The girl is mature and smart for her age, with a natural intelligence and, above all, politically reliable, as is Mr. Seidenberger, a former Social Democrat, and his wife, a lively anti-Nazi, socialist-thinking countrywoman. [Maria] agreed to develop and enlarge my photographs, even those of illegal origin like photos of the prisoners and buildings in the camp."[78] Seidenberger stored his photographs as well as letters from other Dachau prisoners in her family's beehive. The photos she hid for Kasak show his fellow prisoners, Dachau camp buildings, and a hanged Soviet partisan. During the final weeks of the war, she also secretly photographed the death march from Buchenwald to Dachau from inside her home in Hebertshausen. One photograph shows her mother, Katharina, distributing potatoes to the prisoners. After the war, Seidenberger accompanied Kasak back to Czechoslovakia before returning to Hebertshausen in 1959.[79]

Other prisoners even managed to photograph the camp grounds on their own. One example consists of two clandestine images taken by the Polish prisoner Jerzy Tomaszewski at the Cieszanów labor camp in Poland. The photos show an SS guard beating a prisoner as three other SS guards and a crowd of several dozen fellow prisoners look on.[80] At Buchenwald, Georges Angéli discovered in the attic of the photo department a box of cameras that had been confiscated from newly arrived prisoners and took one to photograph the camp. According to Angéli, since it was a Sunday, most of the camp SS men were absent. He solicited the help of three fellow prisoners to shield him from view as he snapped his pictures. "One Sunday afternoon, June 1944," Angéli recounted,

I decided to take photographs in the camp and came back from the laboratory with the camera wrapped in newspaper. I asked my Belgian comrade José Fosty to serve as a screen and Raymond Montégut and André Maes to follow us from afar and possibly distract attention [from us]. The camera was wrapped in a newspaper that I had torn at the location of the lens. I held the package under my arm or on my stomach and pointed it, without having to look in the viewfinder, at what I wanted to photograph. I had also torn the newspaper to reach the winding wheel that I turned to make the next shot.[81]

Angéli managed to take twelve photographs of the camp, which depict fellow prisoners assembled in the "little camp" at Buchenwald and in front of Block 46, where medical experiments were conducted.[82]

Prisoners who had no connection to the Erkennungsdienst used photography for similar purposes if they could. The best-known example is the group of four photographs made in August 1944 by prisoners in the Auschwitz Sonderkommando unit who were responsible for disposing of the bodies of gas chamber victims.[83] Alberto Errera, a Greek Jewish naval officer, took the pictures with the help of fellow inmates David Szmulewski and Stanisław Jankowski. Jankowski recalled: "Midway through 1944 we decided to take pictures secretly to record our work. I do not remember precisely all the details, but we managed to get a camera. [Alberto] quickly took out his camera, pointed it toward a heap of burning bodies, and pressed the shutter."[84] Alfred Wóycicki later testified during the Frankfurt Auschwitz trials that he had been the one who secretly developed the film using the darkroom at the Auschwitz Erkennungsidenst.[85] The film was then smuggled out of the camp in a toothpaste tube through the Polish resistance network. Shortly afterwards, Errera was killed trying to escape. In October 1944 at Ravensbrück, a Polish prisoner, Joanna Szydłowska, took a series of clandestine photographs documenting the arrival of a women's transport from Warsaw following the suppression of the Polish Home Army uprising in August. She had traded a piece of bread for a camera with one of the women on the transport who was about to be registered as a new prisoner. After Szydłowska and her fellow prisoners Maria Kusmierczuk and Barbara Pietrzyk had their legs mutilated during sulfanilamide and bone experiments conducted in Ravensbrück, they took pictures showing their injuries. Szydłowska, Kusmierczuk, and Pietrzyk were three of the seventy-four Polish victims experimented on at the camp, dubbed "rabbits" by the SS personnel carrying out the experiments, likening them to laboratory animals used for medical testing.[86] The women discarded the camera but hid the film in their barracks, where it was discovered and taken to France by a French prisoner, Germaine Tillion, upon liberation on April 23, 1945.[87] Tillion had herself hidden a separate roll of film. "I also managed to hide a roll of undeveloped film showing the gangrenous legs of the schoolchildren who had been the subjects of Dr. Karl Gebhardt's experimental operations. I had kept the film in my pocket since January 21, 1944, always wrapped in scraps of filthy cloth to avoid its attracting attention during searches," Tillion wrote in her 1975 memoir.[88] At Dachau, moreover, the Czech prisoner Rudolf Cisar took clandestine photographs as well. Cisar had arrived at Dachau from Mauthausen in November 1942 and was assigned to serve as a nurse in the infirmary. During the spring of 1943, using a camera he had managed to smuggle into the camp, he made a series of photographs depicting prisoners and deportees standing outside awaiting medical treatment. He also took several photographs portraying an execution but was forced by an unidentified person to destroy the negatives before he was able to circulate this information beyond camp walls.[89] Inmates had been expressly forbidden to photograph any deaths or executions in the camps unless explicitly authorized to do so, and Cisar risked his life as well as the lives of his fellow prisoners by disobeying. Had the person who made him destroy the photographs been less tolerant, he likely would have been executed for his actions.

For those prisoners who put their lives on the line by creating photographs of their own, it was the very act of taking pictures rather than the pictures themselves that constituted resistance. Resistance, as the Holocaust survivor and historian Nechama Tec has argued, included all activities "motivated by the desire to thwart, limit, undermine, or end the exercise of oppression over the oppressed."[90] By taking photographs, prisoners aimed to capture, publicize, and stop the violence and suffering that characterized everyday life in the camps. "If I made these pictures and stole others," Angéli recalled, "it was in the hope of being released and giving testimony."[91] The rest of the world, however, was concerned primarily with the images they created. The clandestine nature of their photography obscured much of what they were trying to show. Angéli made one of the photographs in his collection in order to depict the crematorium on Buchenwald grounds, a focus he signaled in the caption, "La Dernière Étape [The Last Stage]: Le Crématoire (juin 44)." On the right-hand side of the photograph are blurred figures lying in the grass, one of whom appears to be a child leaning over an adult. According to Angéli, their presence gave the wrong impression of the camp as a place where prisoners could lounge around and sunbathe rather than one where they were routinely beaten and worked to death. So Angéli retouched the photograph to remove the figures in the grass and show only the crematorium.[92] The hasty composition and consequent blurriness of his photographs not only prevented a clear understanding of his intentions but also threatened to undermine the seriousness of the subject he was trying to capture. It is perhaps a function of the mixed messages he worried about conveying that there was little widespread interest in the collection until the 1990s, long after Angéli's first attempts to show the pictures to the public.

The records prisoners created and preserved would be even more valuable following the chaotic evacuation phase of the camp system. In response to major Allied victories in Italy and France as well as the Soviet entry into German territory, the Nazis emptied one concentration camp after another between the spring of 1944 and the beginning of 1945. The SS pushed all remaining prisoners from camps on the front line to those located farther west, killing most of them along the way on death marches.

As SS personnel destroyed the remaining prisoners, they also tried to destroy all incriminating evidence of the camp system. That included the bodies of hundreds of thousands of victims as well as written documents and photographs.[93] The war itself occasionally accomplished this, as was the case when a British air strike destroyed the photo identification service archive at Buchenwald in August 1944. In camps elsewhere, however, SS men burned the documents and photographs they had spent years creating and gathering, including those recording all "unnatural deaths" and prisoner identification photos. At Mauthausen, when commandant Frank Ziereis received the order to destroy all the negatives, he instructed SS photographer Paul Ricken to complete the destruction process. It took three days for Ricken to destroy the entire camp archive, which he ultimately reported having done successfully.[94] The same was true as Soviet troops approached Auschwitz in January 1945, when Bernhard Walter frantically called to Wilhelm Brasse as he pulled up next to him on his motorcycle, "Brasse, *Ivan kommt*! Destroy and burn all the photos, documents, everything!"[95] Walter told him to continue burning until he had erased every trace of the camp political department, then rode away. As he did, he warned Brasse that he would return the following day to verify that his orders had been properly carried out. But Walter never came back, and six days later, Soviet forces liberated the remaining prisoners at Auschwitz.

Many of the photographs produced in the Erkennungsdienst survived only because of the efforts made by prisoners to save them. Prisoners were careful to store the collections they gathered themselves. Angéli, for instance, had stashed film from the camera he used to take his twelve pictures of Buchenwald in a box, which he hid under the stairs of his barracks. After the photo department was bombed, Angéli's collection was the only photographic record to survive. "The day after our release," he remembered, "I recovered my box, and I kept an eye on it until repatriation without telling anyone what was inside."[96] Prisoners were also careful to preserve the photographs that had been filed in Erkennungsdienst archives. After Bernhard Walter instructed Wilhelm Brasse to destroy all documents held in the Political Department, Brasse and his assistant Bronisław Jureczek purposefully sabotaged the destruction process to save the photos. Jureczek had been sent to Auschwitz as a Polish political prisoner as well, arrested for belonging to a secret Polish organization in Silesia and for listening to the radio. Jureczek spoke fluent German, which in addition to his photographic knowledge may have played some role in his selection for the photo service. "At almost the last moment we were ordered to burn all the negatives and photographs which were in the Erkennungsdienst," Brasse remembered. "First, we put wet photographic paper and photographs and negatives into a tile stove in such large numbers as to block the exhaust outlet. This ensured that when we set fire to the materials in the stove, only the photographs and negatives near the stove door would be consumed, and that the fire would later die out due to the lack of air." After the war ended, he continued, "I learned that our assumption had been right, and that a high percentage of the photographs and negatives had survived and found their way into the right hands. Moreover, under the pretext of haste, I deliberately scattered a number of photographs and negatives in the rooms of the lab. I knew that with the hurried evacuation of the camp, no one would have time to gather them all and that something would survive."[97] Many pictures did. As the camp emptied, survivors like Erwin Olszówka remembered seeing "photographs from the archive of the Erkennungsdienst scattered all over camp streets."[98]

Although it was defined by the Nazis as a social practice reserved for members of the *Volksgemeinschaft*, "true" Germans inadvertently placed photography back in the hands of some they had deemed unfit to participate in it before arriving at the camps. Ultimately the esteem Nazi authorities had for photographic expertise provided experienced prisoners with unique opportunities for survival and resistance. The exceptional case of Inge Schlesinger aside, however, that esteem was still determined by Nazi racial ideology and, once it began in the summer of 1941, the Holocaust. The opportunity to work in official photography in the camps, whether at the Erkennungsdienst or in any other capacity, was typically extended only to non-Jewish prisoners. With their help, SS personnel made and archived pictures of everything from the construction of camp crematoria to the prisoners themselves, whether dead or alive. Some of those photographs made their way beyond camp walls thanks to the efforts of prisoners who used their unique capacity as workers in the Erkennungsdienst to gather official evidence documenting the violence and cruelty of the camps—evidence that SS and Wehrmacht soldiers largely did not include in their personal collections.

As we shall see, whether in the Wehrmacht, the Waffen-SS, or from their posts as SS camp guards, German soldiers understood sharing photographs and compiling photo albums with their families as both a medium of intimate communication and an expression of patriotic duty. On the war front, photography allowed these men to reaffirm their commitment to their fellow soldiers and families, which the Nazis viewed as fundamental to the ability of Germany to win the war. Focused as they were on enacting these ideas, soldiers largely omitted atrocities in the photographs they sent home for their albums. For them, photography was never about exhaustive documentation. Instead, it was about reifying certain narratives about themselves that would help them justify both war and genocide.

Part II

CHAPTER 4

Fabricating Innocence

When the American journalist William Shirer looked out the window of his hotel room in Berlin in 1939, he saw that "thousands of German soldiers on leave were here to rubberneck. I watched them from outside my hotel, staring at the Brandenburg Gate, the Reichstag, and snapping photographs. The Germans, I'm convinced, are the most camera-mad people in the world. I have yet to meet one on the street without a camera slung on his or her shoulder."[1] Shirer could not have known at the time that part of the reason why so many people had cameras had to do with the efforts of Nazi officials to promote photography and make it available to as many non-Jewish Germans as possible—especially soldiers. By the time World War II began in 1939, Nazi authorities had made photography accessible to more Germans than ever before. They also taught Germans two important lessons about photography: first, that only "Aryan" Germans had the right to practice photography, and second, that practicing photography together would connect Germans in a single racial community. Both lessons would acquire new significance as Germany's armed forces went to war and helped carry out the Holocaust.

Wehrmacht soldiers deployed across Europe from 1939 to 1945 witnessed and helped perpetrate unspeakable crimes against prisoners of war, civilians, and Jews. And while they sometimes photographed their atrocities against those deemed "enemies" of the Third Reich, they much more frequently took pictures illustrating leisure, sociability, and comradeship on the war front. Recent scholarship has tended to ignore these photographs, however, perhaps because their banality is perceived as being uninteresting or redundant among historians.[2] But that banality is important, not only because it confirms that the people capable of such crimes were indeed "ordinary men," but also because soldiers themselves used such photographs to craft narratives about one another and the war that helped justify it—as well as the violence and genocide endemic to it—to themselves, their families, and their comrades.[3] Soldiers more often used photography to tell stories about themselves than about their victims. The narratives they created established them as devoted husbands, brave soldiers, honorable patriots, and decent men who fought a civilized fight to protect their families as well as the entire German nation, and they propagated them in their diaries and letters as well.[4] Those portrayals ultimately helped soldiers and their families make sense of war and genocide while justifying both as necessary for their survival.[5] They aligned as well with institutional formulations establishing the German soldier as the model of wartime diligence and duty. Soldiers' photographs allowed them, then, to portray themselves as espousing all the qualities the Nazi regime demanded of its regular armed forces, qualities that they had been instructed by state and military authorities to express in pictures ever since the mid-1930s.

Promoting the use of photography to unite Germans between war and home fronts had characterized Nazi state and corporate efforts since Germany began to remilitarize after 1933.[6] The Reich Propaganda Ministry was already thinking about popular photography in military terms when it began lobbying Germany's "army" of millions of amateur photographers to invest their time and resources in the photographic industry early on in 1933.[7] Major German camera manufacturers like Agfa, Zeiss Ikon, Voigtländer, and Leica started gearing their products and advertisements toward soldiers. Even the American competitor Eastman Kodak followed this marketing strategy in publications and catalogs circulated from branches in Berlin and Stuttgart.[8] In June 1936 Agfa's amateur magazine *Photoblätter* dedicated an entire issue to "photography in our military time." The issue specifically addressed soldiers as amateur photographers, proclaiming, "The modern soldier is not only familiar with weapons, no—he takes photographs!"[9] Camera advertisements featured in the official propaganda newspaper for the Wehrmacht advised: "Don't forget to pack your camera! Being ready is everything, even for the amateur. Be prepared!"[10] Camera retailers packaged war as an adventure to be remembered and chronicled for family members. Zeiss Ikon touted the merits of photographing new places for soldiers' loved ones back home, arguing that they would otherwise be unable to see such things on their own. "There are millions of people who have never been told what it looks like in other countries, among other peoples, and above the clouds if images did not give them these impressions," one advertisement declared. "Everyone experiences and sees every day an endless number of interesting things and everyone can take pictures of them themselves."[11] Rearmament, it seemed, was as much about building up a supply of cameras as it was about stockpiling guns. By September 1936, members of the Hamburg photographic crafts association were crediting a "revival of the photographer's craft" to German rearmament.[12]

Production of cameras, film, and photo paper increased in anticipation of war. Manufacturers designed the latest camera models to appeal to soldiers. Each new model was lighter, smaller, and more durable than the last, an ideal combination for carrying in a soldier's kit. Camera distributors (*Photohändler*) typically recommended the 35 mm models produced by Zeiss Ikon and Leica as best suited for soldiers' use. The Zeiss Super-Ikonta II and Leica III were particularly well regarded in the industry, as they were small, slim enough to fit in a uniform pocket, inexpensive, and reliable.[13] Leica sold 311,000 of its new compact model I/III cameras between 1930 and 1939.[14] To keep pace with its competitors, Agfa released its Billy Clack "soldier camera" model in 1937. Crafted from a new synthetic material and encased in leather-like armor, the Billy Clack was supposedly indestructible.[15] Production of photographic film continued to increase steadily throughout the war, peaking in 1940, when Agfa sold 26 million rolls of film compared to the 14.6 million rolls sold in 1938.[16]

The Second World War began in September 1939. After Germany had successfully annexed Austria and occupied Czechoslovakia without any opposition from the Allied powers, Britain and France finally declared war on Germany when Hitler's troops invaded Poland under the pretext of a defensive maneuver. As hundreds of thousands of German soldiers left home for active duty, they brought their cameras with them. A quarter of the 10 million soldiers who would be stationed in the east already owned cameras.[17]

The outbreak of war compelled Nazi authorities to clarify the purpose of photography. For one thing, taking pictures strengthened the bonds among soldiers by facilitating sociability during leisure time. Camera and photo supply retailers reinforced this message in their advertising. Agfa, for example, urged soldiers to create and share souvenir pictures (*Erinnerungsbilder*) documenting everyday life with their comrades to strengthen camaraderie. In addition to promoting their physical health and hygiene with advertisements for Nivea shaving cream and Sebald's hair tonic, publications of the Wehrmacht High Command (Oberkommando der Wehrmacht, OKW) encouraged soldiers to photograph one another to pass the time while stationed at the front, stressing that the men should nurture their emotional as well as their physical health with books, musical instruments, and cameras. Articles and camera supply ads from the period stressed that the very act of photographing one another individually or in groups during travel or leisure time strengthened the bonds between soldiers and created lasting souvenirs of their time spent together. Showing one another photos from home, too, facilitated male bonding. An Agfa ad from a 1940 issue of *Die Wehrmacht* exemplified this. It features two children playing with their dolls, faces turned upward and gazing into the distance, captioned "Ein Gruß von uns beiden [A greeting from both of us]. In the form of a photo, the soldier carries home with him. He can proudly show his comrades: My children!"[18] Showing one another photos of their children demonstrated who soldiers were and what they had waiting for them back home when the war ended.

Military officials and camera retailers further envisioned that wartime photography would bridge the distance between soldiers and their families at home. Until soldiers could be reunited with their loved ones, officials urged them to curate their own archives from the front by including photographs in letters home. Exchanging letters between soldiers and their families was central to the German armed forces' ability to keep fighting because it perpetuated soldiers' relationships and offered individuals on both fronts hope for an imminent reunion and a better future.[19] Photographs were a crucial aspect of these exchanges, for they allowed recipients to see their loved ones rather than only read their words. The Wehrmacht High Command used the military press to show soldiers how taking pictures could boost morale at home by bringing their experiences to life before their loved ones' eyes. Even more important, pictures could show their families that they were healthy and doing well.[20] An advertisement for Agfa film featured in a March 1940 issue of the official OKW magazine *Die Wehrmacht* shows a soldier eating from his mess kit with the caption "I'm fine!"[21] Another Agfa ad shows an elderly woman looking at photos presumably sent to her by her son with the caption "Every good message brings joy. A picture brings even more happiness. In a photo, the one you love is there before your eyes. Front and *Heimat* are close in pictures. Whatever you photograph, create lifelike pictures with Agfa film."[22] Other companies like Fotowerke Dr. C. Schleussner in Frankfurt emphasized group sociability as part of what it meant to be "doing well."[23] During the war, the firm repeatedly released advertisements touting the wartime benefits of photography as a community-building exercise between fronts. An ad for Adox Film in the June 1940 issue of *Die Wehrmacht* presents a cartoon drawing of six soldiers on leisure time. Two of them are playing an accordion and a harmonica, three others are listening, and a fourth is photographing the scene. All six of them are smiling and smoking contentedly. The advertisement's next panel depicts the home front, where a postal worker delivers the soldier's snapshots of this scene to his family. Women and children gather around to view what appears to be four or five photos in the hands of the soldier's wife. The entire exchange is bound together by the caption "When the front takes pictures . . . the homeland [*Heimat*] rejoices."[24]

Adox ran similar versions of this ad using other leisure scenes. One shows a soldier photographing his comrades swimming in a lake with their horses, and the next panel features the soldier's parents and wife looking at the pictures while seated at their dining room table.[25] Another depicts a soldier having his portrait taken by two fellow soldiers. In the next frame, the postal worker comically enlists the help of a dog to deliver the photo to the soldier's wife, who happily greets its arrival.[26] Another shows a shirtless soldier shaving while standing in a stream. Two other soldiers can be seen nearby, one of whom takes

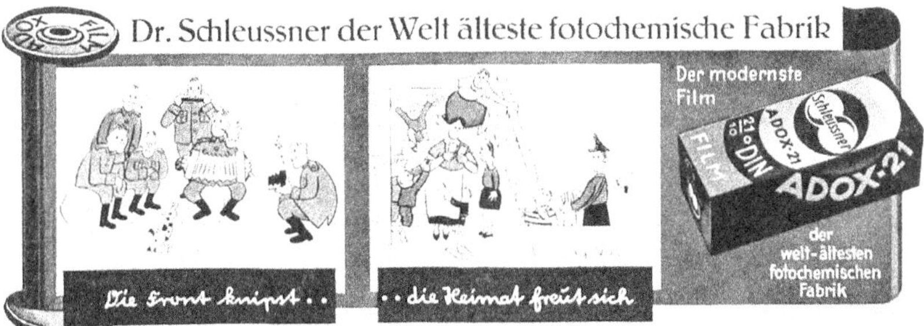

FIGURE 1.   "The front takes pictures . . . the homeland rejoices." Adox film advertisement in *Die Wehrmacht* 4, no. 15 (June 17, 1940): 17.

pictures while the other milks a cow. The next panel shows a group of women, a child, and a man in a hayfield enjoying a meal and sharing the pictures.[27] Adox also ran ads in which civilians at home take pictures and send them to soldiers at the front. In one, a woman takes a picture of her son posing as a scarecrow in a field as birds approach, mistaking him for an actual scarecrow. The next panel of the ad shows the soldier looking through those photos in a surprisingly tranquil setting; he is shirtless, sprawled out on the grass as his fellow soldiers swim together nearby.[28] These kinds of advertisements encouraged soldiers to see photography primarily as a social exercise that could help maintain their relationships with loved ones back home. Highly selective subject matter that showed families only the most idyllic scenes of military service was at the core of that sociability.

State and military officials encouraged civilians on the home front to use photographs to boost soldiers' morale as well. Already in 1934, Major Wilhelm Reibert's popular manual for German soldiers included a section advising soldiers how to keep their pictures from home arranged neatly in their barracks.[29] But it was a task that fell to women as well. While officials instructed men to pursue the photography of adventure, military pursuits, and boisterous social gatherings, they urged women to pursue photography that emphasized quiet domestic life. After the Nazi takeover, there was a noted increase in trade periodicals insisting that women were best suited to domestic photography, a genre that critics argued was particularly important as the war continued. One correspondent for *Photoblätter* declared:

> Above all, women have to put aside that certain shyness toward technology, not to the extent that it would masculinize them, but only to the extent that they absolutely need this technology to reveal their personal idiosyncrasies to the rest of the world. . . . An image can often clarify better than handwriting and give us a deep impression of the creator's inner experience. As a result, the photographing woman becomes the man's teacher again, because she teaches him how beautiful her world is and how right the woman's experiences can be for the womanly sphere he has paid less attention to.[30]

It goes without saying that this assessment of women's relationship to photography was misinformed. To claim that women were "shy" when it came to photographic technology was undoubtedly a pointed rejection of those women who had already taken up hobby photography or achieved remarkable success in their own right as professional photographers during the imperial and Weimar years in travel, fashion, and portrait photography.[31] Women's "natural talents" were now said to reside in the home, a notion framed from 1939 on as a meaningful way for them to contribute to the war effort.[32] Sending pictures documenting

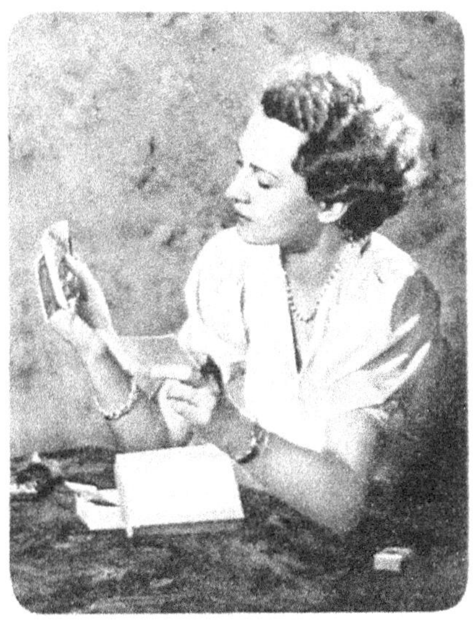

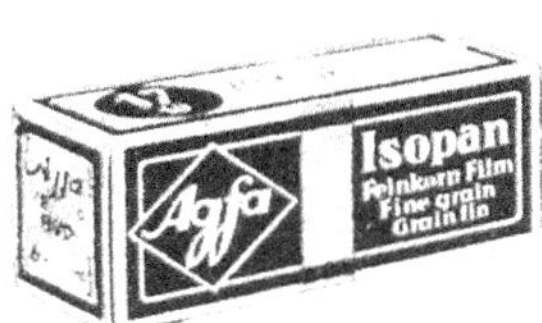

FIGURE 2. "They will give him joy." Agfa film advertisement in *Die Wehrmacht* 4, no. 12 (June 5, 1940): 16.

weddings, birthdays, children, and home interiors would remind soldiers of their lives beyond the war and boost their spirits. Such pictures also served as symbolic links to their fellow *Volksgenossen* and reminders of the normalcy and stability to which they could return after the conflict. A March 1940 Agfa film ad, to take one example, shows a young woman seated at her dining room table examining a box of printed photographs over the caption "They will give him joy. What does he like? What should you send him? Pictures from home are always a bonus. They take up little space, do not cost much and are always pleasing. Well-done photos, however, carry the well-known name: Agfa."[33] Another observer noted how "amateurs take pictures of their homes, women, and children, and now send individual pictures or small, nicely arranged albums to the comrades. Could there be a nicer photographic task today?"[34]

Military authorities likewise considered photo albums to be essential in connecting Germans at war to those at home. The OKW began distributing blank albums titled "My Service Years" (Meine Dienstzeit) and "War Memories" (Kriegserinnerungen) to soldiers for their families to fill with photographs they sent from the front. The albums featured colorful tassels and leather bindings with small helmets attached to or painted on the front cover.

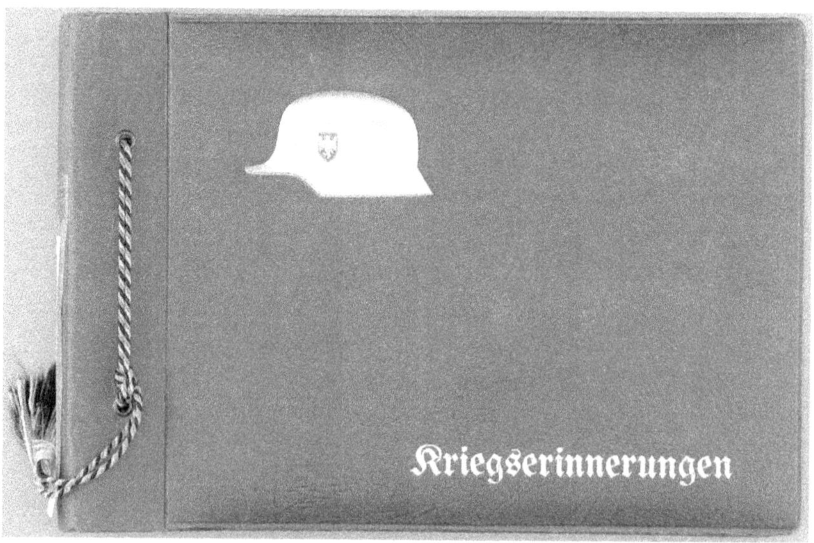

FIGURE 3. Cover of an album compiled by an unidentified soldier, "Kriegserinnerungen, 1940–1941." José María Castañé Collection of War-Related Photograph Albums, ca. 1920–1950 (MS Span 183), vol. 56, Houghton Library, Harvard University.

OKW officials noted that these albums provided opportunities for soldiers to create the "perfect souvenirs" to remember their military service.[35] Album manufacturers introduced new designs on a yearly basis. In the spring of 1940, an album designer sent Reich Marshall Hermann Göring a recent prototype. In the letter that accompanied it, he reminded Göring "how many hours there are in German families, in which the grandfather, father, brother, uncle, etc. tell of their soldiers' time in war and peace. The whole family and guests eagerly listen. But no one, even with the greatest imagination, can imagine everything as it really was. What did you have to remember war and duty? Military papers, yellowed photographs, reserve sticks, beer steins, cartridge cases, or unexploded shells." Only photograph albums, the designer believed, could properly preserve soldiers' memories to share them with family members. "To remedy this," the letter continued, "I have created a real memento that is of great value not only to the owner but also to his family. It is now up to the soldier himself to make the document that gives exhaustive information about the most important time in the life of the German man. If a soldier falls on the field of honor, the Wehrmacht photo album is the thank-you to the family." The album designer further revealed to Göring that wartime album-making fundamentally depended on the women in a soldier's family. "Because of the size, the beauty, and the nature of the Wehrmacht photo album," he wrote, "the album is in most cases presented to the soldier during his leave. The album will not be sent to the front. The mother, wife, and so on will begin [it] by gluing in the pictures sent by the soldier."[36] Given the cumbersome size of Wehrmacht-issued albums, the designer acknowledged, soldiers would ideally receive them while at home on leave rather than keeping them at the front. The soldier's mother or wife would then take charge of the album and arrange the pictures he sent her. Many of the photograph albums housed in archives today, then, were carefully arranged, captioned, and preserved not by the soldiers who took the pictures but by the women assembling them back in Germany.[37]

Photography could therefore help bring soldiers and civilians alike together to constitute what Nazi officials called the *Kampfgemeinschaft*, or the community of struggle. The act of taking pictures and mailing them, whether to soldiers at the front or back home to family members, reinforced the broader language of state and military authorities, who repeatedly defined proper wartime conduct not only as fulfilling one's military duty in a disciplined way but also as maintaining close ties to fellow soldiers and family members. Joseph Goebbels referred to all

Germans at war and on the home front as members of the same national "family" in a 1940 New Year's Eve speech: "The homeland and the front form a big family as we bid farewell to a year that was full of challenges and historic victories."[38] Despite the challenges, Goebbels implied, Germans remained united by their "familial" ties to one another and their faith in victories both secured and anticipated. Franz Hermann Woweries, chief of the Reich leadership office, elaborated on these same ideas in a widely distributed pamphlet he published that same year. Woweries maintained that among the many core principles of proper conduct for soldiers at war, preserving the ties between soldiers and their loved ones back home was particularly important, because relationships with family and with comrades at the front were in fact inextricably linked. "What you or the man alongside you can no longer do, camaraderie will do for you both," Woweries promised. "From small-scale camaraderie grows large-scale camaraderie. From personal camaraderie grows community, the people's community, the German socialism that is the expression of our faith and the goal of our struggle: joyful people, laughing children, men defending a flourishing people and a powerful Reich, stronger than fate, following the supreme law of the community before the self."[39] According to Woweries, protecting the German people's community was the "supreme law" governing the war and military conduct. Only by forging strong ties with their fellow soldiers and families back home, Woweries argued, could Germany's men in uniform have any hope of carrying on the fight and winning the war.

Nazi authorities were also careful to remind soldiers what *not* to photograph. As early as March 1938, high-ranking officers were commenting on an undisciplined "outbreak" of photography among soldiers. At first it was unauthorized photographs of Adolf Hitler that attracted such apprehension. Hitler was notoriously controlling when it came to who was allowed to photograph him, but military officials found the habit distasteful for other reasons. Then serving as the commander of the German army, Walther von Brauchtisch commented on April 13, 1938, that "it is regrettably noted that uniformed Wehrmacht members as well as individual spectators did not shy away from photographing the Führer during his presence in locations or at special events. Those involved have demonstrated by this outrageous behavior that they lack any sense of military tact."[40] A few months later, Admiral Erich Raeder likewise sent a note to the High Command of the German navy expressing concern about soldiers' incessant picture-taking. "Such behavior is unsoldierly and runs counter to a healthy sense of military tact," Raeder wrote.[41] Left too long to their own devices, soldiers and their cameras jeopardized the self-control and discipline that were supposed to characterize the entire German armed forces.

Admiral Raeder further argued that in carrying a camera, soldiers were behaving like common tourists rather than dignified fighters: "It is not compatible with the exemplary demeanor and appearance of a soldier in uniform that he hang a camera on a strap over his shoulder." He advised unit leaders to be vigilant in punishing observed breaches: "I make it obligatory for all commanders, through education and instruction, to ensure that these exhibitions are abolished, to arouse and sharpen the sense of soldierly appearance within the troops, and to vigorously intervene in case of violations. The appearance, attitude, and uniform of the individual soldier are rightly the standard for [judging] the value of a crew or a troop."[42]

After the fighting began, the OKW confronted new fears that soldiers would accidentally disclose strategic military information through their photographs. Photographic associations and trade periodicals chimed in on this issue as well. In September 1939 *Photofreund* cautioned soldiers that they would have to get permission to take pictures from a company commander, who could always be "trusted to teach what was acceptable" to photograph and what was forbidden. "This is no joke, because the laws against the betrayal of military secrets are equally sharp in Germany and abroad."[43] *Die Foto-Schau* advised a year later: "One can formulate briefly: forbidden are all photographs that may be of use to the enemy. In most cases, not only photographing is forbidden but [also] carrying cameras."[44]

The German invasion of the Soviet Union in the summer of 1941 prompted state and military authorities to remind soldiers and civilians about the purpose of photography. At the end of December 1941, Joseph Goebbels, too, would reiterate how critical a united people's community across both the eastern and western fronts was to the German war effort and any hope of success, declaring that the war itself was "a community task of the front and homeland."[45] Reich propagandists like Walter Tießler saw the family as the most practical means to express the principles at the core of a Nazi *Volksgemeinschaft.* Tießler, who had joined the Nazi Party early in 1924, saw the German people's community as it was broadly conceived as essential in shaping how Germans fought the war. "What are you fighting for, German people, men, women, soldiers?," he asked in a pamphlet published in early 1942. "All tasks we face will be dealt with in accordance with a fundamental principle of the National

Socialist worldview: the people's community." But while the people's community lay at the core of the National Socialist worldview, Tießler argued that the very idea of a national community was most effectively and regularly expressed through the family unit. Ultimately it was family that proved the most important aspect of Germany's wartime community spirit precisely because Germans found it to be an idea with immediate and concrete relevance. "Each worldview has eternal value if we experience it not only at great moments and events but also if it is useful in daily life," he wrote. "Just as we experience the loyalty of the whole people as well as the individual at important moments for the nation, we have also in private life the most varied opportunities to prove our loyalty. We must experience all the great National Socialist concepts within the family. Here each can show whether or not he is serious about his worldview. The essential characteristics of the German racial character, simplicity and modesty, are most visible in family life." Demonstrating that each household took the principles of National Socialism seriously, as Tießler saw it, was as much about racial quality as it was about maintaining good relationships between husbands and wives, parents and children. In this way, Tießler concluded, the family constituted another fundamental locus of National Socialism: "If, therefore, we want to root National Socialism in practical life and preserve it, we can best do this by always keeping in mind a fundamental concept of National Socialism: the family. The family is the eternal wellspring of the people. From it the people are constantly renewed. It is thus one of the most essential requirements for an eternal Germany. Family is the most important individual community within the people's community, for all healthy peoples at all times."[46] Like Franz Woweries, Tießler saw firm family ties as the starting point for a broader communal spirit uniting all Germans who belonged to the *Volksgemeinschaft*. The act of taking and exchanging photographs, then, allowed soldiers and their loved ones to strengthen family bonds as well as the broader "communal spirit" these bonds embodied.

As of the 1941 invasion of the Soviet Union, German authorities were also very careful to detail what was not acceptable to photograph, and in particular what constituted pictures that could potentially be "of use to the enemy." The OKW laid out precise prohibitions on photographs depicting railways, artillery, or distinctive terrain in a 1941–42 Wehrmacht intelligence (Abwehr) report. "Unofficial photography by armed forces personnel is permitted under the watchful eye and responsibility of the leaders of units equipped with armored vehicles," the report began, noting further, however, that "all soldiers of the field army and persons who come under the jurisdiction of the military have to exercise the utmost care when photographing outdoors," and forbidding photos that provided any information on weapons and troop locations. Soldiers were required to submit their photos to the disciplinary supervisors and would have their negatives destroyed if they violated any of these provisions, risking the possibility of "sending the cameras home" for good measure.[47]

The OKW further forbade "any photograph that damages the reputation of the Wehrmacht, as well as recordings of accidents, losses, and bombardment effects."[48] This was a thinly veiled reference to the increasing number of mass shootings of Jews, Soviet civilians, and prisoners of war as the "Holocaust by bullets" began during the summer of 1941. Nazi authorities worried that picture-taking by propaganda photographers or other authorized persons at such scenes would prompt rank-and-file soldiers to do the same, thereby creating indiscipline and disobedience. Moreover, they feared that if soldiers did send home pictures showing abuses or executions, the images could be intercepted and used to bolster Allied propaganda.[49] Cases of unauthorized photography at execution sites had been reported to the High Command, and some of the photographs had already been intercepted by the German military mail service (Feldpost) censor's office. Most often the pictures intercepted by this office showed dead Soviet soldiers or "partisans."[50] On December 21, 1941, the censor's office reported two such incriminating negatives sent from the city of Pleskau in Soviet Russia.[51]

To preempt this behavior, Wehrmacht officers repeatedly issued regulations from July 1941 to 1944 reminding soldiers that the production and distribution of "inappropriate" photographs was forbidden.[52] Above all, the photography bans functioned as threats, since prohibiting photography entirely would jeopardize the boost to morale that Reich and OKW authorities knew photography generally offered to soldiers and their families.[53] The officials circulating these orders guaranteed "utmost severity" and "severe punishment" without ever specifying an exact procedure in part to increase soldiers' fears of the potential consequences.[54] The orders were not, of course, uniformly effective or followed, for some soldiers disobeyed them and took pictures anyway.[55]

But in many cases, these prohibitions were enforced. During the Kaunas pogrom in Lithuania, one soldier took two photographs that showed German troops and Lithuanian collaborators beating Lithuanian Jews to death. He was perhaps acting in response to the fact that soldiers in Einsatzgruppen-A in the rear had been cleared to photograph the proceedings at Kaunas if they could convey that "it was the Lithuanians who carried out the first spontaneous executions of the Jews."[56] As the soldier began to take pictures, he later testified, "just then I was confronted by an officer of the Wehrmacht, who told me that it was not permitted to take photographs of such events. I had to give him my particulars and the name of my unit and he confiscated the camera. I was only able to save the pictures because I had already taken the film out of my camera."[57] During a mass shooting of Jews in Zhitomir, Ukraine, another German soldier who witnessed the incident later filed a report in which he observed that "the bodies fell forward into the pit. Several members of the [Einsatzkommando] photographed the matter, but their undeveloped film was destroyed by an officer."[58]

These official communications about what to photograph and what not to photograph while at war shaped German soldiers' approach to photography as a way to sustain their personal relationships with family back home. That included, on the one hand, the very practice of sending photographs in letters home for the family album and, on the other, the content of the photos. The pictures most soldiers sent home in albums and letters showed men eating, drinking, traveling, and resting together rather than taking part in executions or observing deportations. This highly selective view of their military service was both officially acceptable and personally preferred.

As they invaded Poland and western Europe from September 1939 to 1940 and the Soviet Union in the summer of 1941, Wehrmacht soldiers avidly sent pictures back to their families, prompting one observer to note "how lively photography is on the front."[59] Albert Neuhaus, who owned a delicatessen in Münster before he was drafted into the Wehrmacht, told his wife, Agnes, to "save the pictures for your joy and my memory."[60] Agnes happily did so, telling him, "Your pictures are very nice, I've put them all together in the album."[61] Elisabeth Spemann, too, excitedly thanked her husband, Friedrich, in September 1939 for the photo he sent her. "Another letter came from you today," Elisabeth wrote, "which, of course, I opened immediately. You probably guessed my wish that I wanted to have such a picture! How can I thank you. I'm so happy!"[62] In a 1940 letter to her husband, Ernst, while he was stationed in France, Irene Guicking reminded him that she never tired of seeing pictures of him and hoped to compile them in the album some day with the help of Ernst and their two children. "You must always remember," she wrote, "that I cannot have enough pictures of you. When you get home, we'll glue the pictures together. Yes, that's how we'll do it."[63]

Civilians also continued to send soldiers at the front photographs from home at their request. "I am waiting for letters and pictures, please, in every letter," one soldier wrote.[64] While stationed in the Protectorate of Bohemia and Moravia, Sergeant Hellmuth H. wrote to his wife in 1939: "My parents sent me pictures. I am always happy when I show the adorable children's pictures, which are mostly from you, to someone. You have proven yourself to be a very capable photographer."[65] Corporal Paul Strache, who lived in Berlin until he was drafted into the 50th Infantry Regiment in 1939, wrote his wife in the spring of 1940 from occupied Norway, "If I did not have the pictures, I would not even know how it looks at home."[66] Hans Simon, who at eighteen years old had just left the Reich Labor Service (Reichsarbeitsdienst, RAD) for the Wehrmacht, wrote to his mother early in 1941: "Thank you for the beautiful pictures that now decorate my room. Now I have a piece of home [here]."[67]

Wehrmacht soldiers who sent photographs for their albums back home generally focused on the relationships that mattered most to them according to the *Volksgemeinschaft* framework: fellow soldiers and family members. That approach is embodied by the albums reproduced in this chapter.[68] The first is compiled in an official OKW-issued album titled "Kriegserinnerungen."[69] The album holds fifty-three pages of photos and is divided into sections corresponding to the region where the unidentified soldier was serving. The narrative begins with the soldier's training period and covers his participation in campaigns in France, Poland, and Ukraine before ending abruptly in Soviet Russia in November 1941. The second collection is compiled in another OKW-issued album titled "My Service Years" ("Meine Dienstzeit"). The album, which contains twenty-one pages of roughly one hundred photographs, covers this soldier's participation in the Reich Labor Service in 1938 until he was called up for military service. The album ends with the soldier's recovery in the spa town of Marienbad in the Sudetenland after injuries sustained at Stalingrad in 1942.

Soldiers like the men who compiled these albums would have developed their photographs in two main ways. One was by relying on local photography studios in the villages and cities they occupied. An example of this is the photo studio Fotoris, one of the largest photo shops in central Warsaw. The company was staffed by Poles who had worked in the film and photographic industries before the war began, among them Jerzy Tomaszewski, Mieczysław Kucharski, Włodzimierz Baran, and Andrzej Honowski, and was managed by Ludwik Herbert. During the German occupation of Poland, Fotoris was frequented by all ranks of the German armed forces. Soldiers came in to develop their private pictures of family members and fellow soldiers. "The Germans loved photography," Tomaszewski recalled.[70]

Apart from relying on nearby businesses in occupied eastern and western Europe, soldiers also sent their undeveloped film home for their wives or parents to deliver to their local photo shop. This proved to be an even more convenient method for those who hoped their relatives would arrange the printed pictures in albums that were already in their care. Others requested that the prints be sent back to them. "Please be so good as to send me the picture when it has turned out well," Karl Nünninghoff asked his parents after sending them his film.[71] Berliner Martin Meier, who had been a banker before he was deployed with the 14th Panzer Division, wrote to his wife in the summer of 1940: "I sent the film to Bezee [a photography business in Leipzig] yesterday to develop and make prints. The pictures go to you, you can send them to me then please, you keep the film, you can also settle the bill."[72]

Many of the men sent portraits home to establish for their families their transformation from civilians to soldiers.[73] In September 1940, Lieutenant Willi Betz, who took part in the Polish, French, and Soviet campaigns with the 17th Infantry Division until he was killed in Soviet Russia in November 1941, told his girlfriend, "I was photographed here last week and I am enclosing a picture, the first and most beautiful."[74] Soldiers also hoped to reassure their loved ones back home that however much the war might change them, they remained steadfast in their character and, above all, in their love for their family.

Each of the albums shown in this chapter contains several portraits. The first album, "Kriegserinnerungen," includes a portrait of an unidentified soldier, and the album's likely author, standing "on guard in Warsaw," dressed in full uniform. Another depicts him seated in the doorway of a train car "on the way to France," dressed in full uniform and looking off into the distance as if prepared for the next adventure. The second album, "Meine Dienstzeit," also shows several portraits of the soldier who curated it. In one he is dressed in full uniform, standing on the top of a hill with a mountainscape behind him. Another is a formal studio portrait taken of him while he was in training with the Reich Labor Service in 1938–39. The portrait presents him gazing into the distance, prepared for duty, dressed in Wehrmacht uniform with the RAD symbol on his cap. According to the caption, he had been drafted into the Labor Service on October 1, 1938, and released into military service on March 31, 1939.[75]

Soldiers repeatedly photographed their comrades to commemorate the men in their unit and the experiences they shared together. Many mailed these pictures to their families to reassure them that they were not alone.[76] Klaus Becker, for example, who had been a lawyer until he was drafted into the Wehrmacht in 1940, sent a letter to his wife from Poland in January 1941 in which he included two photographs of soldiers from his unit he seems to have written often to her about. He provided their names and additional details on where the photograph was taken so that she could accurately caption the photos for their album. "Today I received two pictures taken on the day of our loading in Rendsburg at the local train station," Becker wrote. "In the one picture I am together with Paulsen Heide and in the other again with him and Eschenhauer from Vienna, about whom I have told you more often."[77] After reading her husband, Roland's, tales of camaraderie in his unit in his latest letter to her, Hilde Laube replied in the spring of 1941: "Now that I have read this, I have become much calmer in my concern for you. I am not only concerned with your physical well-being—also with the soul. I no longer have to worry about it. You are not alone."[78] Such photographs also functioned for those on the home front as reminders of the men who were fighting on behalf of them and the *Volksgemeinschaft.* Camaraderie was central in German soldiers' ability to keep fighting the war, a sentiment Sergeant Karl Schwegler spoke to when he wrote his girlfriend in the winter of 1939 from Poland, "There are few secrets out here among us; because camaraderie is what binds us together out here."[79]

The "Kriegserinnerungen" album reproduced here, just one of the hundreds that have informed this book, is emblematic of the kinds of photography Wehrmacht soldiers emphasized in their collections. The album is dominated by images of its compiler and his fellow soldiers, particularly during leisure time. One photograph, for example, captioned "A Sunday in Luneville," shows soldiers canoeing with a small dog on a sunny day in France in 1940.[80] The person who took the picture made a point of situating the soldier within the wider landscape of lush trees and calm waters behind him, suggesting an interest in showing soldiers engaged with the natural world in a way that was as much aligned with the desire of the Nazi state to strengthen the Germans' love for "*Heimat* and soil" as it was about how soldiers chose to spend their leisure time. The men look relaxed but contemplative, while

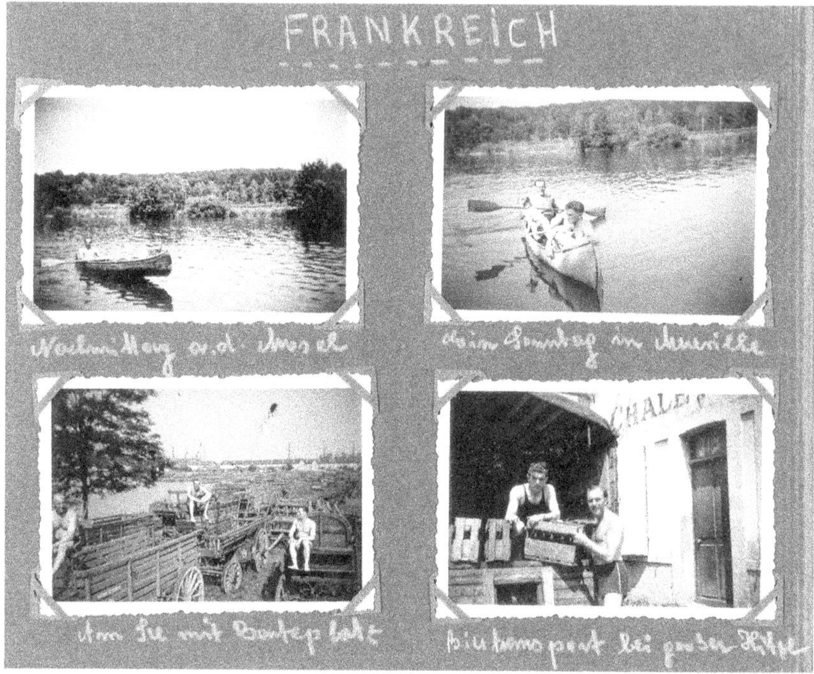

FIGURE 4. Album page with photographs from France, "Kriegserinnerungen, 1940–1941." José María Castañé Collection of War-Related Photograph Albums, ca. 1920–1950 (MS Span 183), vol. 56, Houghton Library, Harvard University.

the dog stands alert, gazing at something in the distance.[81] Engagement with the natural world also manifested itself in scenes emphasizing physical fitness and bodily health.[82] In an effort to portray themselves as striving toward a certain masculine ideal, soldiers routinely displayed their nude bodies in the photographs they sent home, and this album is no exception.[83] A 1940 photo taken in France shows the unidentified soldier wearing only swimming trunks while seated on a hay cart. Another page features a full nude photograph of him apparently taken by a fellow soldier behind him without his knowledge. As the caption explains, the picture was the result of "the act of a comrade while bathing." On the same page he is photographed "in my garden" in the French city of Nancy.[84] Once again, he is wearing only swimming trunks and is reclining in a leisurely pose in a chair beneath the trees and sun, gazing away from the camera toward the sky.[85] These photos, it is also worth noting, are almost exactly the kind of material circulated by Adox Film in their 1940 advertisements encouraging soldiers to photograph one another during leisure time.

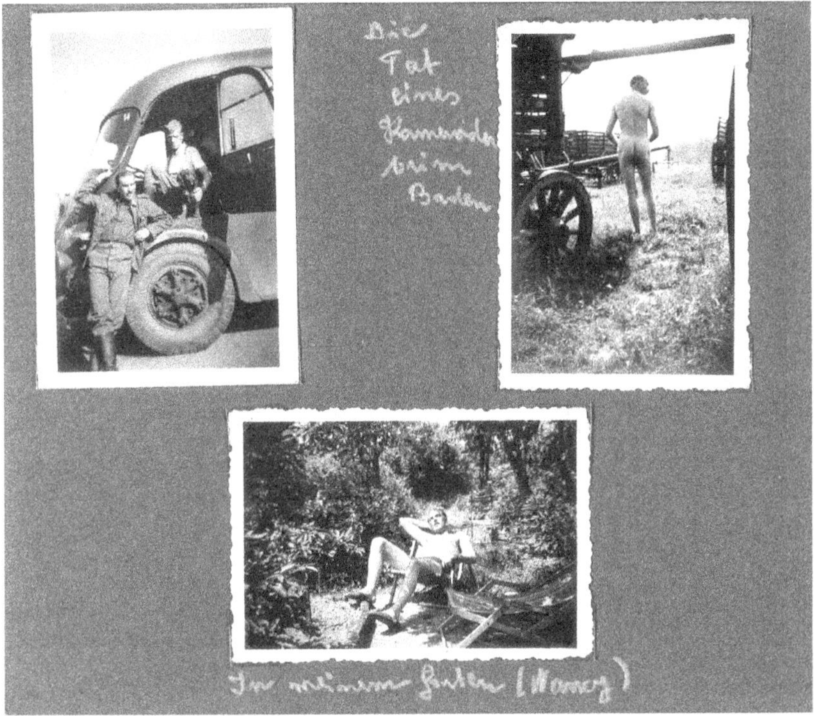

FIGURE 5. Album page with photographs from France, "Kriegserinnerungen, 1940–1941." José María Castañé Collection of War-Related Photograph Albums, ca. 1920–1950 (MS Span 183), vol. 56, Houghton Library, Harvard University.

Other albums prominently feature leisure time with fellow soldiers in the natural world. In the first several pages of the second album, "Meine Dienstzeit," are two copies of the same photograph showing ten men in the soldier's Reich Labor Service unit (Busenberg) sitting on top of a rocky hill. Some of them look at the camera while others stare into the distance. The way they are all positioned suggests their integration into the landscape and the rocks and grass underneath them. That the rocky hillside takes up most of the frame with the men visible only in the top third of the image suggests that it was primarily the landscape that captured the photographer's interest. A few pages later, two photographs illustrate "a rest in the forest" on the way to France and Belgium. The photos show the men milling around behind their tent, pitched beneath several pine trees. In photographs from Ukraine, the soldiers are fishing in a lake while, as the caption tells us, "On June 21, 1941, the war against Russia begins" and "Vast stretches of land were overcome." The

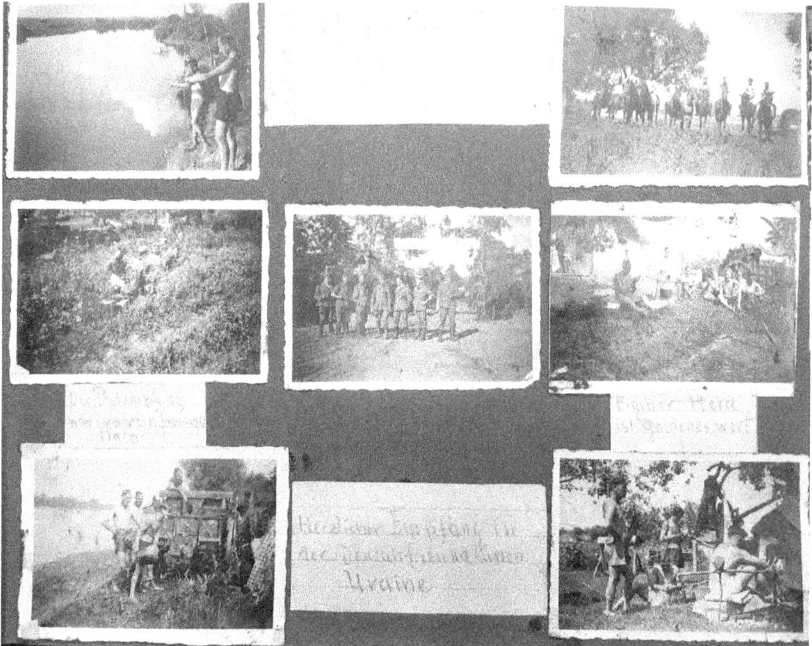

FIGURE 6. Album page with photographs from Soviet Russia and Ukraine, "Meine Dienstzeit, 1939–1942." José María Castañé Collection of War-Related Photograph Albums, ca. 1920–1950 (MS Span 183), vol. 42, Houghton Library, Harvard University.

photograph beside it, presumably from the same day, shows the soldiers riding their horses shirtless, the lake in the background. Soldiers used such photos to record days spent together in communal joy and relaxation with fellow members of a united *Volksgemeinschaft* rather than the death and terror they inflicted on Jewish and non-Jewish Soviet civilians and prisoners of war.[86]

Eating was another popular subject for soldiers sending photographs home. Reassuring their families that they had enough food and water was an essential way of letting them know that they were all right.[87] As Albert Neuhaus put it to his wife, Agnes, in sending her a series of photographs from eastern Europe, "As the picture shows, nobody has to complain about malnutrition."[88] Sharing meals together, moreover, was a crucial aspect of strengthening comradeship. A photo in the "Kriegserinnerungen" album reproduced here presents the men in the unit seated for Christmas dinner in 1940, while two photographs from France show the soldier gathered with comrades over coffee and cake. A few pages later, another meal is pictured in photographs recording the group's departure from France. Too absorbed in his work to look at the camera, the unit's cook is busily unloading a truck filled with food supplies. The next photo shows the troops gathered around what is presumably that same supply truck, pausing for their afternoon meal at one of their last stops in France on their way to Poland. The group of more than fourteen soldiers stand as they eat, many of them smiling at one another or looking, mouths full, into the camera. The tone of this photograph, the warmth and cheer pictured, cannot be attributed to the presence of food alone but to the comradeship depicted as well. The next page shows them gathered for another meal after having reached Warsaw in September 1941. The photo, captioned "Gathering food in Warsaw," shows the album's author and three other men cleaning dishes to serve the meal. In a later photo, he is taking on the role of cook, happily doling out soup to two fellow soldiers with a large ladle. One of the men is looking directly at the camera as if to acknowledge the importance of the moment. Why the album's author has taken on this role is unclear. The former cook may have died or been relocated to another unit. But the focus on taking rests and eating together continues after the unit reaches Soviet territory. One photo depicts the group gathered together to commemorate their "first rest on Russian soil." Three of the soldiers are munching on what looks like bread or fruit. The last photo in the album shows the men of the troop arrayed around a Soviet panzer, captioned "A heavy Soviet tank." A few of them appear to be eating apples.

Other albums similarly emphasize meals. A photograph in the "Meine Dienstzeit" album shows several of the unit's men gathered around a table for a meal on the way to France. Others can be seen carrying their food away from the table, perhaps to be eaten nearby in the grass. The same scene is re-created in additional photographs from the journey, including one showing several soldiers seated around a table while eating, as well as one showing a group of soldiers seated beneath an artillery cart, eating from their tins and reclining on the ground. A photograph from Ukraine shows the men sitting shirtless in the grass around a fire and a boiling kettle, presumably cooking their next meal. The caption reads, "Our own stove is worth its weight in gold," indicating their pride in their ability to prepare meals on their own.[89]

Drinking alcohol is also a common theme, because these scenes allowed soldiers to show their loved ones that the war was going so well for them that they could afford to have some fun.[90] Drinking, moreover, was a community-building activity, though one that also often facilitated violence.[91] For soldiers, alcohol fostered comradeship as well as the feelings of belonging and affection so many of them wanted to commemorate in their photographs. Including pictures showing them drinking with fellow soldiers allowed soldiers to indicate to friends and relatives who received them that they were having a good time together celebrating their victories. A photograph in the album excerpted here portrays soldiers taking a "brandy pause" (*Schnappspause*) in Luxeuil, a small town in eastern France where they stopped on their way to Nancy in the winter of 1940. All the men are warmly clad in winter coats and hats. They are smiling and looking at the camera or at one another, with the exception of one soldier, who instead distractedly buttons up his coat while frowning and smoking a cigar. A particularly striking series features seven photos of the troop members in a stone doorway.

Some of the photos in this group are pasted into the album out of order and appear on different pages. They were clearly taken while

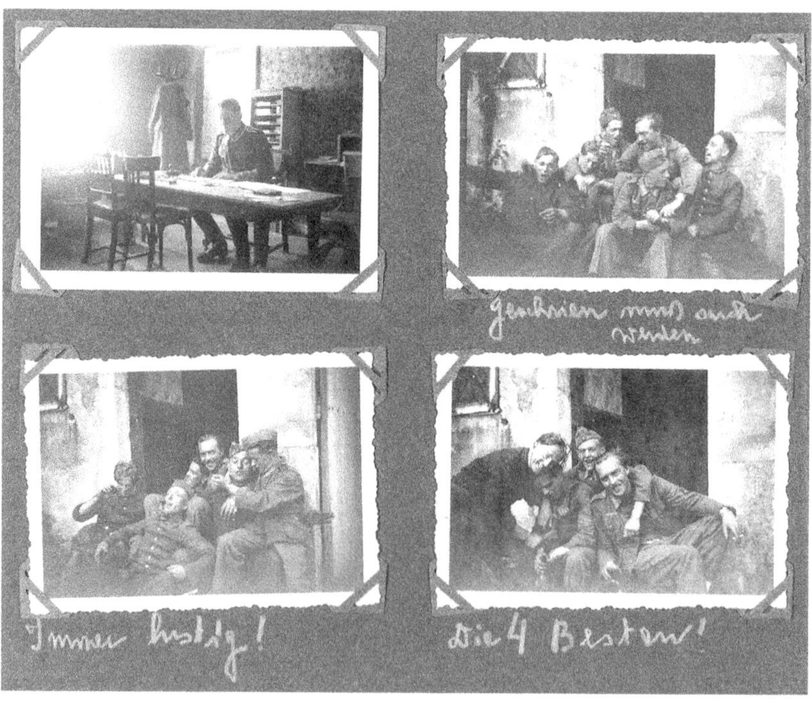

FIGURE 7. Album page, "Kriegserinnerungen, 1940–1941." José María Castañé Collection of War-Related Photograph Albums, ca. 1920–1950 (MS Span 183), vol. 56, Houghton Library, Harvard University.

the soldiers were in the throes of some sort of alcohol-infused celebration. The men are clutching liquor bottles while smoking, laughing, and embracing one another. Some of the revelers appear to have fallen over from drunkenness. There is a lively energy to these photos that is absent in other pictures showing the same soldiers gathered together. This is due in part, of course, to the alcohol. All sense of formality and composure is shattered, capturing them in a moment of spontaneous affection and fun. But that energy can also be attributed to the composition of these photos. The pictures present slightly different versions of the same scene, creating a nearly cinematic effect of movement and suggested sound. The faces of the several individuals who appear to be singing, moreover, are blurred, amplifying those qualities. The photos show, and were meant to show, how close the unit had become and how many good times they shared together. How far these relationships had come is further confirmed by lighthearted but emotional captions like "The four best [friends]" and "Always funny!" to narrate these scenes. A picture in the "Meine Dienstzeit" album, from the soldier's time in the Reich Labor Service, similarly shows nineteen men gathered together indoors, clutching bottles and smoking pipes. One of the men is shirtless, and two in front appear to be in costumes of some kind, which may indicate that this scene is from an evening when some members of the RAD put on a theater or music performance for the other men as part of the RAD's organized leisure programming.[92] Many of them embrace one another, indicating a further evolution of the relationships formed among these men since their service began.

Soldiers frequently documented the chores they performed together to convey a sense of domestic normalcy and show their loved ones that despite the war, they were still taking care of themselves and attending to their health and hygiene.[93] Images of doing laundry and shaving outdoors appear often in soldiers' collections, including the "Kriegserinnerungen" album. The photo of the album's author bathing and being photographed naked by a fellow soldier is one example. Another photograph shows the soldiers seated while looking directly into the camera's lens. The album's author is still brandishing a spoon, suggesting that the men have just finished a meal. Behind them, clean laundry hangs on a clothesline. The soldiers are relaxed, their faces displaying proud, determined expressions. Another photo on the same page taken through the window of a car or truck shows the album's author receiving a shave from another soldier. His face, covered in shaving cream, is tilted back but visible through the open window. The soldier doing the

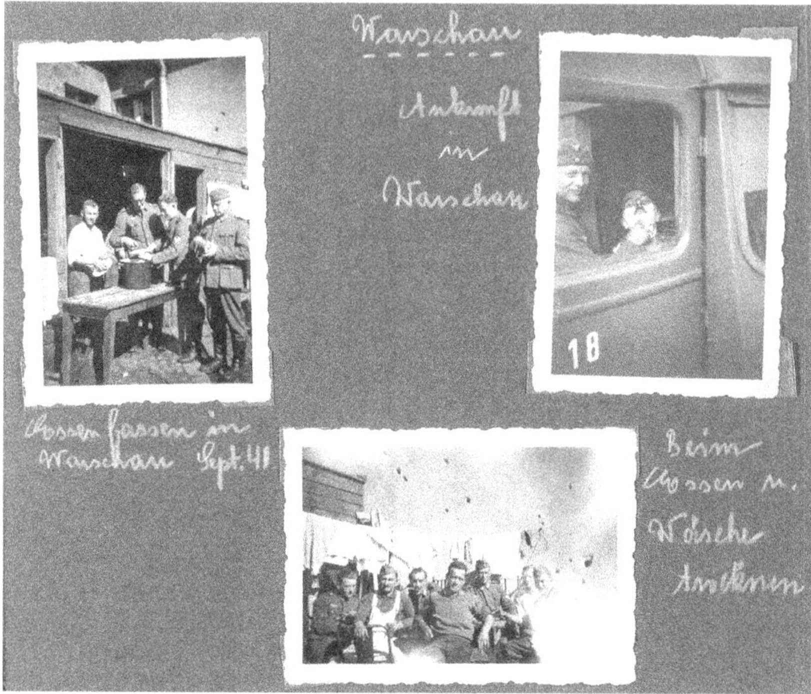

FIGURE 8. Album page with photographs from Warsaw, "Kriegserinnerungen, 1940–1941." José María Castañé Collection of War-Related Photograph Albums, ca. 1920–1950 (MS Span 183), vol. 56, Houghton Library, Harvard University.

shaving is smiling, and both men look at the camera as if to indicate that they are knowingly putting on a show. The possibility, and sometimes the necessity, of shaving outdoors appears to have been a particularly common subject for German soldiers.[94] In addition to reassuring their families that their daily hygiene routines were continuing uninterrupted even under such abnormal conditions, soldiers also may have thought that the novelty of shaving outdoors would bring a smile to their loved ones' faces.

The displays of comradeship and camaraderie in these albums further demonstrate a concerted effort to show that morale remained high for the men despite mounting difficulties for Germany's armed forces after the winter of 1941. One photo in the album depicts four soldiers, including the album's creator, standing in the doorway of their train car on the way to Poland. Each of them is smiling and staring directly at the camera, and the caption reads, "Still in good spirits." That they were "still in good spirits" seems to be one of the more central and lasting points made throughout the whole album. Even the photographs at the very end reinforce this aim. They consist of three group shots showing soldiers standing around burning campfires and a "heavy" Soviet tank. Even though what is being commemorated here is "the first cold" experienced by the unit as they enter the eastern front, the soldiers nevertheless look comfortable and at ease. There remains a sense of camaraderie and affection among them.[95]

Communication with family was critical to soldiers' lives at the front, and pictures with parents, siblings, wives, and children appear often in their albums and loose photo collections.[96] In addition to representing the evolution of soldiers' relationships to one another in their leisure time, soldiers also aimed to demonstrate in their albums their dedication to their families. This focus was often reflected in an emphasis on soldiers opening letters from home. In the "Meine Dienstzeit" album, for example, a photograph presents a group of six soldiers sitting in the grass, opening mail together as they recline. The caption, "Mail arrival—always a happy occasion," testifies to the importance for soldiers of receiving mail from home and the opportunity for togetherness and camaraderie it offered them through opening and reading their letters together.[97] The fact that these albums exist in the first place is a testament to the importance of maintaining family ties while at war, since family members were soldiers' primary audience, and it was often their wives, sisters, or mothers who arranged their photos from the front in albums.[98] But family members are also a prominent presence for the soldier selecting pictures for the first album. Two series of photographs in the "Kriegserinnerungen" album document the soldier's experiences while he was on leave (*Urlaub*). The photos show him surrounded by family. The women and men in the photo all link arms, gazing solemnly at the camera. Another series shows a second leave the soldier took in June 1941, which he spent with his wife and another couple hunting in the countryside. One photo shows him clad in hunting clothing standing in a field of wildflowers, holding a gun. He gazes directly at the camera. Another is a portrait of a woman, who smiles for the camera while kneeling behind two dead deer they must have killed shortly before the photograph was taken. The third shows the album's author, his wife, and a second man seated smiling behind the two deer, their guns pointed upright. The series commemorates what would have been an important moment of togetherness in light of wartime separation. The photo was clearly taken and preserved to recall a day of relaxed, leisurely enjoyment

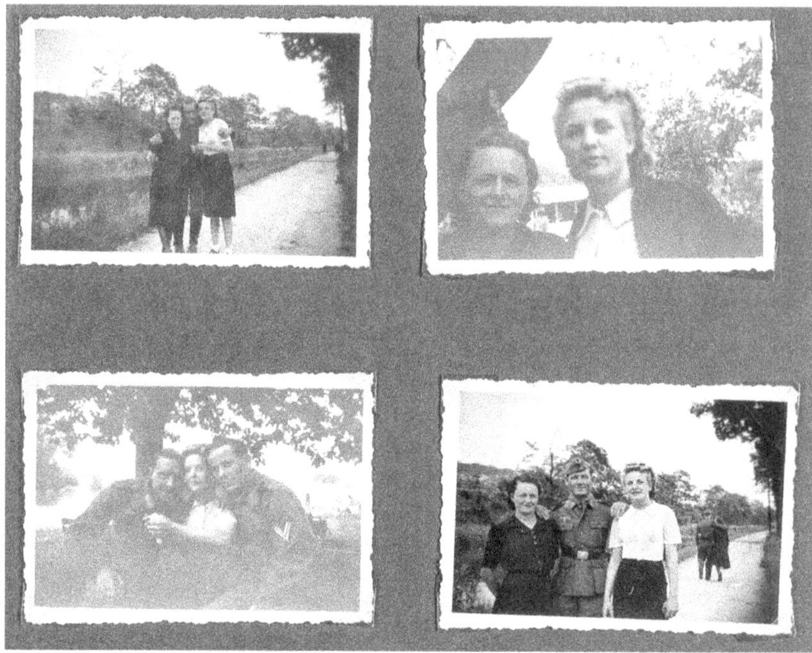

FIGURE 9.   Album page, "Kriegserinnerungen, 1940–1941." José María Castañé Collection of War-Related Photograph Albums, ca. 1920–1950 (MS Span 183), vol. 56, Houghton Library, Harvard University.

amid the sunlit, tranquil surroundings of trees, grass, and nature. Days like these would become increasingly rare for the soldier and his family members as the war continued.

Other photographs in the "Kriegserinnerungen" album document instances in which family members visited the soldier at the front. Seven photographs taken in France in 1940 record a visit from two women, presumably the soldier's wife and mother, while he was stationed in Nancy. In a picture of his wife, mother, and a fellow soldier, another soldier and a woman are visible in the background, their arms around each other, walking away from the person taking the picture, leading to the reasonable assumption that multiple soldiers were being visited by family members on the same day. One photo shows two women standing with the soldier, his arms around them, clutching their shoulders. Another is a portrait of his wife, who, though making eye contact with the lens, is entirely out of focus. The next portrait of her is more successful. She stands beside a tree, arm extended along a branch, laughing, eyes closed, with her face turned away from the camera, her other hand resting on her hip. Other photographs show him and his comrades smoking cigarettes while seated as his wife opens a bottle of champagne.

The bulk of the photographs soldiers preserved commemorated fellow soldiers and loved ones. The nature of what became the "war of annihilation" around them is confined to traces. When this content does come up in photo albums, pictures showing destroyed buildings, artillery, or captured enemy soldiers appear most often.[99] Soldiers were more candid about what they had seen and done in their correspondence. Anton Böhrer, who was born in 1915 and worked as a gardener before he was drafted into the Wehrmacht in early 1941, served in the artillery regiments of the 221st and 294th Infantry Divisions. He told his parents and sister on Christmas Day in 1941 that he had made "nice" pictures of burned-out buildings in eastern Ukraine: "From Charkoff of the burnt-down hotels, I also took very nice pictures. The Jews have now fortunately migrated. The Ukrainian population was very happy about it, because the night shootings have subsided. Of course, many Jewish people did not reach their assigned camp and have already died on the way. We owe the whole war to this rabble and it is good that they are now locked up together and die on their own."[100] Like many others, Böhrer did not bother to take pictures of the atrocities he witnessed, helped perpetrate, and spoke openly about to his family. He was simply glad to be rid of the "rabble" he so resented. Antisemitism, then, did not manifest itself solely in propagandistic images of Jewish ghettoes or scenes of atrocity and torment. It also manifested itself in the very absence of Jews in the pictures soldiers were taking.

Several pictures in the "Kriegserinnerungen" album shown here indicate that the soldier who curated it hoped to emphasize German victories over Soviet troops despite the cold, wet, and muddy conditions his unit encountered. His pictures of such conditions suited Nazi narratives that juxtaposed western civility with eastern backwardness.[101] One photo shows a procession of Soviet prisoners of war "after the battle at Vyazma." The photo of captured Red Army troops depicts the group of men walking between two vehicles. Some of them make direct eye contact with the camera while others look away. Three more pictures show dead Soviet soldiers in the snow with the captions "Three shredded Russians" and "A finished-off beast." Another picture shows a "half-dead Russian" by the side of the road with a group of German soldiers gathered around him. The soldier who curated the album makes eye contact with the camera, as if to indicate his own importance in bringing about

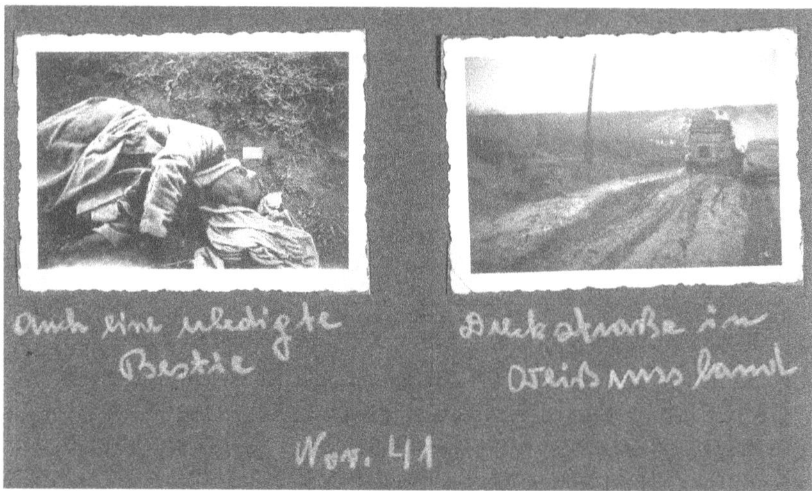

FIGURE 10. Album page with photograph of a dead Soviet soldier, "Kriegserinnerungen, 1940–1941." José María Castañé Collection of War-Related Photograph Albums, ca. 1920–1950 (MS Span 183), vol. 56, Houghton Library, Harvard University.

the Soviet soldier's demise. Overall, however, the photos selected for this album are more suggestive than explicit about the violence on the eastern front.

The album also includes a photograph showing French African soldiers, a common theme in the photography of German troops stationed in France. This photograph, though, is very different in tone from the photos one might expect.[102] Three African prisoners of war stand in the foreground, their faces turned downward toward some sort of activity on the ground that they are performing together. Four German soldiers pose awkwardly at a distance in the background, looking on and smiling at the camera but unnoticed by the African soldiers. Though the album's creator may have intended it to function like one, this is hardly the kind of gruesome trophy photograph that would be expected of German soldiers, given their involvement in horrific massacres of French African soldiers on the western front.[103]

Like many others, the two albums presented here are silent on the Holocaust. The photographs in the "Kriegserinnerungen" album that hint at what Raul Hilberg called the "ghettoization" stage of the Holocaust are just as selective in showing what the Germans and their collaborators were doing to Europe's Jews.[104] The photos depart from pictures created by some soldiers who ignored official bans to

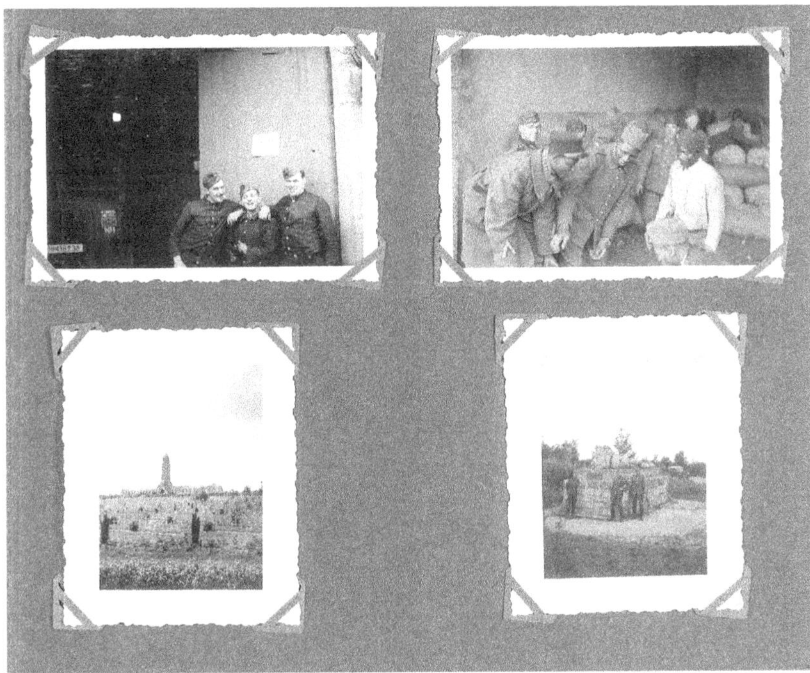

FIGURE 11. Album page with photograph of French African POWs, "Kriegserinnerungen, 1940–1941." José María Castañé Collection of War-Related Photograph Albums, ca. 1920–1950 (MS Span 183), vol. 56, Houghton Library, Harvard University.

photograph ghetto streets and residents.[105] For the soldier who created this album, however, the experience of the ghetto consists of only two photographs, one of which does not actually show the ghetto at all. It is an interior scene, dimly lit by a curtained window. Like so many other pictures in the album, the photograph shows the soldier seated with his comrades at a table drinking, laughing, singing, and raising their glasses to the camera.

The other photograph shows buildings crammed together beyond the ghetto wall. It is a blurry photograph, shot slightly askew, as if the soldier took it in a hurry or from a moving vehicle. It is only when we read the caption that our attention is redirected to the ghetto wall and the person walking beneath it in the bottom right corner. The figure is wearing a hat and staring back at the camera. This, then, is a person living in Warsaw, or perhaps someone the album's author thought was a ghetto resident. That the soldier took the time to create these pictures as well as the self-portrait while on duty indicates that he was aware of

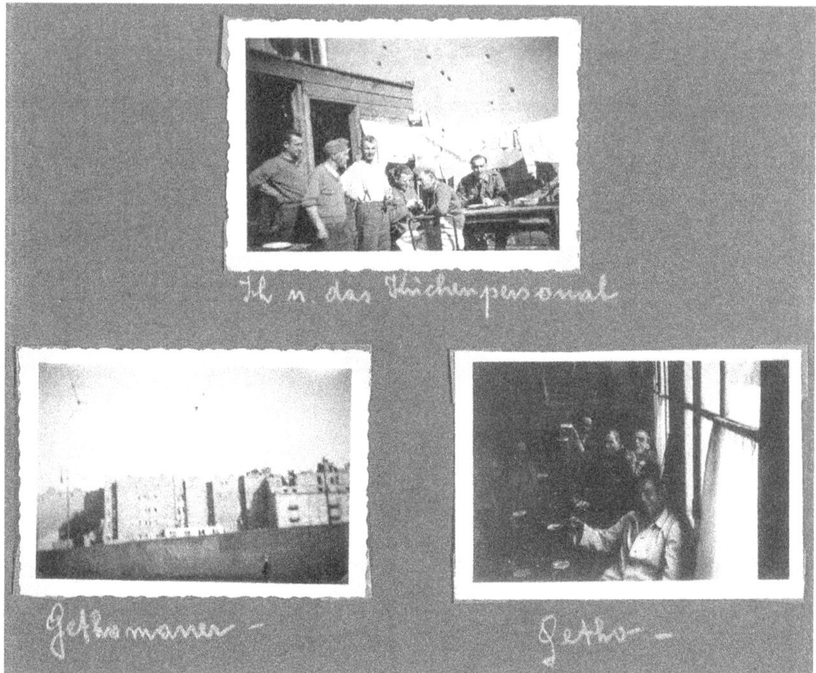

FIGURE 12.   Album page with photographs taken near the Warsaw ghetto, "Kriegserinnerungen, 1940–1941." José María Castañé Collection of War-Related Photograph Albums, ca. 1920–1950 (MS Span 183), vol. 56, Houghton Library, Harvard University.

what was happening inside its walls. In both captions the word "ghetto" is misspelled, reflecting an unfamiliarity with the term but an acknowledgment of the place and its purpose as another site where German troops were helping to defeat more of their alleged "enemies." Taking these pictures allowed the soldier to summon memories of what he had seen and known in the war, even if the photographs themselves are more suggestive than explicit.

The German army's failed attempt to take Moscow in the winter of 1941–42 and the Battle of Stalingrad from the summer of 1942 to the winter of 1943 shifted the tide of the war against Germany. During this time, soldiers continued to send home pictures of themselves and their comrades to lift their loved ones' spirits and reassure them that what they were doing was justified for the sake of their fellow soldiers and family back home. The "Kriegserinnerungen" album is emblematic of this focus. After two final pictures that portray soldiers gathered happily around a fire for "the first cold," the album ends—a reflection, perhaps, of the new challenges to photography experienced by this particular unit in eastern Europe. The second album, "Meine Dienstzeit," presents a highly sanitized account of the unit's experiences in Stalingrad. Rather than depicting cold, hunger, and defeat, this soldier portrays camaraderie, comfort, and persistence. A shadowy photograph on the page shows four of the soldiers seated at a table, eating and drinking as they stare into the camera's lens. Another photograph shows the men gathered for a Christmas party. Ten of them stand in front of a Christmas tree, and one has a bottle of champagne or schnapps peeking out from his coat. Another photograph shows the soldier smiling for the camera as he fixes the engine of a truck. Only a caption on the page beneath a snowy landscape with several men moving a wagon and horse indicates that the author of the album "was wounded and went to Marienbad," which may be an oblique reference to the Soviet advance in the area between the Ukrainian cities of Slawjansk and Kursk in the winter of 1942.[106]

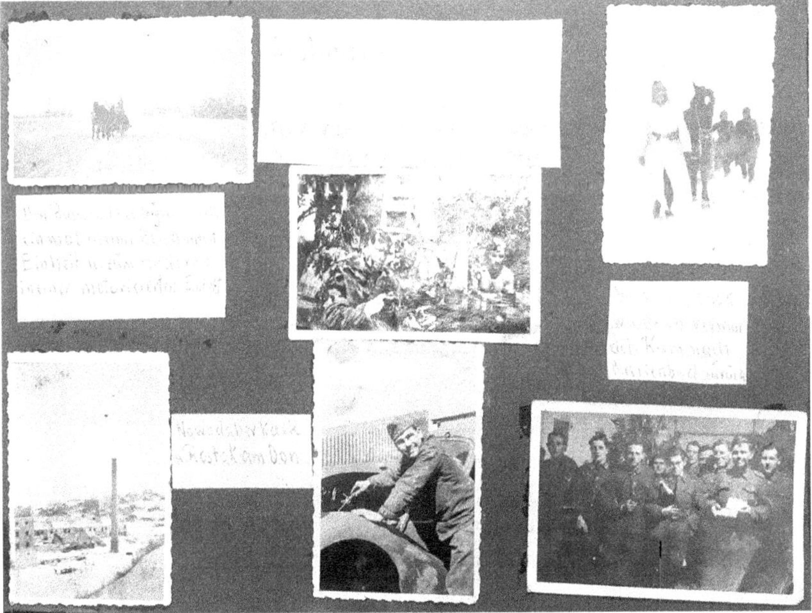

FIGURE 13.   Album page with photographs from Stalingrad, "Meine Dienstzeit, 1939–1942." José María Castañé Collection of War-Related Photograph Albums, ca. 1920–1950 (MS Span 183), vol. 42, Houghton Library, Harvard University.

As wartime crises mounted, soldiers continued to request the same family photos they had asked for before the war started to turn against Germany. "I'm really looking forward to your photos," former architect Adalbert Huber wrote to his wife, Trudl, in the spring of 1942 while stationed in Ukraine.[107] Franz Schmidt, too, a carpenter before he was drafted into the Wehrmacht in 1942, wrote to his brother Reinhard back home with a request for photographs of them with their mother: "Send a few pictures where we stand with Mom, you with Mom, me with Mom, and all three of us."[108] Wolfgang Panzer was likewise heartened when he received the family photos he had requested from Berlin in October 1942. Panzer had been an academic in Heidelberg before joining the staff of the Berlin High Command. After he was wounded during an Allied airstrike in 1944, he was released from service. In the letter of thanks to his family, Panzer affectionately referred to his wife and three sons as a military unit of their own. "I just received the lovely family pictures," Panzer wrote. "For that you must have a very special thank-you from my heart! The 'Panzer company' is very special and makes me proud!"[109]

Many soldiers came to see these pictures as more than just cheery reminders of home. Pictures took on a talismanic role for them, providing comfort and hope for survival and eventual victory. Keeping pictures of their loves ones next to them reminded soldiers of what and who they were fighting for back home. As one soldier wrote in the winter of 1943, "At least I have you figuratively with me!"[110] A soldier identified as Hans Joachim S. told his wife while stationed in France that he kept pictures of her close to him: "I only have the beautiful pictures of you, which are always on my desk, but only increase my longing for you."[111] Ludwig Kierstens wrote to his mother about the photo of her he carried with him during his service in eastern Europe: "A small picture of you accompanies me now for my entire time as a soldier [*Soldatenzeit*], again and again it falls into my hand and my eyes linger on it. We're fine, do not worry about us. Everywhere there is still a spark of beauty in life, worth the joy. So you are in this picture."[112] For Kierstens, the picture of his mother was the "spark of beauty" that gave him hope to keep fighting. The image of a soldier looking at small photographs (*Bildchen*) from home became so familiar that it cropped up often in soldiers' writings. It inspired Gerd Schnieder, for one, to write a poem, "Der Soldat mit dem Bildwerk," in his 1942 war diary:

> The soldier stops and thinks
> a small picture from Lon

a mother with her tiny child, this is her son
The soldier's gaze bowed over the mother
The soldier has the mother and his child in his hand
and the rain falls on the hard helmet and runs over the edge.[113]

Schneider's dreary interpretation of wartime photographic correspondence emphasized the sense of distance between soldiers and their loved ones that photographs could reinforce.

Until the very end, Germans on the home front continued sending pictures and parcels to soldiers at the front to keep their spirits up. The regime and its corporate partners encouraged this activity. As late as November 1944, to take one example, Agfa was still calling photography "a bridge between front and homeland."[114] Soldiers continued to request pictures from home. After yet another year spent apart, police regiment officer Walter Kappmeier wrote to his wife in December 1944: "I have a request, take some pictures with the children and send me the pictures for my birthday. There were different comrades who received pictures from their women for Christmas, I found that very nice."[115] Kappmeier was not alone in making such requests. Michael Wutz thanked his wife in March 1945 for sending him pictures from their last Easter vacation. "Lovely pictures from our Easter trip," Wutz wrote. "Could it not be peace! I have such a longing for rest. However, I know that you also have to endure hardships at home."[116]

In contrast, far fewer soldiers were producing photos for albums by 1944 and 1945. The two albums reproduced in this chapter, for instance, end in 1941 and 1942. Increasingly difficult conditions, mounting defeats for German troops, and the deterioration of the war's novelty led soldiers to stop documenting their war experiences as excitedly as they had during its initial phase. By late 1944, photographic materials were in much shorter supply, too. Equipment had been either damaged, lost, or stolen. Joseph Goebbels's declaration of the "Total War Effort" on February 18, 1943, moreover, limited non-military consumer industries and any labor that was not directly benefiting the war effort, though he made some exceptions when it came to morale-related products for soldiers.[117] Cameras were one of the products to suffer shortages, though film continued to be produced in large quantities. Düsseldorf-born Horst Feldbusch, who was nineteen when he served in Ukraine and Soviet Russia in June 1943, told his parents in a letter shortly before his death in 1944: "It is to be regretted that we hardly have the opportunity to take photographs, for you would marvel at my artist's mane. No trace of a military haircut. So very slowly we approach the prototype of a typical front soldier outwardly as well as inwardly."[118] Hans Karl Schmidt, too, remarked sadly in a letter to his parents from January 1945: "Unfortunately, I cannot present you with a picture of me. Nobody ever carries around valuable things like a camera anymore."[119]

The purpose of photography as a community-building practice shaped the content that soldiers selected for their photographs as well as the act of taking pictures itself. But their pictures hardly constituted "exhaustive" information about "the most important time in the life of the German man," as the album designer envisioned in his 1940 letter to Hermann Göring. Instead soldiers carefully selected the images to prove that their devotion to their comrades, families, and the Reich remained steadfast during the war. As they carried out Nazi Germany's war against their military and civilian racial enemies, SS men also used photography to depict and enact their ties to fellow soldiers and family members. That emphasis appears in the personal photograph albums made by Waffen-SS soldiers stationed on the eastern front as well as SS personnel staffing Nazi concentration camps and killing centers.

CHAPTER 5

Concocting Decency

Like Wehrmacht soldiers, SS men also turned to photography for opportunities to create wartime narratives about themselves. They compiled photo albums commemorating their wartime employment in Waffen-SS combat units as well as the SS-Totenkopfverbände (SS-TV), the Death's Head regiments that staffed the Nazi concentration and killing centers. SS men, like Wehrmacht soldiers, sometimes photographed the acts of violence, mass murder, and abuse they oversaw and committed but far more often used photography to help justify war and genocide and establish their importance in carrying out both. They portrayed themselves through their pictures as devoted husbands, determined soldiers, and decent men who fought an honorable fight to protect their families and all other members of the German *Volksgemeinschaft* from the Third Reich's imagined racial enemies. Those narratives enabled SS men to see themselves as possessing all the qualities the Nazi regime demanded of them, and to show their loved ones that they possessed these qualities too.

SS photograph albums have a great deal in common with their Wehrmacht counterparts despite the distinct training and wartime roles of their makers. The Nazi regime primarily tasked Wehrmacht troops with fighting the Allied powers and winning the war. Indoctrinating Wehrmacht soldiers in Nazi antisemitism and anti-Slavism remained an uneven and therefore secondary goal until the summer 1941 invasion of the Soviet Union.[1] In contrast, since the inception of the SS as one of two paramilitary wings of the Nazi Party, membership in it depended on a full ideological commitment to Nazi racism and antisemitism before enforcing it in various roles and settings. As SS-Reichsführer Heinrich Himmler put it, "Everyone is first and foremost an SS man; after that he belongs to the General SS, the Waffen-SS, the Death's Head units, or the SD."[2]

The SS men examined in this chapter received additional training that was specific to their wartime function. Waffen-SS men, for example, underwent strenuous combat training in addition to ideological indoctrination. Himmler had established the Waffen-SS to strengthen the position of the SS in Germany's armed forces. Initially restricted to four divisions, under Himmler's guidance the Waffen-SS eventually grew to encompass thirty-eight divisions comprising about half a million men with a command and operations structure that rivaled that of the German army. The Waffen-SS participated in most of the major military campaigns of World War II and perpetrated countless war crimes in this capacity. Waffen-SS units also directly implemented the Holocaust through mass shootings. Members of the Waffen-SS who were discharged for medical reasons ended up as guards in Nazi concentration camps. Many had also previously served as camp guards before the war began. Those stationed as guards in concentration camps underwent further ideological training. As the SS newspaper *Das Schwarze Korps* put it: "The essence of the camp indoctrination was threefold. The SS recruit was drilled to obey without question every order, no matter how harsh. He learned to hate absolutely the enemies behind the wire as subhumans who were a lethal political and racial threat to the security of the Reich."[3] SS men further acquired the belief that the Death's Head regiment, tasked with the responsibility of guarding "the most dangerous enemies of the state and the racial community," constituted an elite formation within the SS.[4]

At the war front and in the camps, SS troops operated at the epicenter of the violence that underwrote the Nazi vision of a racially united national community. Those staffing the concentration camps abused and starved prisoners while also selecting and delivering Jews and other victims of Nazism to the gas chambers. Those in combat units were responsible for countless atrocities against prisoners of war, civilians, and Jews. But their photographs tend only to hint at this. Like Wehrmacht soldiers, SS men too had been trained to see their personal relationships with fellow soldiers and family members on the home front as integral to their wartime duties. Ever since the mid-1930s they had been taught to use wartime photography to strengthen both, bringing together members of the *Volk* as they attempted to make the *Volksgemeinschaft* concept a reality through war.[5]

The SS and the Wehrmacht were united in the belief that photography could help boost morale across fronts, a rare point of agreement in an otherwise competitive and contentious relationship. Like the members of the Wehrmacht High Command (Oberkommando der Wehrmacht, OKW), the SS also distributed special albums to the men in their combat units, featuring covers identifying which branch of the SS they belonged to, for them to fill with photographs "in memory" of their service.[6] Wehrmacht and SS officials were also united on what constituted proper photographic behavior. Even as Allied forces began to close in on Germany's troops in the spring of 1944, the Waffen-SS Hohenstaufen Panzer division put together a photo diary using images made by the division's amateur photographers. The division had been activated in December 1942 to provide support for German forces in battles on the eastern and western fronts until their surrender in Austria to the US Army in May 1945. Several men in the division considered themselves amateur photographers and would contribute the photographs.[7] The division's leaders circulated a memorandum to all combat soldiers who owned cameras inviting them to submit their pictures while also reminding them what constituted appropriate behavior. According to the memo, soldiers had to secure official certification or else their cameras would be confiscated. They had to be careful, moreover, about what they decided to photograph. "Good pictures," the memo continued, "are made only of such occasions and objects which have real memory value."[8] The unit replied with a list of all SS officers who owned cameras.[9] These officers were instructed to fill out certification forms declaring the make and model of their camera.[10] "Every camera owner must be in possession of a certificate," the instructions stated. "If [anybody] is found without this certificate, the apparatus will be collected and sent to the Sennheim camp. The person is also punished."[11] In the end, the regiment decided to use a few of the photographs the soldiers had submitted to them in their regiment report, including pictures of Christmas celebrations, urban landscapes, and a burial ceremony for a fellow SS-Unterscharführer.[12] Before they made their selections, the regiment reminded them, the content they submitted had to be "well chosen," explaining: "Since film and printing papers are no longer unlimited in the fifth year of the war, it is a matter of course that good pictures are made only of such occasions and objects that have real memory value. Attention is also drawn to the ban on photographing military items from which the enemy can benefit."[13] Pictures summoning powerful memories of comradeship, service, and ties to the German *Volk*, in other words, were far more desirable for placement in the regiment's illustrated report than any pictures showing executions, violence, or other content that could be useful to the Allies.

As the Hohenstaufen case further indicates, the SS had also routinely issued regulations reminding SS troops what not to photograph. SS chief Heinrich Himmler was particularly fixated on the possibility of pictures falling into enemy hands and repeatedly warned SS troops about this risk. "It is forbidden to take photographs of executions," he wrote in orders circulated in 1942 and again in 1944. "Permission to produce recordings for official purposes can be given only by the heads of the state police. If necessary, previously made photographs must be filed then destroyed. Executions are unfortunately necessary in a war. It is as tasteless as it is harmful to our fatherland, as the opponent abuses such photographs in his propaganda."[14] In April 1942 Reinhard Heydrich, chief of the Reich Security Main Office, also distributed orders prohibiting such images to all SS and police units.[15]

The exceptional trial of Max Täubner was staged as dramatically as possible to prevent other SS men from disobeying these orders. Täubner was an SS-Untersturmführer with the 1st SS Infantry Brigade, a division of the Waffen-SS that had been formed in April 1941 from former concentration camp guards. The division took part in numerous mass shootings of Jews and prisoners of war during its operation until 1944, when it was absorbed into the Horst Wessel Division. Täubner's is the only known case of the Supreme SS and Police Court going so far as to punish unauthorized photography by trial, which ultimately resulted in Täubner's expulsion from the SS and a short term in Dachau.[16] Judges Günther Reinecke, Hans Brauße, and Heinz Meurin rebuked Täubner for committing "deplorable excesses" against Ukrainian Jews in 1941. In at least a dozen different towns between September and November that year, Täubner and his men subjected Jewish men, women, and children to merciless abuse before forcing them to dig their own graves and shooting them. Reinecke, Brauße, and Meurin concluded that Täubner's unit acted "with such vicious brutality that they conducted themselves under his command like a savage horde." The court declared Täubner to be a "fanatical enemy of the Jews." But the case was not about punishing

Täubner and his men for murdering Jews. Far from it. In the end, all three judges justified Täubner's actions on the grounds that "the Jews have to be exterminated and none of the Jews killed is any great loss." For them, this was a disciplinary issue about photography.[17]

It was their discovery that Täubner had made "shameless and utterly revolting" photographs of the executions that particularly unnerved Reinecke, Brauße, and Meurin. "Taking pictures under circumstances where photographing secret official procedures is forbidden cannot be viewed lightly," they cautioned. "[It] is the expression of an inferior character." To make matters worse, Täubner had shared his pictures with fellow soldiers as well as friends and family back in Germany. He did so, the judges argued, knowing that such behavior was prohibited and that it could pose serious risks "to the security of the Reich if [the pictures] fell into the wrong hands."[18] The court found Täubner guilty of "particularly severe" disobedience. After the trial, SS chief Heinrich Himmler ordered three officers to burn all sixty-nine of Täubner's photographs, including the negatives.[19]

In response to these regulations and what officials considered appropriate content, Waffen-SS men generally emphasized family and fellow soldiers in their photo albums. One example is the album made by SS-Sturmmann Adolf Fritz, a member of the 3rd SS Panzer Division Totenkopf.[20] The division was an elite one within the Waffen-SS, formed mainly from members of concentration camp guard units. The division saw action in western and eastern Europe and became known for its brutality and numerous war crimes in France and Poland. During the May 1940 Le Paradis massacre, for example, Waffen-SS troops slaughtered British soldiers with the Royal Norfolk Regiment after the regiment had surrendered. The division also executed hundreds of captured French African troops and took part in the suppression of the 1943 Warsaw ghetto uprising.

Fritz's album shows none of these atrocities. Instead, it is dominated by images of himself as well as family and fellow soldiers. The very first page of the album features a portrait of Fritz in his Waffen-SS uniform with the words "In memory of my service in the SS Totenkopf Division— my honor means loyalty." One page shows a picture of Wilfried Richter, whom Fritz refers to as "my boss." Pictures from Fritz's time in France show the Eiffel Tower in Paris and the "training of a young recruit" who stands beside Fritz for the photographer. The album also contains a full page devoted to a woman named Malle, who may have been his wife, filled with portraits of her at various ages. Two pictures from

Ukraine show Fritz and a fellow Waffen-SS man washing themselves outdoors with clean laundry hanging in the background. Another page from Kharkov, Ukraine, shows the Hiwis (*Hilfswilliger*), or eastern European recruits who voluntarily assisted German forces in combat and in enforcing Nazi racial law.[21] A page from July 1941 in Porkhov, northwest Russia, moreover, shows five pictures of Fritz gathered with fellow soldiers. In one photograph they go for a swim; in others they are assembled shirtless in the back of a truck, uniformed in front of a building, or repairing equipment in a courtyard. Another photo shows someone standing over a steaming cauldron distributing soup with the caption "At last a full mess kit again," an image that Adolf Fritz likely intended to demonstrate to his loved ones back home that he was getting enough to eat and taking care of himself. The subject matter emphasized here, from the faces of Fritz's loved ones and fellow soldiers to the idyllic scenes of comradeship and leisurely sociability, came together to convey an image of himself as an honorable husband, soldier, and friend who devoted himself to killing and destruction on their behalf.

SS photograph collections, like their Wehrmacht counterparts, contain only hints of that destruction and killing. Fritz's album is no exception. One page shows several images of German soldiers' graves with the caption "Who died for Germany."[22] The album also contains pictures of assembled Soviet prisoners of war and of destroyed planes and other war matériel. Two photos, for instance, show damaged train cars with the caption "Partisan work." Pictures from Demjansk depict muddy roads and troop movements in the snow, and the album ends with a portrait of Fritz as a prisoner of war "in captivity" standing in front of a tree with a fence in the background. His clearance certificate is also included on the page, documenting his release on December 18, 1949. Fritz, like most German soldiers, relegated the reality of what they did to prisoners of war, Jews, and other civilians to a few suggestive images that hinted at but did not exhaustively depict the true nature of Hitler's "war of annihilation." That silence not only was embodied by the photographs soldiers made at the war front but also defined collections made by SS personnel staffing Nazi concentration and killing centers.

Waffen-SS men were not the only members of the SS who created and circulated photographs for family albums back home. Members of the Death's Head units, the SS-TV (Totenkopfverbände), also participated in this practice. Founded in 1933, the SS-TV was responsible for administering the Nazi concentration camps and killing centers. After war broke out in 1939, many of the men who staffed the camps would be reassigned to active duty with Waffen-SS units in western and eastern Europe. In concentration camps SS men largely made their personal photographs using the resources of the Gestapo-operated photo identification service discussed in chapter 3, the Erkennungsdienst. Although the service had been set up in camps throughout the Reich for administrative and official photography, it was also available for the use of SS men. In fact the SS men frequented the photo identification service so often that camp commandants were troubled by the possible security threat, and the threat to control and order, such access posed. At Auschwitz, for example, Rudolf Höss, who had been commandant at the camp since the spring of 1940, repeatedly tried to prohibit SS men from using the resources of the Erkennungsdienst for their private photography between 1942 and 1944. Having circulated these orders in October 1942, Höss felt compelled to repeat them the following February, warning: "Once again I point out that photography in the camp area is forbidden. I will severely punish offenders."[23] At the end of July 1944 Höss circulated these guidelines yet again, declaring that only photographs produced for official purposes were permitted. All other requests had to be cleared by the commandant's office before being fulfilled: "For the last time, I point out the prohibition, which has already been enacted in passing, according to which any photographing in the camp area is prohibited. The Erkennungsdienst has been instructed not to make any more private pictures except for the necessary passport photos. Insofar as individual SS members request pictures in small numbers and in the simplest form for special reasons, a request must be submitted here."[24] The same orders prohibiting pictures of executions or other content that could be "of use to the enemy" that applied to Wehrmacht soldiers also applied to the SS. In August 1942, Höss explicitly forbade SS men from "photographing executions in and outside Reich territory. . . . It is also forbidden to induce non-members of the Waffen-SS to take pictures of executions," adding that taking such pictures required official permission and that without it, any pictures would be destroyed.[25]

As was the case with Wehrmacht soldiers, the restrictions on what SS men could take pictures of in the camps shaped their collections. But they also primarily sought to establish themselves as the protagonists of certain narratives for loved ones back home. Camp SS men had families to whom they hoped to return after the war, and they used their photography to maintain these ties from a distance while the war continued.[26] The fifty-six-year-old Neuengamme guard Hugo Behncke was still convinced that Germany could win the war when he wrote a letter to his wife in the summer of 1944: "So we're hoping we'll have victory soon, first over the Russians and then over the Western powers. After we've won my comrades want to carry on . . . as soldiers but not me! I want to get home to you and my children."[27] SS camp guards used photographs to show family members that they were thinking of them from a distance. The photo that Herta (last name unknown) sent to her parents while she was an overseer for the SS (*Aufseherin*) at the Ravensbrück women's camp is a good example of this. The photo is captioned "In memory of my pleasant service in Grüneberg, to my dear parents, your Herta, 24 March 1944. This is my dear and loyal dog Greif."[28] The photo shows Herta standing proudly with a German shepherd at Grüneberg, a subcamp of Ravensbrück, which housed over a thousand prisoners engaged in forced ammunitions labor. She is neatly dressed in full uniform standing at the edge of a forest. She does not make direct eye contact with the camera. Instead she gazes into the near distance while holding the leash of the dog, who is wearing a uniform of his own, a light jacket with the SS logo stitched on the left-hand side. Herta clearly intended this photo to commemorate her "war service" and present herself to her parents as professional, polished, happy, and integral to camp operations. Seen in this light, the camp is picturesque, planted with trees, allowing her opportunities not only for career advancement but for emotional fulfillment as well.

Such photographic self-fashioning in the camps also applied to SS-Hauptscharführer Werner Fricke, who was born in 1908 in Britz and was the head of the civil registry office Weimar II in the political department at Buchenwald. In 1941 Fricke took several personal photographs to commemorate the house he and his wife lived in at the SS settlement near the camp, just eight kilometers away in Kleinobringen. One of these is a portrait of Fricke and his wife, Dini, likely meant for his parents or friends, captioned "a memento of Dini and Werner Fricke. Weimar, March 30, 1941."[29] Three other photographs show Fricke and his wife entertaining guests, Anne and Hugo Seehof, on the outdoor terrace at their home. They drink coffee, smoke cigarettes, and smile fondly at one another, a picturesque leisure scene on the grounds of a house that Fricke and his wife were clearly proud to live in. A fourth photograph testifies to this as well, since it shows only the exterior of the house and its terrace, with no people present, perhaps meant to document their fondness for the house and the opportunities for entertaining and leisure to be found there.[30]

Entire SS photograph albums retain an overwhelming emphasis on these kinds of convivial scenes. Georg Brendle, for example, put together an album while he was an SS recruit in Dachau and then a member of Totenkopf-Standarte 14 in Buchenwald from 1939 to 1940.[31] The SS established Buchenwald in July 1937 to house male political prisoners. At the time Brendle took his photographs, from 1939 to 1940, the camp had begun accepting Jews, Jehovah's Witnesses, Roma, and Sinti. Brendle's album, which is compiled in an album titled "Memories of My Service Years," records the time he spent as an SS recruit in Buchenwald and Dachau until his unit was sent to the front in the winter of 1940. Even though SS Death's Head regiments often created official albums of their own, Brendle put the collection he amassed from his years at Buchenwald into an OKW-issued album. This was no accident. Brendle's unit had been called up to the front in 1940, so he would have been eligible to receive such an album. In addition, it represented a fundamental understanding of both front-line service and camp guard duty as integral components in the war effort. After Brendle's death the album passed into the possession of his son, who gave the collection to the Buchenwald Memorial archives in June 2008.

Brendle included several self-portraits to mark his transformation from civilian to SS soldier. One photo is captioned "On a glorious winter's day in Dachau." It was taken in 1939 and shows Brendle standing in front of one of the camp's watchtowers. In the photo, Brendle stares at the camera dressed in full uniform with hat and boots, arms by his sides and knee bent in a determined but relaxed pose. A second photo shows Brendle on guard duty at Buchenwald in 1940. It is captioned "At the Weimar watch, 1940. On guard" and shows Brendle in full uniform, this time with a rifle strapped on and wearing a helmet, standing rigidly upright at the ready and looking directly at the camera. The seriousness of Brendle's pose is shattered by the SS man behind him, who is leaning out of the window, his face propped on his curled hand as if he was bored by the scene, the job, or the photographer's presence. A third shows Brendle, according to the caption, "on a Sunday afternoon in Buchenwald near Weimar" in 1940. Brendle holds his rifle against his shoulder, dressed in full uniform and helmet, with a slight smile on his lips. The photo is composed at a rather crooked angle, perhaps to situate Brendle parallel to the tree trunks and SS barracks in the background. A fourth portrait shows SS-Obersturmführer Hans-Joachim Mützelfeldt, regiment adjutant of Brendle's Death's Head regiment, walking across a grassy meadow on the southern slope of the Ettersberg hill on which Buchenwald was built in the summer of 1940. It is the only portrait of a man other than Brendle himself in the collection, which suggests that this person was someone Brendle expressly chose to remember as one of his most important colleagues and comrades.

The transformation from civilian to political soldier could not have been complete without military discipline and training, subjects represented in Brendle's album as well. A series of four photos shows Brendle's first practice march with his unit, fully equipped with weapons and packs and supervised by an officer identified as Untersturmführer Döring on horseback. Other photos show the unit engaged in other marches and exercises on the Ettersberg hills, practicing formations on the main square of Buchenwald, and learning how to operate a machine gun in the summer of 1940. Two photos stress the importance of physical fitness by showing members of the unit playing sports and doing exercise drills together "with funny faces" from the strain. Brendle's collection has a great deal in common in this regard with other collections compiled by SS recruits, one being an album made by an unknown SS man in 1943 during his training period. The collection displays a similarly conspicuous focus on his fellow SS recruits and comradeship, with five pictures indicating that he was being trained in motorcycle handling and repair. In addition to group shots with his comrades, the collection holds four pictures of the young man with his motorcycle. In two of these pictures, he is performing balancing tricks on it, riding backwards and then standing on the seat.[32]

As was also the case for Wehrmacht soldiers at the front, it was important for SS men to showcase in their albums their ties to fellow soldiers and the comradeship the SS offered them. After all, it was not cold-blooded ruthlessness alone but camaraderie as well that the SS envisioned as constituting proper SS spirit. In June 1934, shortly before Heinrich Himmler appointed him chief of the Concentration Camps Inspectorate (Inspektion der Konzentrationslager), Theodor Eicke reminded his men that "in service there is only merciless severity and hardness, outside service hours there is heartwarming comradeship."[33] SS men used their pictures and albums to interpret the official goals of military bearing and fellowship in personally relevant but officially tolerable ways.

Brendle included over a dozen pictures with his fellow SS recruits in his album. One photo, captioned "Our favorites," shows Brendle with three others in front of the barracks at Buchenwald, smoking cigarettes. Whether the caption refers to the men or the cigarettes is unclear. Only

Brendle looks at the camera as if to indicate that the picture is being taken for the chief purpose of showing himself, while the three other men look to the side in the distance. A second photo, captioned "Nothing can shake us," shows sixteen men including Brendle seated for a rest on logs in the woods; some of them are smoking cigarettes. Another depicts the same group at a Christmas party, captioned "Christmas 1939, a fun get-together." A fourth shows Brendle with three other men gathered around a table inside their Buchenwald barracks in 1940. It is one of only a few photos that do not show Brendle in uniform. Instead, all four of the men are wearing pajamas. They appear to be in the middle of a conversation as they open the mail before them and write letters of their own. In the background, attached to the wall and balanced on one of the bunk beds, are two pictures of women, presumably the girlfriends, wives, or mothers of the men pictured, intended as reminders of home and of the ties being maintained between "fronts" ever since the war began. A fifth shows Brendle and four men on a cigarette break, captioned "On a Sunday in Buchenwald, 1940. My comrades. My roommates." The group is sitting on a fence, looking into the sun with determined expressions on their faces.

Brendle also included pictures of senior SS officers in the album. One picture shows SS-Obersturmbannführer Georg Martin, the commander of Brendle's regiment, during a field exercise in 1940. Martin is talking to another person, not paying attention to the camera. But Brendle's proximity to him was clearly something Brendle wanted to capture, only bolstering the feelings of comradeship and importance he felt not just while surrounded by men of his own rank but in the presence of men of even higher standing as well. Another shows four SS officers, including Georg Martin as well as SS-Hauptsturmführer Heinrich Heinke, walking toward Brendle in front of the Buchenwald casino. The four men are talking to one another but smiling for the camera, preserving a moment of affection and comradeship that transcended the hierarchies between them.

The "comradeship evenings" held at Buchenwald are also pictured in Brendle's collection. A series of three photos depict Brendle and his fellow SS recruits, according to the caption, at "a regiment evening" in the Buchenwald casino in 1940. The regiment appears to have put on a performance there, as two of the pictures show the men onstage in costume. The third photo, captioned "A regimental evening in Buchenwald. 1940. A good place," shows them at a celebratory party after the performance, surrounded by bottles of alcohol and one another. They hold full glasses, smoke cigarettes, laugh and talk together, some with their hands affectionately touching the shoulders of the other men present.

Brendle's album contains nothing related to concentration camp inmates or the suffering and cruelty the men who compiled such souvenirs helped inflict on camp prisoners. His album, like the bulk of Wehrmacht and Waffen-SS soldiers' albums and loose photographs, is largely devoted to himself. That was in part due to strict regulations prohibiting SS men from unauthorized interactions with prisoners or from photographing them in the main camp area.[34] But it was above all because for these men, the purpose of photography was to chronicle themselves and their own personal relationships, not the "enemy" behind the wire.

The personal photograph albums curated by SS men staffing the killing centers disclose similar themes and subject matter as those curated from the eastern front or in concentration camps.[35] From the killing centers, SS men compiled photograph albums using their own materials, for unlike in the concentration camps, there was no official photography department there. With the exception of those prisoners temporarily selected for forced labor in the Sonderkommando units, all those who were sent there would be gassed on arrival rather than registered.[36] The significance of these collections goes well beyond which known perpetrators can be identified in the collections.[37] They also attest to the Nazi configuration of photography as a pastime meant for non-Jewish German members of the *Volksgemeinschaft* to build a racially exclusive community.

The photo albums created by Johann Niemann while he was deputy commandant of the Sobibor killing center testifies to that purpose.[38] The SS opened Sobibor to carry out Operation Reinhard, the codename used to arrange for the extermination of Polish Jews in German-occupied Poland from October 1941 to November 1943. The deadliest phase of the Holocaust, it marked the introduction of three main killing centers—Belzec, Sobibor, and Treblinka—that were purpose-built to murder millions of Jews in gas chambers.

Niemann filled a black leather album titled "SS Totenkopfverband Brandenburg" emblazoned with SS insignia, covering the years 1934–1941, with pictures from his time at the Esterwegen, Sachsenhausen, and Bernberg concentration camps and the Sobibor killing center.[39] Niemann joined the Nazi Party in 1931 at the age of eighteen. He first served as an SA guard at Esterwegen before he joined the SS and became a guard at Sachsenhausen. In 1939 he started working for the T4 "euthanasia" project and was assigned to the Grafeneck, Brandenburg, and Bernburg facilities, where his duties included moving the murdered victims

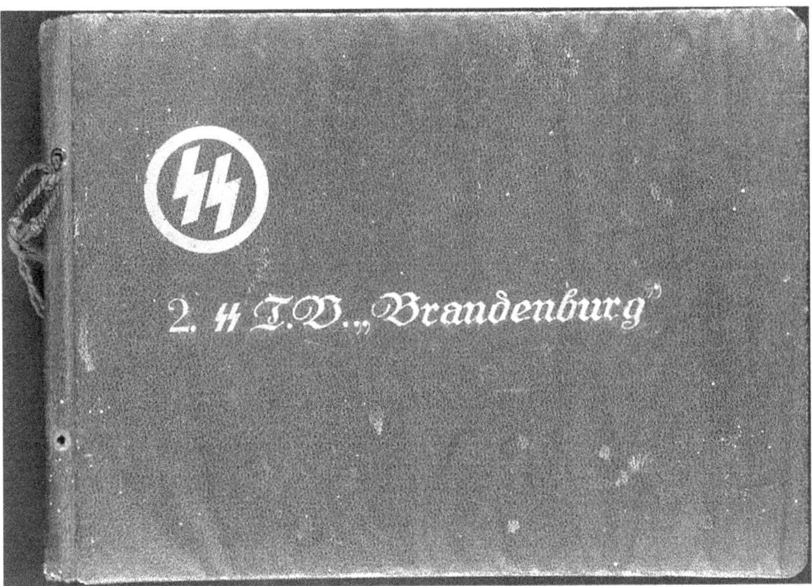

FIGURE 14.   Cover of album compiled by Johann Niemann, Album 1, "2. SS-T.V. Totenkopfverband Brandenburg" [original order], 1934–1941. United States Holocaust Memorial Museum Archives, 2020.8.1, series 1, file 14, photograph 1. Copyright of United States Holocaust Memorial Museum.

from the gas chambers to the crematoria. He was promoted to SS-Oberscharführer in August 1941. Niemann next helped establish the Belzec killing center, where he commanded Camp II, the location of the camp's killing facilities. He then helped establish the Sobibor killing center in spring 1942, was posted there as deputy commander in the summer, and was promoted to SS-Hauptscharführer. He held the rank of SS staff sergeant at Belzec until his transfer to Sobibor. Heinrich Himmler promoted Niemann to SS-Untersturmführer and gave him the permanent position of deputy commander in 1943 under the primary leadership of commandant Franz Reichleitner. Niemann served in that position until he was killed with an axe to the head during the October 14, 1943, Sobibor prisoner revolt.[40] His large collection of photographs includes loose photos and two albums, one containing eighty photographs and the other a little over one hundred. After Niemann's death, these items as well as a series of photographs documenting his burial and funeral services were sent to his widow, Henriette. In 2015, Niemann's grandson donated the photographs and documents to Bildungswerk Stanislaw-Hantz, and the United States Holocaust Memorial Museum acquired the collection in January 2020.

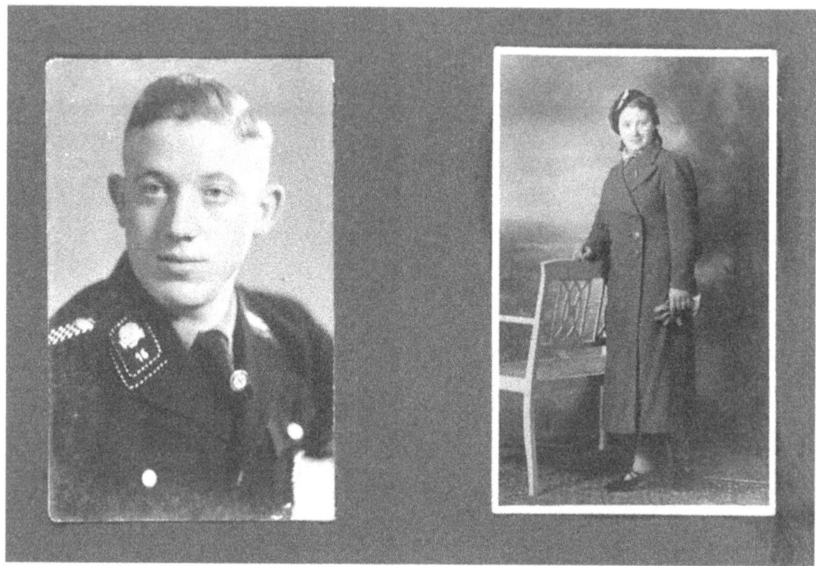

FIGURE 15.   Page from album compiled by Johann Niemann, Album 1, "2. SS-T.V. Totenkopfverband Brandenburg" [original order], 1934–1941. United States Holocaust Memorial Museum Archives, 2020.8.1, series 1, file 14, photograph 3. Copyright of United States Holocaust Memorial Museum.

In his album, Johann Niemann styles himself, as other Wehrmacht and SS men did, as a determined soldier and devoted father and husband. Several photographs are studio portraits of him dressed in SS uniform, the skull and bones insignia of the SS Death's Head embroidered on his collar. Another photograph taken while he was the deputy commandant at Sobibor shows him riding a horse, taken from the ground to make him look larger, more authoritative and in charge. Other portraits showing him in more relaxed positions were meant to convey his understanding of himself as a devoted father and husband. In one photograph he is lying in bed reading beside a framed picture of himself, his wife, and his son on the nightstand. Another shows Niemann dressed in SS athletic apparel intently writing while seated at a desk. The photograph is captioned "Writing a letter to my wife." Photographs like these conveyed his desire to both depict and enact his self-perception as a dutiful SS man while also preserving the softer contours of his identity as a father and husband.

The importance of comradeship and relationships with fellow SS men is another common theme of the albums. That Niemann fills so much of his albums with photographs that testify to these ties

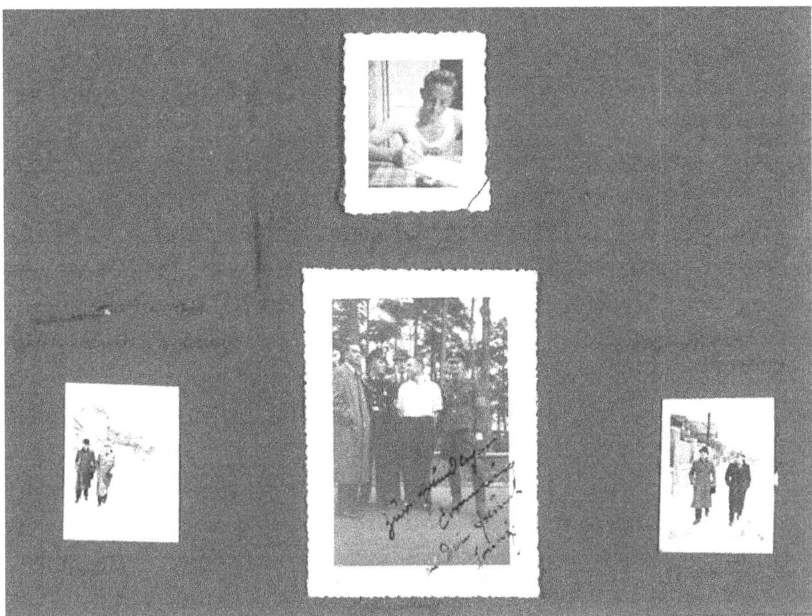

FIGURE 16. Page from album compiled by Johann Niemann, Album 1, "2. SS-T.V. Totenkopfverband Brandenburg" [original order], 1934–1941. United States Holocaust Memorial Museum
Archives, 2020.8.1, series 1, file 14, photograph 160. Copyright of United States Holocaust Memorial Museum.

indicates, on the one hand, his adherence to using photography to
showcase his devotion and loyalty to fellow *Volksgemeinschaft* members
and, on the other, an emphasis on portraying himself as an important
and valued member of that community. A number of these record SS
training exercises, which was an important bonding moment for men
in the SS as well as soldiers in the Wehrmacht.[41] Some of Niemann's
photographs show his unit in formation at NS-Ordensburg Vogelsang,
the Nazi estate established at the Eifel National Park in North Rhine–
Westphalia to train SS leaders.[42] Others record the men on a march at
KZ Esterwegen, the concentration camp established early in the summer of 1933 in lower Saxony to detain political prisoners, among them
the Nobel laureate journalist Carl von Ossietzky.[43] Still others show
them cleaning and practicing with their rifles. Niemann frequently
included pictures of top Nazis like Hitler, Rudolf Höss, and Heinrich
Himmler in his album as well. Several photos show Höss and Hitler
present during SS training exercises at Vogelsang or Hitler greeting SS
men and their wives and children. Other photos show Himmler visiting

Esterwegen. His own proximity to Nazi leaders was clearly something Niemann wanted to display and remember from his years as an SS officer, memories that appear to have been so special to him as to warrant such a series.

Other photographs show Niemann and his fellow recruits engaged in leisure activities together.[44] One photograph shows Niemann drinking beer with a fellow SS officer, staring at the camera. In other photographs Niemann is goofing around in staged scenes with fellow recruits or enjoying "bachelor evenings" with his fellow SS recruits, drinking beer, playing musical instruments, and laughing. Additional loose photographs from Niemann's tenure at Sobibor depict him relaxing on the patio of SS quarters, eating, smoking, drinking, playing chess, and listening to music with other SS guards.

Such scenes had the effect of demonstrating to the album's audience—primarily his family and children—that not only did these men matter greatly to Niemann but also he mattered greatly to them. One photograph included at the very end of the album is a signed photograph showing Niemann surrounded by four fellow SS men. On the

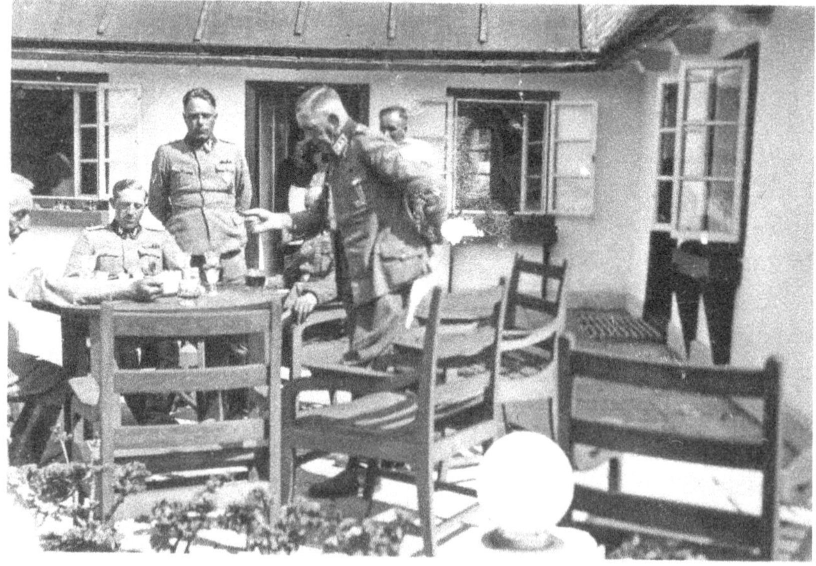

FIGURE 17. Photograph of Niemann socializing with fellow SS men, "Sobibor, loose photographs, 1942–1943," United States Holocaust Memorial Museum Archives, 2020.8.1, series 1 file 9, photograph 58. Copyright of United States Holocaust Memorial Museum.

photograph is written a dedication, "a friendly reminder of your friend Franz," a possible reference to Franz Reichleitner, the commandant of Sobibor.[45] In the photo, Niemann and "Franz" look at each other fondly, while the other three men pictured look at the camera or into the distance.

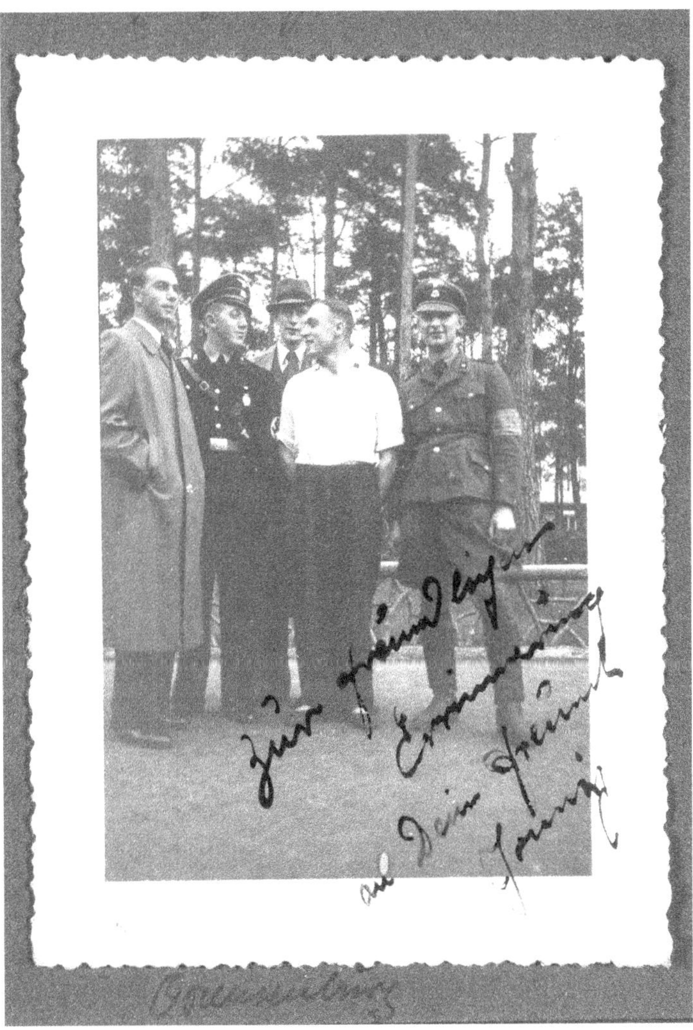

FIGURE 18.   Signed photograph, possibly from Commandant Franz Reichleitner, showing himself with Niemann, Album 1, "2. SS-T.V. Totenkopfverband Brandenburg" [original order], 1934–1941. United States Holocaust Memorial Museum Archives, 2020.8.1, series 1, file 14, photograph 163. Copyright of United States Holocaust Memorial Museum.

The importance of Niemann's relationships with fellow SS men is further documented in an official album created to chronicle a Sobibor staff visit to Berlin and Potsdam in 1943.[46] The album was distributed to camp staff as a reward, though it is unclear how many of the SS men present on the trip received the album other than Niemann. The album shows each stage of the group's trip, from preparing the bus for departure and the journey to their arrival and sightseeing. Several photographs show the SS men stopping for meals and rest, posing for group photos while reclining in the grass. Other photographs show the group arrayed in front of landmarks or seated at outdoor cafés over meals and glasses of beer.

Like the Wehrmacht soldiers and SS personnel staffing concentrations camps, killing center guards also sought to depict and enact their relationships with loved ones and family members even from a distance. This is especially true for Niemann, who includes in his albums several pictures of his wife and two children, who lived in Vollen while Niemann was away in the 16th Death's Head Regiment. On the second page of the album is a studio portrait of Niemann's wife, Henriette, taken by

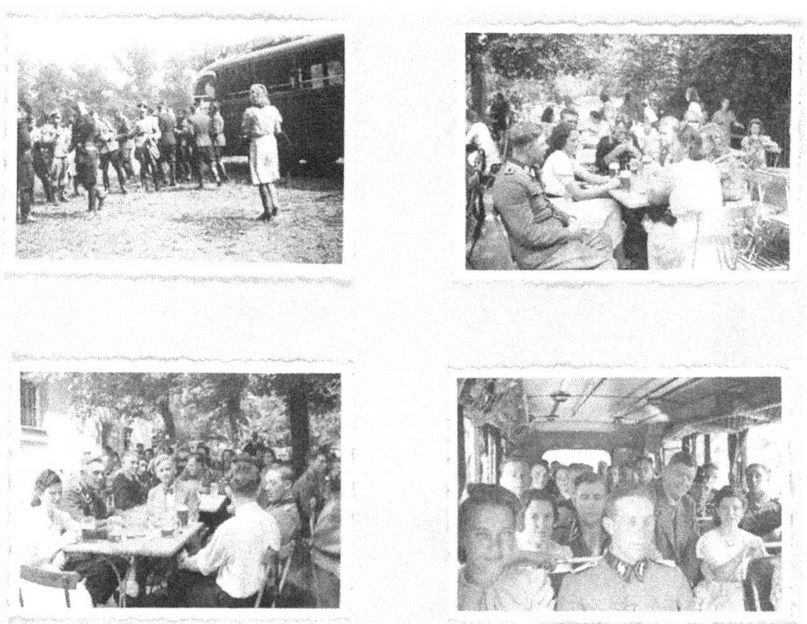

FIGURE 19. Page from album commemorating trip to Berlin and Potsdam, "Sobibor personnel official trip to Berlin and Potsdam, 1943." United States Holocaust Memorial Museum Archives, 2020.8.1, series 1, file 15, photograph 21. Copyright of United States Holocaust Memorial Museum.

the photographer Johannes Ehrlich, who operated a portrait studio four miles away from Vollen in Papenburg.[47] That her picture appears so prominently at the beginning of the album suggests that Niemann primarily compiled the album for her, but it also suggests that the "service" he chronicled in the course of the album was done for her too. Several more portraits of Henriette appear in the second half of the album. One shows her hanging clothes to dry, while in another she is carrying milk pails on her shoulders across the yard. The album includes pictures of Niemann's two children as well. A portrait of his son August shows him wearing a Hitler Youth uniform, and a picture of his daughter Johanne, who was born in the spring of 1942, shows her asleep in a stroller.[48] Much in Niemann's albums expresses how integrated his wife was in the world of the SS. That is evident in the first album, in a picture of her standing between two SS men, one of whom looks fondly at her while she looks at the camera. It is even more evident, however, in the album documenting the 1943 visit of Sobibor camp staff to Berlin and Potsdam, since the wives of some of the SS men in attendance had been invited along on the trip.[49] Picture after picture in the album show SS officers' wives seated beside them on the bus, at outdoor cafés, or standing next to them beneath city landmarks. Henriette makes direct eye contact with the camera in several of these, indicating what may have been her desire to render herself important in these scenes and make her presence known in the pictures taken.

Like the albums curated by Wehrmacht soldiers and SS men guarding concentration camps, the albums created by killing center personnel are silent about the Holocaust. The only hints offered in Niemann's albums are the pictures that nominally show the crematoria and other buildings designed for mass murder at Sobibor.[50] Such omissions are not coincidental, for silence characterizes more broadly the wartime photography and album-making practiced by German soldiers in the Wehrmacht and the SS. A closer look at what unites their collections reveals that the subject matter they did concentrate on, pictures showing fellow soldiers, family, and leisure scenes, reified the overarching narrative of "Aryan" German men and women coming together to create a united racial community. Germans had learned how to see photography along those lines ever since the Nazi takeover in 1933 and put those teachings into practice as war and genocide continued.

Epilogue

The general absence of atrocity photographs in private collections curated by German soldiers and their families would shape the refusal of many Germans to accept their own or their family's complicity in Nazi crimes in the aftermath of World War II, culminating in the explosive reaction to the traveling photographic exhibition "War of Annihilation: Crimes of the Wehrmacht, 1941–1944." When Germany's parliamentary representatives gathered for the 163rd session of the Bundestag in Bonn on March 13, 1997, no other item on their agenda stimulated as much heated debate as this exhibition. After Alfred Dregger, himself a Wehrmacht veteran, took the podium on behalf of the Christian Democratic Union and declared that "German soldiers risked life and limb for their country" but "were not involved in Hitler's war crimes," Gerald Häfner from Alliance 90/The Greens interjected, "Never did this exhibition seem more necessary than during your speech!"[1] At first glance it would seem strange that an exhibition would make the Bundestag's agenda that spring and provoke such fiery remarks, especially in the aftermath of the fall of the Berlin Wall just seven years prior. But in the 1990s, Germans were not just preoccupied by the challenges of navigating a newly reunified country. They were also still grappling with key aspects of the Nazi past. And toward this end, the exhibition was as consequential as it was turbulent.

Produced by the Hamburg Institute for Social Research, the Wehrmacht exhibition documented the war crimes committed by members of the regular German armed forces during World War II. An estimated 800,000 people visited the exhibition as it traveled to thirty-three German and Austrian cities from 1995 to 1999. The purpose of the exhibition made it deeply controversial. Scholars from the Hamburg Institute hoped that it would overturn the myth of a "clean" Wehrmacht, the fictitious notion that only the SS and Einsatzgruppen had perpetrated the Holocaust and other war crimes during the Second World War, and that members of Germany's regular armed forces were not involved. The myth originated during the war itself as German soldiers and military leadership alike insisted on their respectability despite their active participation in a criminal operation.[2] It persisted into the postwar years. During the Nuremberg trials, for example, former Wehrmacht leaders compiled a memorandum titled "The German Army from 1920 to 1945," which drew on those wartime narratives of innocence and respectability to exculpate the regular German armed forces from complicity in the Holocaust. For decades after the war ended, Germans widely clung to this myth, and its hold lasted well into the 1990s despite the efforts of historians since the 1960s to challenge the myth using documents that detailed the scope of the Wehrmacht's involvement in war crimes and genocide.[3]

No less controversial were the source materials used in the exhibition. On display to detail the Wehrmacht's participation in Hitler's "war of annihilation" were written documents as well as hundreds of photographs showing executions, mass graves, and other atrocity scenes that had been found in the pockets of captured or killed German soldiers. But just as organizers prepared to open the exhibition in New York, the Polish historian Bogdan Musiał announced that ten of the featured photographs had been mislabeled and showed atrocities perpetrated by the Soviet secret police (People's Commissariat of Internal Affairs, NKVD), not the Wehrmacht. The Hamburg Institute canceled all further displays pending a thorough review, and a revised version appeared in 2001.[4]

When the exhibition first opened, the historian Hannes Heer, who helped organize it, said that he and his colleagues hoped "to force a debate . . . to blow up this wall of silence and denial."[5] He got what he wished for. Like Gerald Häfner, some Germans viewed the exhibition as a necessary reckoning with this aspect of the nation's past.[6] "Now I see what it meant when my father talked proudly about his war experiences. Thank you for this long-overdue lesson," one visitor wrote in the exhibition's guest book. "It's the truth, what's being shown here," a former soldier with the 6th Army under the command of General Friedrich Paulus remarked.[7] Like Alfred Dregger, however, others saw it as an insult to the men who they believed had only been fighting for their country. "Those were the doings of the troops in the rear echelons and not those of the true fighting soldier," many insisted, repeating the mistaken belief that it had been only Nazi SS, SD, and Einsatzgruppen units who were responsible for the violence against civilians.[8] Protesters routinely gathered outside the buildings that housed the exhibition, and in March 1999 right-wing terrorists bombed the high school in which the exhibition appeared in Saarbrücken, Austria.[9] Descendants of Wehrmacht soldiers, too, denied the possibility that their fathers, grandfathers, and uncles were murderers. The granddaughter of one veteran commented, "I simply cannot believe that [my grandfather] would have participated in such atrocities."[10]

Larger confrontations with key aspects of Germany's past during the 1990s shaped this sharply divided response to the exhibition. Recent scholarship had raised new questions about how "ordinary Germans" could become perpetrators.[11] More important, however, were the conversations that took place in private between former soldiers and their families. According to the social psychologist Harald Welzer, those private conversations shaped public opinion more than any other source. Germans primarily relied on two key frameworks to remember the war years, Welzer argued. The first was the "lexicon," as it was known, which stood for the information and knowledge disseminated through school curricula, the media, and other public outlets for cultural memory. The other was what Welzer called the "family album," a metaphor for communicative memory. The metaphor denoted unique family memories that had been condensed into stories that provided identity and meaning, like an album in which family photographs tell stories in chronological as well as emotional terms. After conducting hundreds of interviews with war veterans and their families, Welzer concluded that the family album framework overrode the lexicon in shaping individual memories. Moreover, it allowed soldiers to exclude key parts of their war experiences to maintain the memories that informed the "family album." The Holocaust, as a result, rarely if ever appeared in the memories and conversations that took place in private between former soldiers and their families.[12]

But the "family album" can and should serve as more than just a metaphor, for photographs were central to those conversations and in postwar communicative memory.[13] When grandfathers, uncles, and fathers shared their stories with their families, they relied on the photographs and photo albums they had created during the war to help them do so. Their relatives, moreover, continued to use those same photographs to investigate these family histories. In his memoir recounting how he discovered that his grandfather Rudolf Langbein had been an SS officer, BBC editor Martin Davidson relied on "the prewar and wartime photographs" his mother still kept in a "large, heavy photo album" to retrace his life and career.[14] To piece together the life of her own grandfather SA-Obergruppenführer Hanns Ludin, the writer Alexandra Senfft also relied on his personal photographs from the war years.[15] The psychologist Roger Frie likewise used his family's photograph albums from the prewar and war years to reconstruct the life and experiences of his grandfather.[16]

Observers at the Wehrmacht exhibition noticed that many veterans and their families responded to the pictures on display as if they had never seen anything like them, despite their reliance on photographs and albums to share their own war stories. As she recorded heated exchanges between veterans and civilians once the exhibition reached Vienna, the filmmaker Ruth Beckermann tried to understand why the images provoked such shock and hostility when their albums and letters during the war years must have been filled with photographs just like them. The pictures of executions and hangings used in the exhibit, Beckermann assumed, surely dominated private collections as well.[17]

But the albums German soldiers compiled with their families during the Second World War generally did not contain these kinds of photographs. As this book has shown, the pictures former soldiers selected to tell their war stories did not depict mass executions, shootings, and hangings. Instead, they showed family members and fellow soldiers, visits home on military leave, and meals shared among comrades at the front. After he found out that his grandfather had been a member of the SS, Roger Frie wrote that he had been struck by the "everydayness of the images" in his grandfather's album, where he expected to find more incriminating material.[18] And in the 2011 film *Hitler's Children*, Rainer Höss, grandson of Rudolf Höss, the former commandant of Auschwitz who was hanged there in 1945, said he "was sure" that he would see "photos of the horrors" upon inspecting his grandfather's collection of photographs and memorabilia. Instead, he encountered picture after picture of Höss's children playing in the home he and his family inhabited just steps away. "Obviously no photos show—you can't actually see anything from the camp," the journalist Eldad Beck, who assisted Rainer Höss in his archival search, noted, visibly stunned by this realization.[19]

The photograph albums German soldiers made with their families during the war helped them substantiate an altogether different narrative from the one shown in the "War of Annihilation" exhibition.[20] Instead of corroborating stories of their own complicity in war crimes and genocide, most of the photographs soldiers sent home depicted mundane scenes that revealed more about soldiers' personal relationships with friends, family, and fellow soldiers than the suffering, cruelty, and mass murder for which they were responsible. There are photographs in some personal collections that reveal the violence, and the growing literature on photography during the Nazi era has offered important insights into some of these shocking pictures produced by German troops as they invaded and occupied Europe.[21] But as the photographs and albums that fill archives today indicate, such images are extremely rare. Personal photograph collections are instead dominated by innocuous scenes of leisure, friendship, and sociability. More than the misidentification of a dozen or so of the exhibition's photographs, it was that discrepancy that made the exhibition so controversial. And it is that discrepancy that is part of the reason why it took Germany so long to develop the candid memory culture for which it is now widely known and respected. As this book has shown, that emphasis was precisely what photography meant under Nazism. On the one hand, photography under the Nazis was about achieving the absence of Jews both in front of and behind the camera. Nazi officials prohibited Jews from practicing photography as a hobby and dispossessed the Jewish men and women who worked professionally in the industry. But on the other hand, that dispossession was facilitated by the larger purpose for photography that the Nazis envisioned. To them, photography was a transformative act that could unite non-Jewish Germans as members of the same racially exclusive community. The dictatorship promoted photography for those who belonged to that community and prohibited those who did not from practicing it. That configuration in turn guided German soldiers and their families as they created wartime photograph albums that were largely about themselves rather than the victims of Germany's armed forces.

What was most "Nazi" about the wartime albums made by German soldiers and their families, then, was the set of ideas that informed their creation rather than their content. The vigorous involvement of the Nazi state transformed photography into a racially exclusive pastime that could maintain and strengthen the bonds among Germans, especially while at war. The absence and exclusion of Jews from the practice was critical to this formulation. What makes German World War II albums distinctive, then, is the context that is not always visible in the images themselves.[22] This context goes beyond the state of the war, the atrocities German troops committed, or the other written and visual materials they produced. It is also about the practice of photography itself: why so many Germans took it up on the eve of the Second World War, and why the Nazi regime felt that there was so much to be achieved through it.

The idea of selective memory is often invoked to explain how Germans came to terms with this history after 1945.[23] But this framework falls short when the aim is to explain not just whether but *how* Germans constructed their claims of wartime innocence.[24] Remembering and forgetting are not only psychological and emotional acts but material ones as well, and photographs must be included in any investigation of either process. Returning German soldiers used the photographs they sent home from the front to reinforce memories of their devotion to their comrades, families, and the idea of a *Volksgemeinschaft* during the war rather than memories of executing civilians and razing villages to the ground. The family members soldiers returned to, moreover, used the photographs they sent to the front to reinforce memories of their own devotion to fighting sons and husbands as well as their children and friends rather than memories of the Jewish neighbors they denounced or watched suffer. The tenets of family, comradeship, and community that lay beneath these "redemptive memories" also lay at the core of postwar efforts to reconstruct the German nation.[25] And they were the very same principles that had guided German soldiers' photography and album-making all along.

Descendants and researchers who expect to find detailed evidence of the horrors carried out by German soldiers during the war in their personal photographs will in all likelihood be disappointed. But the relative absence of atrocity photos in these collections does not mean that the soldiers who made them were innocent, nor does it signify anything less than their total devotion to the war effort. Instead of corroborating stories of their own complicity in war crimes, soldiers and their families used photography to uphold their membership in and service to the *Volksgemeinschaft,* the Nazis' utopian concept of a racially united people's community. Visitors themselves invoked it at the "War of Annihilation" exhibition to defend their fathers and grandfathers. "We saw it all differently from how it is shown here," a former leader of the League of German Girls (Bund Deutscher Mädel), a Nazi youth organization, objected. "We were taught to be idealistic and be there for others. . . . [Y]ou got a sense of family instilled in you, otherwise you couldn't have gotten through that time."[26] Maintaining their relationships to loved ones, fellow soldiers, and other members of that community was a critical requirement for membership in it. The popular conviction that it could become a reality had helped propel the Nazis to victory in 1933, turn Germans against their Jewish neighbors, mobilize them for war, and, even when the war began to favor the Allies after 1942, motivate them to keep fighting. Ultimately, photography's close relationship to the *Volksgemeinschaft* idea holds important historical lessons for understanding everyday life during the Third Reich as well as the many photographs and albums to emerge from it. But it holds further lessons still for the countless grandchildren and great-grandchildren who continue to search their family photograph collections to make sense of who their ancestors were and why their photographs reveal only a glimpse of what they saw and did during their years under Nazism.

Notes

Introduction

1. USHMM Henry Landman Papers RG-10.476, "A Return Home: The Henry Landman Story," 1992, 286.

2. For more on German Jewish soldiers in the US Army during World War II, see Bruce Henderson, *Sons and Soldiers: The Untold Story of the Jews Who Escaped the Nazis and Returned with the U.S. Army to Fight Hitler* (New York: HarperCollins, 2017); and Werner T. Angress, *Witness to the Storm: A Jewish Journey from Nazi Berlin to the 82nd Airborne, 1920–1945* (Bloomington: Indiana University Press, 2019).

3. USHMM Henry Landman Papers RG-10.476, box 1, folder 13, "Lists of Holocaust Victims Related to the Landman Family," 1990.

4. Landman Papers, "A Return Home," 227.

5. Landman Papers, "A Return Home," 6, 286.

6. USHMM Henry Landman Papers RG-10.476, Correspondence, box 1, folder 20.

7. The dispossession of German and European Jews is a recent emphasis within the scholarship on Nazi Germany which emphasizes the importance of theft and profit to Nazi antisemitic policy. See Jonathan R. Zatlin and Christoph Kreutzmüller, eds., *Dispossession: Plundering German Jewry, 1933–1953* (Ann Arbor: University of Michigan Press, 2020).

8. The subject of resistance during the Holocaust is a well-known subject in the literature on Nazi Germany but tends to emphasize armed resistance rather than written or visual documentation. A useful introduction to the subject is Patrick Henry, *Jewish Resistance to the Nazis* (Washington, D.C.: Catholic University of America Press, 2014).

9. "The concept of the *Volksgemeinschaft* drew its political power not from a social reality achieved but rather from its promise, and the mobilization it inspired," as Michael Wildt has pointed out. Michael Wildt, "Volksgemeinschaft: A Modern Perspective on National Socialist Society," in *Visions of Community in Nazi Germany: Social Engineering and Private Lives*, ed. Martina Steber and Bernhard Gotto (Oxford: Oxford University Press, 2018), 49. See also Robert Gellately, *The Gestapo and German Society: Enforcing Racial Policy, 1933–1945* (Oxford: Clarendon Press, 1990); Dietmar Süß, *Tod aus der Luft: Kriegsgesellschaft und Luftkrieg in Deutschland und England* (Munich: Siedler Verlag, 2011); Michael Wildt, *Hitler's Volksgemeinschaft and the Dynamics of Racial Exclusion: Violence against Jews in Provincial Germany, 1919–1939* (New York: Berghahn, 2012); Frank Bajohr and Michael Wildt, eds., *Volksgemeinschaft: Neue Forschungen zur Gesellschaft des Nationalsozialismus* (Frankfurt am Main: Fischer Taschenbuch Verlag, 2009); Norbert

Frei, "'Volksgemeinschaft': Erfahrungsgeschichte und Lebenswirklichkeit der Hitler-Zeit," in *1945 und wir: Das Dritte Reich im Bewußtsein der Deutschen* (Munich: Deutscher Taschenbuch Verlag, 2005); Ian Kershaw, "Volksgemeinschaft: Potential and Limitations of the Concept," in Steber and Gotto, *Visions of Community in Nazi Germany*.

10. For a particularly thoughtful overview of the use of photography to negotiate German national identity, see Andrés Mario Zervigón, *Photography and Germany* (London: Reaktion Books, 2017). On the practice of compiling photobooks in central Europe during the late nineteenth and early twentieth centuries, see Steven Samols, "Capturing Difference: The Wurstelprater Photobook in Turn-of-the-Century Vienna," *Leo Baeck Institute Year Book* 67, no. 1 (2022): 55–76.

11. Eva Giloi, *Monarchy, Myth and Material Culture in Germany, 1750–1950* (Cambridge: Cambridge University Press, 2011), 244. See also chaps. 10 and 11, in which Giloi explains the shaping of photographic culture under Kaisers Wilhelm I and Wilhelm II.

12. Lorena Rizzo, *Photography and History in Colonial Southern Africa: Shades of Empire* (Abingdon: Routledge, 2019).

13. Giloi, *Monarchy, Myth and Material Culture in Germany*, 253.

14. Justin Court, "Picturing History, Remembering Soldiers: World War I Photography between the Public and the Private," *History and Memory* 29, no. 1 (2017): 72–103. See also Bodo von Dewitz, *So wird bei uns der Krieg geführt: Amateurfotografie im Ersten Weltkrieg* (Munich: Tuduv-Verlagsgesellschaft, 1989); Stiftung Deutsches Historisches Museum, *Der Erste Weltkrieg in 100 Objekten* (Darmstadt: Theiss-Verlag, 2014); and Dean Putney, ed., *Walter Koessler, 1914–1918: The Personal Photo Journal of a German Officer in World War I* (San Francisco: Dean Putney, 2013).

15. Zervigón, *Photography and Germany*, 83–120.

16. See Daniel Magilow, *The Photography of Crisis: The Photo Essays of Weimar Germany* (University Park: Pennsylvania State University Press, 2012), 122.

17. Michael Berkowitz, "Photography as Jewish Space," in *Space and Spatiality in Modern German-Jewish History*, ed. Simone Lässig and Miriam Rürup (New York: Berghahn, 2019), 246–62.

18. *Völkisch* photography, or the use of photography for pseudoscientific explorations of Germanic racial superiority and non-Aryan degeneracy, has its roots in the imperial period but became more widely considered during the Weimar years. See Magilow, *Photography of Crisis*, 93–98; Amos Morris Reich, *Racial Photography as Scientific Evidence, 1876–1980* (Chicago: University of Chicago Press, 2016).

19. Elizabeth Cronin, *Heimat Photography in Austria: A Politicized Vision of Peasants and Skiers* (Vienna: Photoinstitut Bonartes; Salzburg: Fotohof Edition, 2015).

20. Matthew Jefferies, "Die Schöne Heimat? Depictions of Germany in a Popular Photobook from the Second Empire to the Federal Republic," *New German Critique* 46 (2019): 35–63. See also Erna Lendvai-Dircksen, *Das deutsche Volksgesicht* (Berlin: Kulturelle Verlagsgesellschaft, 1932).

21. Cronin, *Heimat Photography in Austria*, 21.

22. See Christina Irrgang, *Hitlers Fotograf: Heinrich Hoffmann und die nationalsozialistische Bildpolitik* (Bielefield: Transcript Verlag, 2020); and Rudolf Herz, *Hoffmann & Hitler: Fotografie als Medium des Führer-Mythos* (Munich: Klinkhardt & Biermann, 1994).

23. See Maria A. Pelizzari, *Photography and Italy* (London: Reaktion Books, 2011); Emily Evans, "Soviet Photo and the Search for Proletarian Photography, 1926–1937" (PhD diss., University of Illinois at Urbana-Champaign, 2014).

24. See Julia S. Torrie, "Visible Trophies of War: German Occupiers' Photographic Perceptions of France, 1940–44," in *The Ethics of Seeing: Photography in Twentieth-Century German History*, ed. Jennifer Evans, Paul Betts and Stefan Hoffman (New York: Berghahn, 2018), 108–37; Alexander B. Rossino, "Eastern Europe through German Eyes: Soldiers' Photographs, 1939–42," *History of Photography* 23, no. 4 (2015): 313–21; Petra Bopp and Andreas Koch, *Fremde im Visier: Fotoalben aus dem Zweiten Weltkrieg* (Bielefeld: Kerber, 2009); Petra Bopp, "Images of Violence in Wehrmacht Soldiers' Private Photo Albums," in *Violence and Visibility in Modern History*, ed. Jürgen Martschukat and Silvan Niedermeier (New York: Palgrave Macmillan, 2013), 181–97; Wendy Lower, *The Ravine: A Family, a Photograph, a Holocaust Massacre Revealed* (London: Head of Zeus, 2021).

25. Christopher R. Browning, Ordinary *Men: Reserve Police Battalion 101 and the Final Solution in Poland* (New York: Harper Perennial, 2017).

1. The People's Art

1. G. A. Kanitzberg, "Der Neue Weg," *Photofreund* 13 (1933): 259–60.

2. Peter Fritzsche, *Germans into Nazis* (Cambridge: Harvard University Press, 2003); Robert Gellately, *Backing Hitler: Consent and Coercion in Nazi Germany* (Oxford: Oxford University Press, 2013).

3. *Rede des Reichsministers Dr. Goebbels bei der Eröffnung der Reichskulturkammer am 15. November 1933* (Frankfurt am Main: Brönner's, 1933), 21–24.

4. Richard J. Evans, *The Third Reich in Power, 1933–1939* (London: Penguin, 2006), 118. Joseph Goebbels acknowledged in an early March 1933 speech, "The present government must . . . see its task as making all the necessary propaganda preparations to win the whole people over to its side in the long term." Joseph Goebbels, "Rede vor der Presse über die Errichtung des Reichspropagandaministeriums," in *Goebbels-Reden*, vol. 1, *1931–1939*, ed. Helmut Heiber (Düsseldorf: Droste Verlag, 1971), 90.

5. For a useful overview of the state of research on the concept of *Volksgemeinschaft*, see Martina Steber and Bernhard Gotto, eds., *Visions of Community in Nazi Germany: Social Engineering and Private Lives* (Oxford: Oxford University Press, 2018); Frank Bajohr and Michael Wildt, eds., *Volksgemeinschaft: Neue Forschungen zur Gesellschaft des Nationalsozialismus* (Frankfurt am Main: Fischer Taschenbuch Verlag, 2009).

6. Detlev Peukert, *The Weimar Republic: The Crisis of Classical Modernity* (New York: Hill and Wang, 2008); Walter Laqueur, *Weimar: A Cultural History, 1918–1933* (London: Phoenix Press, 2000); Peter Gay, *Weimar Culture: The Outsider as Insider* (New York: Norton, 2001).

7. Alan E. Steinweis, "Weimar Culture and the Rise of National Socialism: The Kampfbund für Deutsche Kultur," *Central European History* 24, no. 4 (1991): 402–23; Jeffrey Herf, *Reactionary Modernism: Technology, Culture, and Politics in Weimar and the Third Reich* (Cambridge: Cambridge University Press, 1984), 31.

8. Top Nazis like Joseph Goebbels, Hermann Göring, and others amassed substantial private art collections to portray themselves as cultural as well as political elites. See Jonathan Petropoulos, *Art as Politics in the Third Reich* (Chapel Hill: University of North Carolina Press, 1999). Propaganda remains the prevailing interest for scholars writing about the visual arts under Nazism. See David Welch, *The Third Reich: Politics and Propaganda* (London: Routledge, 2006).

9. Hitler's speech at the opening of the "Great German Art" exhibition in the House of German Art, Munich, July 18, 1937, *Völkischer Beobachter*, July 19, 1937, 1.

10. Horst Andress Dressler, *Three Years of the National-Socialist Community "Kraft durch Freude": Aims and Achievements* (Berlin: Verlag der deutschen Arbeitsfront, 1937), 4.

11. The exhibitions of 1937, for instance, dominate the literature on popular participation in the visual arts under Nazism. See Michael Tymkiw, *Nazi Exhibition Design and Modernism* (Minneapolis: University of Minnesota Press, 2018); Ines Schlenker, *Hitler's Salon: The Grosse Deutsche Kunstausstellung at the Haus der Deutschen Kunst in Munich, 1937–1944* (Bern: P. Lang, 2007); Stephanie Barron, ed., *"Degenerate Art": The Fate of the Avant-Garde in Nazi Germany* (Los Angeles: Los Angeles County Museum of Art, 1991). More recently, there has been a focus on art exhibitions in factories and workplaces. See Michael Tymkiw, "Art to the Worker! National Socialist Fabrikausstellungen, Slippery Household Goods and Volksgemeinschaft," *Journal of Design History / Design History Society* 26 (2013): 362–80.

12. Shelley Baranowski, "Family Vacation for Workers: The Strength through Joy Resort at Prora," *German History* 25, no. 4 (October 2007): 539–59.

13. Celia Applegate and Pamela Potter have pointed out that historians of Nazi culture tend to rely on the regime's own administrative structure to decipher which arts are worthy of historical inquiry. This chapter heeds their suggestion to "go beyond the surface" and "look closely at the internal composition" of this structure. See Celia Applegate and Pamela Potter, "Cultural History: Where It Has Been and Where It Is Going," *Central European History* 51, no. 1 (2018): 81. For examples of works on culture under Nazism that reflect this structure, see Jost Hermand, *Kultur in finsteren Zeiten: Nazifaschismus, Innere Emigration, Exil* (Cologne: Böhlau, 2010); Lisa Pine, *Hitler's "National Community": Society and Culture in Nazi Germany* (London: Bloomsbury Academic, 2017); Alan Steinweis, *Art, Ideology, and Economics in Nazi Germany: The Reich Chambers of Music, Theater, and the Visual Arts* (Chapel Hill: University of North Carolina Press, 1993); Jonathan Huener and Francis R. Nicosia, eds., *The Arts in Nazi Germany: Continuity, Conformity, Change*, Vermont Studies on Nazi Germany and the Holocaust (New York: Berghahn, 2006).

14. Tim Starl, *Knipser: Die Bildgeschichte der privaten Fotografie in Deutschland und Österreich von 1880 bis 1980* (Munich: Koehler & Amelang, 1995).

15. See Theodor W. Adorno and Max Horkheimer, "The Culture Industry," in *Dialectic of Enlightenment* (New York: Continuum, 1972), 120–67; Walter Benjamin, "The Work of Art in the Age of Mechanical Reproduction," in *Walter Benjamin: Selected Writings*, ed. Howard Eiland and Michael W. Jennings (Cambridge: Belknap Press of Harvard University Press, 2006).

16. Glenn Cuomo, ed., *National Socialist Cultural Policy* (New York: St. Martin's Press, 1995).

17. Avraham Barkai, *Nazi Economics: Ideology, Theory, and Policy* (New Haven: Yale University Press, 1990); S. Jonathan Wiesen, *Creating the Nazi Marketplace: Commerce and Consumption in the Third Reich* (Cambridge: Cambridge University Press, 2011); Hartmut Berghoff and Uwe Spiekermann, eds., *Decoding Modern Consumer Societies* (New York: Palgrave Macmillan, 2012); Tim Mason, "The Legacy of 1918 for National Socialism," in *German Democracy and the Triumph of Hitler: Essays in Recent German History*, ed. Anthony Nicholls and Eric Matthias (London: Allen and Unwin, 1971), 215–40.

18. Hartmut Berghoff and Berti Kolbow, "Flourishing in a Dictatorship: Agfa's Marketing and the Nazi Regime," *Journal of Historical Research in Marketing* 5, no. 1 (2013): 71–96.

19. Shearer West, *The Visual Arts in Germany, 1890–1937: Utopia and Despair* (New Brunswick: Rutgers University Press, 2001), 160.

20. Peter Longerich, *Hitler: A Biography* (Oxford: Oxford University Press, 2019), 486.

21. Schlenker, *Hitler's Salon*, 154. This was an observation made by Peter Guenther as well, who was only seventeen when he visited the exhibition. Peter Guenther, "Three Days in Munich, July 1937," in *"Degenerate Art,"* 34–35. It was also not a coincidence that Hitler selected his personal photographer and confidant Heinrich Hoffmann to help him select the paintings for the 1937 exhibition. Although Hoffmann is typically dismissed as the "court jester" of Hitler's inner circle, his proximity to Hitler raises questions about the full scope of his involvement in Nazi crimes, particularly in the dispossession of German Jews. Hoffmann dodges many of these questions in his self-exculpatory memoir, *Hitler Was My Friend* (London: Burke, 1955). Instead, Hoffmann's photographs are better known than the man himself. See Rudolf Herz, *Hoffmann & Hitler: Fotografie als Medium des Führer-Mythos* (Munich: Klinkhardt & Biermann, 1994).

22. See Devin O. Pendas, Mark Roseman, and Richard F. Wetzell, eds., *Beyond the Racial State: Rethinking Nazi Germany* (Washington, D.C.: German Historical Institute, 2017), in response to Michael Burleigh and Wolfgang Wipperman, *The Racial State: Germany, 1933–1945* (Cambridge: Cambridge University Press, 2005).

23. Richard W. Darré, *Neuadel aus Blut und Boden* (Munich: J. F. Lehmann, 1930).

24. Examples include the photographs used in Willy Stiewe and Heiner Kurzbein, *Foto und Volk* (Halle: Knapp, 1933); Hans F. K. Günther, *Kleine Rassenkunde des deutschen Volkes* (Munich: Lehmann, 1929); and *Der ewige Jude* (The Eternal Jew), dir. Fritz Eppler (Chicago: International Historic Films, 1940).

25. Peter Burke, *Eyewitnessing: The Use of Images as Historical Evidence* (Ithaca: Cornell University Press, 2008), 25.

26. David M. Kennedy, *Freedom from Fear: The American People in Depression and War, 1929–1945* (New York: Oxford University Press, 2005), 255–56; Kerry Ross, *Photography for Everyone: The Cultural Lives of Cameras and Consumers in Early Twentieth-Century Japan* (Stanford: Stanford University Press, 2015); Anne Maxwell, *Picture Imperfect: Photography and Eugenics, 1870–1940* (London: Eastbourne Sussex Press, 2010).

27. Victoria de Grazia, *The Culture of Consent: Mass Organization of Leisure in Fascist Italy* (Cambridge: Cambridge University Press, 1981); Maria A. Pelizzari, *Photography and Italy* (London: Reaktion Books, 2011).

28. Sheila Fitzpatrick, *Everyday Stalinism: Ordinary Life in Extraordinary Times: Soviet Russia in the 1930s* (Oxford: Oxford University Press, 1999), 79.

29. Emily Evans shows how the journal *Soviet Photo* defined and sought to create a truly proletarian photography. Photography was supposed to fulfill certain ideological goals in the early Soviet Union, among them socialist realism and the integration of worker and peasant amateur photographers into the press and institutional structures. Ultimately, the mass character of the project was in name only, for unlike the Nazis, the Soviet leaders did not follow through on this endeavor. See Emily Evans, "Soviet Photo and the Search for Proletarian Photography, 1926–1937" (PhD diss., University of Illinois at Urbana-Champaign, 2014), 227.

30. One of Germany's many photographic associations for professional photographers, the CVDP was founded in 1902 to protect photographers following the establishment of new copyright laws. See John Hannavy, *Encyclopedia of Nineteenth-Century Photography* (New York: Routledge, 2008), 1296.

31. Harold James, *Deutschland in der Weltwirtschaftskrise, 1924–1936* (Stuttgart: Deutsche Verlags-Anstalt, 1988).

32. Bundesarchiv Berlin Lichterfelde (BArchB) R3101/14071; "Was tut der Central Verband?," *Photographische Chronik*, no. 14 (July 4, 1933).

33. BArchB R 3101/14071, Schreiben von die Central Verband Deutscher Photographen-Verein und Innung an das Reichswirtschaftsministerium, Berlin, July 15, 1933, 4, 6–7.

34. See the entry by Rolf Sachsse in Hannavy, *Encyclopedia of Nineteenth-Century Photography*, 1296.

35. Joseph Goebbels quoted in Willy Frerk, "Das Erlebnis des Einzelnen ist zu einem Volkserlebnis geworden und das durch die Kamera," *Photofreund* (1933): 417–18, cited in Timm Starl, *Knipser*, 19.

36. Berghoff and Kolbow, "Flourishing in a Dictatorship," 78.

37. BArchB R 3101/14071, Schreiben von dem Central Verband Deutscher Photographen-Vereine und Innung an das Reichswirtschaftsministerium, Berlin, July 15, 1933, 2–3.

38. Photo identification was new to Germany, introduced only in the 1920s. See Andreas Reisen, *Der Passexpedient: Geschichte der Reisepässe und Ausweisdokumente—vom Mittelalter bis zum Personalausweis im Scheckkartenformat* (Baden-Baden: Nomos, 2012).

39. BArchB R3101/14071, Bezirksinnungsmeister and Obermeister der Photographen-Innung Dortmund (signatures illegible) to Adolf Hitler, 1935, emphasis added.

40. LOC Prints and Photographs Division LC-B2- 4295-16, photograph of Anatol Josepho, inventor of the "Photomaton" photo booth, March 29, 1927.

41. BArchB R3101/14071, Central Verband Deutscher Photographen-Vereine und Innung to Reichswirtschaftsministerium, Berlin, July 15, 1933, 3, 10.

42. BArchB R 3101/14071 no. 10693/33, Abschrift an das Referat IB2, Reichswirtschaftministerium, September 11, 1933.

43. Speech to the press on the establishment of a Reich Ministry of Popular Enlightenment and Propaganda, March 15, 1933, in Joseph Goebbels, *Revolution der Deutschen: 14 Jahre Nationalsozialismus* (Oldenburg: Gerhard Stalling, 1933), 135–50.

44. Reichskulturkammer, *Handbuch der Reichskulturkammer* (Berlin: Deutscher Verlag für Politik und Wirtschaft, 1937).

45. Irene Ziehe and Ulrich Hägele, *Fotografien vom Alltag—Fotografieren als Alltag: Tagung der Kommission Fotografie der deutschen Gesellschaft für Volkskunde und der Sektion Geschichte und Archive der deutschen Gesellschaft für Photographie im Museum Europäischer Kulturen—Staatliche Museen zu Berlin vom 15. bis 17. November 2002* (Münster: Lit, 2004), 230.

46. Heiner Kurzbein, "Reichsverband Deutscher Amateurfotografen," *Photographie für Alle: Zeitschrift für alle Zweige der Photographie,* no. 13 (July 1, 1933): 325.

47. When the war ended, Kurzbein worked as a sales clerk until his death in 1957 in Essen. See Rolf Sachsse, *Die Erziehung zum Wegsehen: Fotografie im NS-Staat* (Dresden: Philo Fine Arts, 2003), 403.

48. Heiner Kurzbein, "Unsere Kamera ist einzuspannen in das politische Leven und Treiben unserer Zeit," *Photofreund* no. 21 (1933): 397.

49. Heiner Kurzbein, "Die deutsche Amateurphotographie und ihre Organisation," *Photographie für Alle: Zeitschrift für alle Zweige der Photographie* 1, 21 (November 1933): 346.

50. Kurzbein, "Die deutsche Amateurphotographie und ihre Organisation," 346.

51. Kurzbein, "Reichsverband Deutscher Amateurfotografen," 325.

52. Kurzbein, "Die deutsche Amateurphotographie und ihre Organisation," 346.

53. Kurzbein, "Reichsverband Deutscher Amateurfotografen," 325. See also Frances Guerin, *Through Amateur Eyes: Film and Photography in Nazi Germany* (Minneapolis: University of Minnesota Press, 2011), 58.

54. U.A., "Dr. Goebbels und die Amateurfotografie," *Photofreund* 15 (1935): 199.

55. Kurzbein, "Reichsverband Deutscher Amateurfotografen," 325.

56. Walter Uka, "Zur Austellung 'Die Kamera' im November 1933," in *Zur Geschichte der Pressefotografie, 1930–36: Die Gleichschaltung der Bilder,* ed. Diethart Kerbs, Walter Uka, and Brigitte Walz-Richter (Berlin: Frölich & Kaufmann, 1983), 156.

57. Petropoulos, *Art as Politics,* 151.

58. Joseph Goebbels, "Eröffnungsansprache zur Austellung 'die Kamera,'" *Völkischer Beobachter,* November 4, 1933.

59. Press release for the exhibition "Die Kamera," Ausstellungshallen am Funkturn, Berlin, November 4–19, 1933, in *Public Photographic Spaces: Exhibitions of Propaganda, from Pressa to the Family of Man, 1928–55* (Barcelona: MACBA, 2009), 263.

60. Universität der Künste Berlin Bibliothek, NX 1422, Heiner Kurzbein, "Die Fotografie im nationalen Deutschland," in *Die Kamera: Ausstellung für Fotografie, Druck und Reproduktion, amtlicher Katalog und Führer, Berlin 1933, 4. bis 19. November* (Berlin, 1933), 9–10.

61. Whether photography was more art than craft was a debate as old as photography itself. See Alan Trachtenberg, *Classic Essays on Photography* (New Haven: Leete's Island Books, 1980); Albert Dresdner, "German Commercial Photography," *Commercial Art* 4 (April 1928): 173–76; Steffen Siegel, *First Exposures: Writings from the Beginnings of Photography* (Los Angeles: J. Paul Getty Museum, 2017).

62. Kurzbein, "Die Fotografie im nationalen Deutschland," 9–10.

63. Tour of "Die Kamera" in press release for the exhibition.

64. Hans Biallas, "Die Deutsche Arbeitsfront und 'Die Kamera,'" in *Die Kamera amtlicher Katalog,* 13–14.

65. Biallas, "Die Deutsche Arbeitsfront und 'Die Kamera,'" 13.

66. Wolfgang König, "Der Volksempfänger und die Radioindustrie: Ein Beitrag zum Verhältnis von Wirtschaft und Politik im Nationalsozialismus," *VSWG: Vierteljahrschrift für Sozial- und Wirtschaftsgeschichte* 90, no. 3 (2003): 269–89.

67. Karl Weiß, "Die Wirtschaftliche Bedeutung der Deutschen Fotografischen Industrie," in *Die Kamera amtlicher Katalog,* 73–76.

68. Wilhelm Niemann, "Berufsfotographie," in *Die Kamera amtlicher Katalog,* 27–28.

69. Heiner Kurzbein, "Die Fotografie im nationalen Deutschland," 10.

70. BArchB R3101/14071 Anordnung 286, Betr,. Belampfung der Schwarzarbeit im Photographenhandwerk, June 12, 1934, 82; Sturmbefehl Nr. 8/34 von Der Führer des Sturms Gunzenhauser, Ziffer 7: Lichtbilder für Ausweise; Brief von Reichspräsidenten der Abteilung, Sandes von Hoffmann, May 29, 1934, "Auf das Schreibens von 16 Mai 1934."

71. BArchB R3101/14071, Schreiben Betr: Lichtbilder für amtliche Ausweise von der Reichs und Preußische Minister des Innern, November 8, 1934.

72. Like other Nazi art exhibitions, "Die Kamera" was designed to "stir and convince people, [and] sweep them away." See Albert Wischek, "Deutschland im Spiegel der Ausstellungen und Messen," *Messe und Ausstellung* 18, no. 5 (March 1–15, 1936): 1–2.

73. This may come as somewhat of a surprise, given the emphasis in National Socialism on women as mothers and housewives rather than businesswomen or artists. Claudia Koonz, *Mothers in the Fatherland: Women, the Family, and Nazi Politics* (London: Routledge, 2014); Elizabeth D. Heineman, *What Difference Does a Husband Make? Women and Marital Status in Nazi and Postwar Germany* (Berkeley: University of California Press, 2003).

74. Bertha Zillessen (1872–1936) was a painter and photographer based in Bautzen, Germany, where she opened her own portrait photography studio. Born to a farming family in Pomerania, Liselotte Strelow (1908–1981) moved to Berlin and took photography courses at the Lette-Verein school. She later became an apprentice to Suse Byk in 1932 and eventually stole her business after Byk was dispossessed under Nazi racial law.

75. "Gruppe Amateurfotografie," in *Die Kamera amtlicher Katalog*, 111.

76. Timothy Mason, "Women in Germany, 1925–1940: Family Welfare and Work," *History Workshop* 2 (1976): 5–32; Sybille Steinbacher, ed., *"Volksgenossinnen": Frauen in der NS-Volksgemeinschaft* (Göttingen: Wallstein, 2007); Koonz, *Mothers in the Fatherland*; Heineman, *What Difference Does a Husband Make?*

77. Willy Frerk, "Schenk deiner Frau eine Kamera!," *Photofreund*, December 20, 1933, 457.

78. "Herunter mit der Maske!," *Deutsche Nachrichten*, May 1, 1933, 65–66.

79. Advertisement in *Die Kamera amtlicher Katalog*, 123. On Ullstein, see Herman Ullstein, *The Rise and Fall of the House of Ullstein* (New York: Simon and Schuster, 1943), 277.

80. See chapter 2 of this book.

81. Anthony McElligott and Tim Kirk, eds., *Working towards the Führer: Essays in Honour of Sir Ian Kershaw* (Manchester: Manchester University Press, 2004); Martin Broszat, *Der Staat Hitlers: Grundlegung und Entwicklung seiner inneren Verfassung* (Munich: Deutscher Taschenbuch-Verlag, 1969).

82. Detlev J. K. Peukert, *Inside Nazi Germany: Conformity, Opposition and Racism in Everyday Life* (London: Penguin Books, 1993), 58; Ian Kershaw, *Popular Opinion and Political Dissent in the Third Reich: Bavaria, 1933–1945* (Oxford: Clarendon Press, 2005), 224.

83. Victor Klemperer, *I Shall Bear Witness: The Diaries of Victor Klemperer, 1933–1941* (London: Folio Society, 2006), 16–17.

84. The exhibition moved on to Stuttgart from Berlin, but the assassination of Ernst Röhm, chief of the SA, in July 1934 prematurely ended plans for its continuation in other major cities. Most of the photographs featured in the "History of National Socialism" section featured Hitler and Röhm together and were thus no longer appropriate. Ulrich Pohlmann, "'Not Autonomous Art but a Political Weapon,'" in *Public Photographic Spaces: Exhibitions of Propaganda from Press to the Family of Man, 1928–55*, ed. Jorge Ribalta (Barcelona: Museu d'Art Contemporani de Barcelona, 2008), 291.

85. LOC LOT 2719 (F), "Mit der Kamera durch die 'Kamera'" album, "Lageplan der Ausstellung mit Eintrittspreise," November 1933, fifty-two photographic prints, 34 x 24 cm. My thanks to Jonathan Eaker at the Library of Congress for providing me with digital scans of this album.

86. Adam Tooze estimates the cost of a loaf of brown bread to have been thirty-one pfennigs in the 1930s. Adam Tooze, *The Wages of Destruction: The Making and Breaking of the Nazi Economy* (London: Allen Lane, 2006), 142.

87. *Photographie für Alle: Zeitschrift für alle Zweige der Photographie* 29, no. 13 (July 1, 1933): 316.

88. LAB A Rep 250-04-21 Nr. 45, Merkblätter des Verbandes Deutscher Amateur-Photographen-Vereine E.V., June 8, 1933.

89. "Zur Ausstellung 'die Kamera,'" *Photographie für Alle: Zeitschrift für alle Zweige der Photographie,* no. 21 (November 1, 1933): 334. Voigtländer was renowned for making quality cameras and lenses and exporting them all over the world, emblematic of the economic as well as cultural grounds on which the Nazis based their advocacy for promoting the practice of photography and protection of the industry.

90. Herbert Starke, "Was der Amateur auf der Ausstellung 'die Kamera' sah und lernte," *Photographie für Alle: Zeitschrift für alle Zweige der Photographie,* no. 23 (December 1, 1933): 369. During the Second World War, Starke led training classes for PK (*Propagandakompanien)* photographers. See Sachsse, *Die Erziehung zum Wegsehen,* 439. See also Daniel Magilow's discussion on how the photographer Albert Renger-Patzsch responded to the exhibition in Daniel Magilow, ed., *The Absolute Realist: Collected Writings of Albert Renger-Patzsch, 1923–1967* (Los Angeles: Getty Research Institute, 2023), 21-23.

91. "Voigtländer auf der Ausstellung 'Die Kamera,'" *Photographie für Alle: Zeitschrift für alle Zweige der Photographie* 29, no. 24 (December 15, 1933): 394.

92. Hubert Mikeffa, "'Erinnern Sie auch noch . . . ?'" *Revue des Monats* 8, no. 2 (December 1933): 135.

93. "Mit der Kamera durch die 'Kamera'" album.

94. F. Martin, "Die Zukünftigen Ziele der Deutschen Amateur-Photographen," *Photographie für Alle: Zeitschrift für alle Zweige der Photographie* no. 24 (December 15, 1933): 383-84.

95. Shelley Baranowski, *Strength through Joy: Consumerism and Mass Tourism in the Third Reich* (Cambridge: Cambridge University Press, 2004). For a concise overview of the organization, see Evans, *The Third Reich in Power,* 465-66.

96. Carl Seitz, "Freizeitgestaltung und Amateurfotografie," *Agfa Fotoblätter* 11 (1934): 2.

97. Timothy Mason, "Labour in the Third Reich, 1933-1939," *Past & Present* (1966): 121-22.

98. Alexander de la Croix, "Lerne Photographieren bei 'Kraft durch Freude,'" *Photofreund* 16, no. 2 (1936): 21-22.

99. BArchB R 8128/17263, Bruno Uhl to Robert Ley, January 31, 1934, cited in Berghoff and Kolbow, "Flourishing in a Dictatorship," 79.

100. BArchB R 8128/ 20576, Bruno Uhl to staff, July 23, 1937, 18, cited in Berghoff and Kolbow, "Flourishing in a Dictatorship," 80.

101. Berghoff and Kolbow, "Flourishing in a Dictatorship," 81.

102. Sachsse, *Die Erziehung zum Wegsehen,* 377.

103. Alexander de la Croix, "Lerne Photographieren bei 'Kraft durch Freude,'" *Photofreund* 16, no. 2 (1936): 21-22.

104. BArchB NSD 50/750, Carl Seitz, "Kraft durch Freude und Amateurfotografie," *Die Liebhaberlichtbildnergilde,* no. 11 (1934): 124-30. Seitz would join the Nazi Party relatively late, in 1940.

105. J. B. Ring, "'Kraft durch Freude,' auch im neuen Jahr schöpferisch: KDF-Foto-Kurse für Anfänger," *Arbeitertum* 5, no. 21 (1935-36): 28.

106. RK, "Die Photolehrgänge der Deutschen Arbeitsfront NS-Gemeinschaft 'Kraft durch Freude,'" *Photofreund* 16, no. 7 (1936): 29.

107. Sozialdemokratische Partei Deutschlands, *Deutschland-Bericht der Sopade, Apr./Mai 1934–Dez. 1936*, 34–35.

108. De la Croix, "Lerne photographieren bei 'Kraft durch Freude,'" 21–22.

109. Stephen Broadberry and Carsten Burhop, "Real Wages and Labor Productivity in Britain and Germany, 1871–1938: A Unified Approach to the International Comparison of Living Standards," *Journal of Economic History* 70, no. 2 (2010): 400–427.

110. BArchB R8128/17344, Wilhelm Otto, Besprechung im Reichswirtschaftsministerium, file note of September 11, 1936, also cited in Berghoff and Kolbow, "Flourishing in a Dictatorship," 85.

111. Between 1934 and 1938, the number of participants who attended KdF events grew from over 9 million to more than 54 million. Baranowski, "Family Vacation for Workers."

112. RK, "Die Photolehrgänge der Deutschen Arbeitsfront NS-Gemeinschaft 'Kraft durch Freude,'" 29.

113. Carl Seitz, "Gründet Werksphotogruppen," *Photographie für Alle* 33, no. 2 (January 15, 1937): 28. See also Horst Dressler-Andress, *Three Years of the National-Socialist Community "Kraft durch Freude": Aims and Achievements* (Berlin: Verlag der deutschen Arbeitsfront, 1937), 4.

114. Sozialdemokratische Partei Deutschlands, *Deutschland-Bericht der Sopade, September–Oktober 1934*, November 6, 1934, 23–25.

115. Baranowski, *Strength through Joy*, 198.

116. Figures for the years 1939–1941 adapted from IG Farben Detaillierter Geschaeftsbericht (1940–41), in Berghoff and Kolbow, "Flourishing in a Dictatorship," 76.

2. "Taking What Belongs to Us"

1. USHMM Rafael and Nelly Brenner Family Papers 1995.61, box 1, folder 6; Charles Lehman, "Berlin to Rome to Washington, D.C.. Saga of Rafael Brenner," *Photographic Trade News* (June 1946): 1–2.

2. USHMM Rafael and Nelly Brenner Family Papers 1995.61, box 1, folder 8, *Westdeutscher Beobachter,* July 4, 1933.

3. See, for example, Alan Steinweis, *Art, Ideology, and Economics in Nazi Germany: The Reich Chambers of Music, Theater, and the Visual Arts* (Chapel Hill: University of North Carolina Press, 1993); Jonathan Huener and Francis R. Nicosia, eds., *The Arts in Nazi Germany: Continuity, Conformity, Change,* Vermont Studies on Nazi Germany and the Holocaust (New York: Berghahn, 2006); Glenn Cuomo, ed., *National Socialist Cultural Policy* (New York: St. Martin's Press, 1995); Jonathan Petropoulos, *Artists under Hitler: Collaboration and Survival in Nazi Germany* (New Haven: Yale University Press, 2015).

4. See Marion Beckers and Elisabeth Moortgat, *Yva: Photographien, 1925–1938 = Yva: Photographies, 1925–1938* (Tübingen: Wasmuth, 2001); Marion Beckers and Elisabeth Moortgat, *Atelier Lotte Jacobi, Berlin, New York* (Berlin: Verborgene Museum, 1997); Wilfried Weinke, *Verdrängt, vertrieben, aber nicht vergessen: Die Fotografen Emil Bieber, Max Halberstadt, Erich Kastan und Kurt Schallenberg* (Weingarten: Kunstverlag Weingarten, 2003).

5. Steinweis, *Art, Ideology, and Economics in Nazi Germany*, chap. 2.

6. Nazi functionaries and civilian enthusiasts also used photography during this and other spontaneous antisemitic "boycotts" to publicly denounce and shame non-Jewish Germans who continued to patronize Jewish-owned businesses. See Julie R. Keresztes, "Shaming through Photographic Denunciation in Nazi Germany, 1933–1938," *Contemporary European History* (2023): 1–12.

7. Diethart Kerbs, *Auf den Straßen von Berlin: der Fotograf Willy Römer, 1887–1979* (Bönen: Deutsches Historisches Museum, 2004); Diethart Kerbs, "Kalte Zeit: Über die zweite Lebenshälfte (1933–1979) des Berliner Pressefotografen Willy Römer," *Fotogeschichte* 24, no. 94 (2004): 68–70.

8. Weinke, *Verdrängt, vertrieben, aber nicht vergessen*, 249. Nazi photographers staged the April 1, 1933, blockade to disguise the violent and destructive nature of it. See Christoph Kreutzmüller, "Staging a Boycott: Photographs of the Nazi Attack on Jewish-Owned Businesses in April 1933," *Holocaust and Genocide Studies* 38, no. 1 (Spring 2024): 1–17.

9. Photographers themselves during these years distinguished between specialties in press, portrait, architecture, commercial, landscape, and even postcard photography. See BArchB R3101/14071, Schreiben von der Central Verband Deutscher Photographen-Verein und Innungen, July 10, 1933, 1–10.

10. "Herunter mit der Maske!," *Deutsche Nachrichten*, May 1, 1933.

11. During the late 1920s, women had found unprecedented professional opportunities in the industry, particularly in portrait, fashion, and commercial photography. Educational opportunities for aspiring female photographers had emerged even earlier. Atina Grossman, "Berufswahl-ein Privileg der bürgerlichen Frauen," in *Fotografieren hieß teilnehmen: Fotografinnen der Weimarer Republik*, exhibition catalog, ed. Ute Eskildsen (Dusseldorf: Richter, 1994), 11; Ingrid Sharp, "Gender Relations in Weimar Berlin," in *Practicing Modernity: Female Creativity in the Weimar Republic*, ed. Christiane Schönfeld and Carmel Finnan (Würzburg: Königshausen und Neumann, 2006), 2.

12. Beckers and Moortgat, *Yva*, 210.

13. Albert Dresdner, "German Commercial Photography," *Commercial Art* 4 (April 1928): 173–76.

14. Lotte König, "Die Frau als Photographin," in *Die Kultur der Frau: eine Lebenssymphonie der Frau des XX. Jahrhunderts*, ed. Ada Schmidt-Beil (Berlin: Verlag fur Kultur und Wissenschaft), 292. See also Sophie Rycroft, "Self-Expression and Profession: Female Photographers' Self-Portraits in Berlin, 1929–1933" (MPhil thesis, University of Birmingham, 2013).

15. A business was deemed "Jewish" if one or more managers of the studio could be identified as such, usually on the basis of surnames. This practice was standard in the exclusion of Jewish business owners from German economic life overall. See Christoph Kreutzmüller, *Final Sale in Berlin: The Destruction of Jewish Commercial Activity, 1930–1945* (New York: Berghahn, 2017), 4–6.

16. "Herunter mit der Maske!"

17. *Die Dame* was a prominent women's fashion magazine published by Ullstein. For the excerpt from *Deutsche Kultur-Wacht: Blätter des Kampfbundes fur deutsche Kultur*, see Beckers and Moortgat, *Yva*, 211.

18. "Herunter mit der Maske!"

19. Heiner Kurzbein, "Die Fotografie im nationalen Deutschland," in *Die Kamera: Ausstellung für Fotografie, Druck und Reproduktion, amtlicher Katalog und Führer, Berlin 1933, 4. bis 19. November* (Berlin, 1933), 9–10.

20. BArch-BL R3101/14071, Alexander Schwarz to Wirtschaftsministerium, Berlin, December 10, 1933.

21. BArch-BL R3101/14071, Reichswirtschaftsministerium, Berlin, to Alexander Schwarz, December 23, 1933.

22. BArch-BL R3101/14071, Reichswirtschaftsministerium, Berlin, to Alexander Schwarz, January 10, 1934.

23. United States Foreign Claims Settlement Commission, "Programs Completed in 1981," *Annual Report, 1981* (Washington, D.C., 1981), 67–68.

24. See the obituary for Benno's son Bernward Thorsch, who was also a photographer, *Santa Barbara Independent*, August 11, 2015.

25. Douglas Martin, "John Noble, Gulag Survivor, Dies at 84," *New York Times*, November 26, 2007.

26. Der Stuermer Archive (Stadtarchiv Nuernberg), E39 Nr. 2448/3, photo store in Mannheim, ca. 1933–1939.

27. LAB A Pr Br Rep 030-04 Nr. 746, Membership statutes for the Berlin-Kreuzberg Amateur Photographers' Association (Amateurphotographen Verein Berlin-Kreuzberg) by association leader (Vereinsführer) Karl Langner, December 20, 1934, 3, 4, 11.

28. Christoph Kreutzmüller and Theresia Ziehe, "Crossing Borders in the Summer of 1935: Fritz Fürstenberg's Photographs of Persecution in National Socialist Germany," *Leo Baeck Institute Year Book* (2019): 73–89. See also Ofer Ashkenazi, "Exile at Home: Jewish Amateur Photography under National Socialism, 1933–1939," *Leo Baeck Institute Year Book* (2019): 115–40; Ofer Ashkenazi, "Reading Private Photography," *American Historical Review* 127, no. 4 (December 2022): 1606–34. On the broader subject of Jewish resistance to Nazi policies and restrictions, see Wolf Gruner, *Resisters: How Ordinary Jews Fought Persecution in Hitler's Germany* (New Haven: Yale University Press, 2023).

29. Jonathan Petropoulos, *Art as Politics in the Third Reich* (Chapel Hill: University of North Carolina Press, 1999), 47.

30. Steinweis, *Art, Ideology, and Economics in Nazi Germany*, 141.

31. Irme Schaber, "Fotografie," in *Handbuch der deutschsprachigen Emigration, 1933–1945*, ed. Claus-Dieter Krohn (Darmstadt: Wissenschaftliche Buchgesellschaft, 2008), 971.

32. Weinke, *Verdrängt, vertrieben, aber nicht vergessen*, 249.

33. Industrie und Handelskammer zu Berlin, *Wirtschaftsblatt der Industrie und Handelskammer zu Berlin: Organ D. Wirtschaftskammer Berlin-Brandenburg* (Berlin: IHK, 1934–1943).

34. Kreutzmüller, *Final Sale in Berlin*, 16.

35. The role of German craftsmen and artisans in bringing the Nazis to power has been well documented. See Frederick L. McKitrick, *From Craftsmen to Capitalists: German Artisans from the Third Reich to the Federal Republic, 1939–1953* (New York: Berghahn, 2016).

36. BArch-BL. R3101/14071, Central Verband Deutscher Photographen-Vereine und Innung to Reichswirtschaftsministerium, Berlin, July 15, 1933, 2.

37. USHMM Archives, Gustav Rohmer, *Die neue Innungsordnung: Erste Verordnung über den vorläufigen Aufbau des Deutschen Handwerks vom 15. Juni 1934 nebst Ausführungsbestimmungen* (Munich: Beck, 1934).

38. See Lotte Jacobi's *Handwerkskarte,* dated October 1, 1934, box 32, folder 28, Lotte Jacobi Papers, 1898–2000, MC-58, Milne Special Collections and Archives, University of New Hampshire Library, Durham.

39. See Margaret Rosenberg's *Handwerkskarte,* dated April 1, 1935, Margaret and Kurt Rosenberg Family Collection, AR 25280, box 2, folder 3.

40. LBI, Margaret and Kurt Rosenberg Family Collection, AR 25280, box 2, folder 3, Kurt Rosenberg, "Berufsgegenstände meiner Ehefrau," 4.

41. StAH 135-1 I-IV 609 Blatt 12, Vermerk von Herrn Oberreigierungsrat Dr. Lindemann, August 9, 1935.

42. Marion Beckers, Hannelore Fischer, and Elisabeth Moortgat, eds., *Lotte Jacobi: Photographien* (Cologne: Wienand, 2012).

43. MSCA-UNH, MC-58, folder 30, box 32, Lotte Jacobi Papers, 1898–2000, Fachverband der Reichspressekammer in der Reichskulturkammer to Firma Bender und Jacobi, June 6, 1935.

44. Reichsschule des Deutschen Buchhandels, *Das Reichskulturkammergesetz* (Berlin, 1933), 1–2.

45. Fachverband der Reichspressekammer in der Reichskulturkammer to Firma Bender und. Jacobi, June 6, 1935, 2.

46. This was standard practice in the general dispossession process. See Kreutzmüller, *Final Sale in Berlin,* 267.

47. Fachverband der Reichspressekammer in der Reichskulturkammer to Firma Bender und Jacobi, June 6, 1935, 2.

48. MSCA-UNH, MC-58, folder 30, box 32, Lotte Jacobi Papers, 1898–2000, Reichverbandes to Bender und Jacobi, September 7, 1935, 2.

49. MSCA-UNH, MC-58, folder 9, box 31, Lotte Jacobi Papers, 1898–2000, diary [loose leaves], 1935–1976.

50. MSCA-UNH, MC-58, folder 12, box 2, Lotte Jacobi Papers, 1898–2000, correspondence from Alexander Bender to Lotte Jacobi, 1935–1970.

51. H.M. Koetzle, *Das Lexikon der Fotografen 1900 bis heute* (Munich: Knaur, 2002), 174.

52. LAB A Rep 342-02 Nr. 36765 Blatt 1–2b, 4, May 27, 1919.

53. Hanni Schwarz, "Photographie als Frauenberuf," *Photographische Mitteilungen,* June 1, 1905, 161–65.

54. LAB A Rep 342-02 Nr. 36765, Survey for the district court of Charlottenburg with the business number 90HRA 50560 +37, August 19, 1919.

55. LAB A Rep 342-02 Nr. 36765, Industry und Handelskammer zu Berlin to Amstgericht Berlin, March 23, 1936, 3.

56. Walter H. Pehle, *November 1938: From "Reichskristallnacht" to Genocide* (New York: Berg, 1991).

57. Christoph Kreutzmüller, *Ein Pogrom im Juni: Fotos antisemitischer Schmierereien in Berlin, 1938* (Berlin: Hentrich & Hentrich, 2013). Wolf Gruner also

discussed the confiscation of cameras in his talk "Total Devastation: The Forgotten Mass Destruction of Jewish Homes during Kristallnacht, 1938," at the University of Pennsylvania on November 14, 2019.

58. See Schreiben an Kurt Schallenberg von Handwerkskammer Hamburg, gez. A. Petersen & Dr. Rieser, December 1, 1938, Amt für Wiedergutmachung Hamburg, reproduced in Weinke, *Verdrängt, vertrieben, aber nicht vergessen*, 291.

59. Heike Stange, "Yva Photographic Studio," in *Final Sale: The End of Jewish Owned Businesses in Nazi Berlin*, ed. Christoph Kreutzmüller, Kaspar Nürnberg, and Charlotte Hughes-Kreutzmüller (Berlin: Aktives Museum Faschismus und Widerstand in Berlin, 2010), 68–71.

60. Bundesarchiv Gedenkbuch, entry for Simon, Else Ernestine (Yva).

61. "Herunter mit der Maske!"

62. Rolf Sachsse, *Die Erziehung zum Wegsehen: Fotografie im NS-Staat* (Dresden: Philo Fine Arts, 2003), 382.

63. USHMM Survivors and Victims Database, entry for Elisabeth von Stengel, https://www.ushmm.org/online/hsv/person_view.php?PersonId=6921922.

64. LBI, ME 880, Inge Schlesinger memoirs.

65. This was a highly unusual and exceptional case. Jewish prisoners were not normally selected to do photographic work in concentration camps. See chapter 3 of this book.

66. USHMM Survivors and Victims Database, entry for Elisabeth von Stengel.

67. Byk was the daughter of the chemist and manufacturer Dr. Siegmund Byk and his wife, Clara.

68. LBI S 2226 K8 A4, *Monatsblätter/Jüdischer Kulturbund Berlin* (Berlin: Schmoller & Gordon, 1935).

69. Landesarchiv Berlin, A Rep 342-02 Nr. 44143, Suse Byk to the Amtsgericht Berlin-Mitte, June 18, 1938, 4.

70. Klaus Honnef et al., *Liselotte Strelow: Retrospektive, 1908–1981* (Ostfildern: Hatje Cantz, 2008), 229.

71. Detlef Gosselk, ed., *Liselotte Strelow (1908–1981): Erinnerungen. Ausstellung, Herz-Kreislauf-Klinik Bad Bevensen* (Bad Bevensen: Herz-Kreislauf-Klinik, 1989).

72. StAH, 314–15 F 132, Abschrift von Achim Lingner an den Herrn Oberfinanzpräsidenten Devisenstelle betr. Auswanderung des Herrn Emil Berlin mit Frau und Kindern, February 11, 1938.

73. Weinke, *Verdrängt, vertrieben, aber nicht vergessen*, 46.

74. Weinke, *Verdrängt, vertrieben, aber nicht vergessen*, 47.

75. StA HH, 314–15 F 45, Hans Schönborn to Devisenstelle, Herrn Benthien, Hamburg, June 30, 1938.

76. Weinke, *Verdrängt, vertrieben, aber nicht vergessen*, 46.

77. StA HH 731-8_A 768, Gisela Schütte, "Auf der Suche nach dem wahren Gesicht," *Die Welt*, September 9, 1978.

78. Klaus Honnef, *Ausstellung Liselotte Strelow, Retrospektive, 1908–1981* (Ostfildern: Hatje Cantz, 2008), 227.

79. Liselotte Strelow, "Das Volksgesicht in der Fotografie," *Photofreund* no. 14 (1934): 68–69.

80. Anja Hellhammer, "Nini Hess," in *Jewish Women: A Comprehensive Historical Encyclopedia*, Jewish Women's Archive, March 1, 2009, viewed June 7, 2018, https://jwa.org/encyclopedia/article/hess-nini-and-carry-hess.

81. On the political conflict between Nazis and Austrofascists leading up to the 1938 annexation, see Eric Grube, "Borderland Brothers: Austrofascist Competition and Cooperation with National Socialists, 1936–1938," *Journal of Austrian Studies* 56, no. 1 (2023): 1–24. On the return of Jews to Vienna after the Holocaust, see Elizabeth Anthony, *The Compromise of Return: Viennese Jews after the Holocaust* (Detroit: Wayne State University Press, 2021).

82. LBI JMB MM III 17, Harvey Fireside né Heinz Wallner, "Delusions and Denials: Viennese Life under the Nazis," 2004, 52.

83. Wallner, "Delusions and Denials."

84. Current provenance debates address paintings, sculptures, and tapestries but not photographs. See, for example, Andrea Bambi and Axel Drecoll, *Alfred Flechtheim: Raubkunst und Restitution* (Berlin: De Gruyter, 2015); Melissa Müller and Monika Tatzkow, *Lost Lives, Lost Art: Jewish Collectors, Nazi Art Theft, and the Quest for Justice* (New York: Vendome Press, 2010); Martin Dean, *Robbing the Jews: The Confiscation of Jewish Property in the Holocaust, 1933–1945* (Cambridge: Cambridge University Press, 2011).

85. BArch-BL. R55/1146-03, Heiner Kurzbein to Herrn Staatssekretär and Herrn Min. Rat Dr. Ott, July 4, 1934, 13–14.

86. Beckers and Moortgat, *Atelier Lotte Jacobi, Berlin, New York*, 134.

87. StA HH, OFP 314-15_F1070 Nr. 15, Bescheinigung Meldeschein vom 30.3.1933 der Polizeibehörde Hamburg, Öffentlich Auskunft und Beratungsstelle für Ausgewanderte Hamburg an Dev. Nr. 43/39.

88. StA HH, OFP 314-15_F1070 Nr. 17, Zollfahndungsstelle Hamburg, February 25, 1939. "If they wanted to take abroad valuable items like photographic, medical, or technical equipment," the historian Susanne Meinl has written, "Jewish emigrants usually had to pay to the Deutsche Golddiskontbank an export fee (Dego-Abgade)." Susanne Meinl, "The Expropriation of Jewish Emigrants from Hessen during the 1930s," in *Confiscation of Jewish Property in Europe, 1933–1945: New Sources and Perspectives; Symposium Proceedings* (Washington, D.C.: Center for Advanced Holocaust Studies, United States Holocaust Memorial Museum, 2003), 97.

89. StA HH/OFP 314-15/FvG2918/30 Blatt 20, Ermittlungsbericht von Zollfahndungsstelle Hamburg, November 11, 1938.

90. StA HH, OFP 314-15/FvG2918/30 Blatt 15, Leiter A. Schwoerer, Hamburger Fotoschule, to Zollfahndungsstelle Hamburg, November 2, 1938.

91. Recent scholarship has painted an overly rosy portrayal of Jewish photographers once they left Germany. See Annette Vowinckel, "German (Jewish) Photojournalists in Exile: A Story of Networks and Success," *German History* 31, no. 4 (2013): 473–96. Only those photographers who were already internationally recognized had a relatively easy time establishing themselves elsewhere. Lesser-known photographers faced many more challenges. The case of Ursula Nachlicht, who repeatedly tried to find work as a photographer and was denied, is one example. LBI AR 25031, folder 5, box 1, Nachlicht Family Collection, 2-34, job applications for Ursula Nachlicht.

3. Gathering Evidence

1. USHMM, Rafael and Nelly Brenner Family Papers 1995.61, folder 6, box 1; Charles Lehman, "Berlin to Rome to Washington, D.C.: Saga of Rafael Brenner," *Photographic Trade News,* June 1946.

2. A powerful example beyond the camps is the case of the Jewish prisoner and electrician David Zivcon, who discovered twelve photographs of the 1941 massacre of Jews at Šķēde beach in Latvia in a drawer when he was sent to do repairs at an SS officer's apartment. See Valerie Hébert, ed., *Framing the Holocaust: Photographs of a Mass Shooting in Latvia, 1941* (Madison: University of Wisconsin Press, Published in Association with the United States Holocaust Memorial Museum, 2023).

3. This was also true to a limited extent in Nazi ghettoes like Łódź and Warsaw, where the SS recruited photographers to assist them in compiling administrative records on all residents as well as identifying the dead. All other photography was strictly forbidden. See YIVO RG 241, folder 433, November 7, 1941, and folder 380, no. 265, May 11, 1941: "Since it is prohibited to take photographs in the ghetto, all new arrivals must offer their cameras for sale by November 23. Violators will be punished and their cameras confiscated." See also the correspondence on training three members of the Jewish police to photograph corpses in the Warsaw ghetto. BArchB R70/581 no. 909-02, Sicherheitspolizei für den Distrikt Warschau to Transferstelle vom Herrn Steinert, April 16, 1941; BArchB R70/581 no. 909-03, Warschau Abteilung Umsiedlung, Transferstelle, to Obmann des Judenrates Warschau, April 17, 1941.

4. Testimony of Francisco Boix, January 28–29, 1946, in *Trial of the Major War Criminals before the International Military Tribunal,* 42 vols. (Nuremberg, 1947–1949), 6:263–67.

5. 1. Fritz Bauer Institut Archiv, 4 Ks 2/63, Frankfurt Auschwitz Trial interrogation of the witness Alfred Wóycicki, May 29, 1964.

6. Marianne Hirsch, "Surviving Images: Holocaust Photographs and the Work of Postmemory," in *Visual Culture and the Holocaust,* ed. Barbie Zelizer (London: Athlone Press, 2001), 215.

7. Susan Sontag, *On Photography* (New York: Farrar, Straus & Giroux, 1977), 20.

8. See, for example, Elissa Mailänder Koslov, *Female SS Guards and Workaday Violence: The Majdanek Concentration Camp, 1942–1944* (East Lansing: Michigan State University Press, 2015); Witold Pilecki, *Freiwillig nach Auschwitz: Die geheimen Aufzeichnungen des Häftlings Witold Pilecki,* trans. Dagmar Mallett (Zurich: Orell Füssli, 2013).

9. Ruth P. Chaves et al., *Fotografien aus den Lagern des NS-Regimes: Beweissicherung und Ästhetische Praxis* (Göttingen: Vandenhoeck & Ruprecht, 2018).

10. Where concentration camp photography is mentioned, it is usually in the context of individual camps, images, or photographers. There has been little synthetic analysis on how photography was practiced in the KL system. See Janina Struk, *Photographing the Holocaust: Interpretations of the Evidence* (London: I. B. Tauris, 2004); Georges Didi-Huberman, *Images in Spite of All: Four Photographs from Auschwitz* (Chicago: University of Chicago Press, 2008); Günter Morsch,

Von der Sachsenburg nach Sachsenhausen: Bilder aus dem Fotoalbum eines KZ-Kommandanten (Berlin: Metropol, 2007).

11. Nikolaus Wachsmann, *KL: A History of the Nazi Concentration Camps* (London: Little, Brown Book Group, 2015), 98.

12. The long legacy of police photography in western Europe contributed to this reputable image. See Alphonse Bertillon, *La Photographie Judiciaire: Avec un Appendice sur la Classification et l'Identification Anthropométriques* (Paris: Gauthier-Villars, 1890). In the German context, see Friedrich Paul, *Handbuch der kriminalistischen Photographie für Beamte der Gerichte, der Staatsanwaltschaften und der Sicherheitsbehörden* (Berlin: J. Guttentag, 1900); Zachary R. Hagins, "Fashioning the 'Born Criminal' on the Beat: Juridical Photography and the Police Municipale in Fin-de-Siècle Paris," *Modern & Contemporary France* 21, no. 3 (2013): 281–96; Mark Michaelson and Steven Kasher, *Least Wanted: A Century of American Mugshots* (New York: Galerie Steven Kasher, 2006); John Tagg, *The Burden of Representation* (Minneapolis: University of Minnesota Press, 1988). One of the only pieces dealing with the German case is Jens Jäger, "Photography: A Means of Surveillance? Judicial Photography, 1850 to 1900," *Crime, Histoire & Sociétés* 5, no. 1 (2001): 27–51.

13. Robert Heindl, "The Technique of Criminal Investigation in Germany," *Annals of the American Academy of Political and Social Science* 146 (November 1929): 223–36. Schneickert, the head of the Berlin Erkennungsdienst, at one point tried to make the case for creating records on all civilians, whether or not they were convicted criminals, to expedite the search and arrest process for the Berlin Criminal Police. He would later look approvingly on Nazi crime-fighting tactics. See Hans Schneickert, "Erkennungsdienstliche Zukunftsfragen," in *Grosse Polizei-Ausstellung Berlin in Wort und Bild: internationaler Polizeikongress in Berlin*, ed. Oskar Dressler (Vienna: Internationale öffentliche Sicherheit, 1927), 242–43.

14. Freiherr von Ledebur, "Die Kinemotography im Dienste der Polizei, Die Polizei," *Zeitschrift für das gesamte Polizei-Polizei-Und Kriminalwesen* 10–12 (September 29, 1921): 248, cited in Sara Hall, "Moving Images and the Policing of Political Action in the Early Weimar Period," *German Studies Review* 31, no. 2 (2008): 285–302.

15. BArchB R 4701/11554 Erkennungsdienstes Düsseldorf an die Oberpostdirektion, December 4, 1926, 1–2.

16. Robert Gerwarth, *Hitler's Hangman: The Life of Heydrich* (New Haven: Yale University Press, 2012), 87.

17. BArchB R 4701/11554 Geheimes Staatspolizeiamt Berlin an das Reichspostministerium Berlin, July 29, 1933.

18. Several of these albums can be viewed at the Landesarchiv Berlin, LAB A Pr Br Rep 030-01 Nr. 18–23. Also see Bodie A. Ashton, "The Parallel Lives of Liddy Bacroff: Transgender (Pre)History and the Tyranny of the Archive in Twentieth-Century Germany," *German History* 42, no. 1 (March 2024): 79–100.

19. Evidence for the existence of a photo identification department also comes from the Ravensbrück and Stutthof camps, though the available records are more sparse in these cases. See USHMM RG-04.058 M Stutthof

Concentration Camp Records, 1939–1945, especially Group II Sygn. I-IID, photo documents of prisoners.

20. "Ein Konzentrationslager für politische Gegner": In der Nähe von Dachau, *Münchner Neueste Nachrichten*, March 21, 1933.

21. Wachsmann, *KL*, 97.

22. See his testimony in Fritz Bauer Institut Archiv, 4 Ks 2/63, Frankfurt Auschwitz trial interrogation of the witness Bernhard Walter, August 13, 1964, and August 14, 1964. See also Fritz Bauer Institut Archiv, 4 Ks 2/63, Frankfurt Auschwitz trial interrogation of the witness Hans Hoffmann, December 11, 1964.

23. Wilhelm Brasse, *Wilhelm Brasse: Photographer 3444, Auschwitz, 1940–1945* (Eastbourne: Sussex Academic Press, 2012), 111; Fritz Bauer Institut, Frankfurter Auschwitz Prozess "Strafsache gegen Mulka u.a.," 4 Ks 2/63 Landgericht Frankfurt am Main 76, Verhandlungstag, 13.8.1964 and 77, Verhandlungstag, 14.8.1964 Vernehmung des Zeugen Bernhard Walter S.2.

24. Jens Jäger, *Gesellschaft und Photographie: Formen und Funktionen der Photographie in England und Deutschland, 1839–1860* (Wiesbaden: VS Verlag für Sozialwissenschaften, 1995). See also several albums that functioned as portable "rogues galleries" for the German criminal police, LAB, A Pr Br Rep 030-01 Nr. 17–23.

25. Brasse, *Wilhelm Brasse*, 120.

26. Auschwitz-Birkenau State Museum Memorial Archives (ABMA), "Zuganglisten Juden- nicht fotografiert vom 12.4.1942," http://auschwitz.org/en/museum/about-the-available-data/new-arrivals-documents/zugang sliste-juden.

27. The Erkennungsdienst at Auschwitz developed and enlarged photos for the Zentralbauleitung der Waffen-SS for the photo department headed by SS-Unterscharführer Dietrich Kamann. See the correspondence regarding enlarged black-and-white copies of photos Kamann took of the camp environment, the prisoner of war camp at Birkenau, workshops, and agriculture in USHMM, Zentralbauleitung der Waffen-SS und Polizei Auschwitz (Fond 502), reel 35, Leiter der Zentralbauleitung der Waffen-SS and Polizei Auschwitz to Erkennungsdienst des KL SS Hauptscharfuhrer Bruno Walther, Betr: Anfertigung von Vergrosserungen, June 17 and 26, July 5, August 24, and October 5, 1942.

28. SS photographers staffing the Erkennungsdienst also photographed visits to the camps from high-ranking Nazi officers as well as SS men for their passport and marriage permit photos. USHMM RG-04.006M, reel 1, Kommandantur-Befehl, undated, 2: "Nr. 6, Passbilder: All members of the SS have to be photographed on Friday 2.5.1941 by the identification service. Men and subordinates initial letter A–L in the morning and the rest in the afternoon."

29. Archives of the Association Française Buchenwald Dora, interview with Georges Angéli conducted by Ilsen About and Clément Chéroux, March 2000.

30. Danuta Czech and Jadwiga Bezwińska, eds., *Kl Auschwitz Seen by the SS* (Oświęcim: Auschwitz-Birkenau State Museum, 2003), 143.

31. Christian Goeschel, "Suicide in Nazi Concentration Camps, 1933–1939," *Journal of Contemporary History* 45, no. 3 (July 2010): 628–48.

32. "Dachau Concentration Camp: Report on Its Organisation, Routine and Recent History, Punishment and Ill-Treatment of Prisoners," *The Guardian,* January 1, 1934.

33. Wachsmann, *KL,* 88.

34. Nikolaus Wachsmann, "The Dynamics of Destruction," in *Concentration Camps in Nazi Germany: The New Histories,* ed. Jane Caplan (London: Routledge, 2010), 109.

35. UNH-MI, Lotte Jacobi Papers, 1898–2000, MC-58, box 39, folder 1, catalog for "Das Lichtbild: Internationale Ausstellung Munich, 1930," 6.

36. David W. Pike, *Spaniards in the Holocaust: Mauthausen, the Horror on the Danube* (London: Routledge, 2000), 137.

37. Deutsches Historisches Museum, Berlin Do2 95/2880, "Die Wahrheit über Dachau," *Münchener Illustrierten Presse,* July 16, 1933.

38. Key among these was the widely circulated and translated account written by former Dachau inmate Hans Beimler, who detailed the murder of the Communist Party activist Fritz Dressel. Hans Beimler, *Im Mörderlager Dachau* (Moscow: Verlag Genossenschaft ausländischer Arbeiter in der UdSSR, 1933).

39. Bundesarchiv Bild 152-02-01-38, Friedrich Franz Bauer, KZ Dachau Häftlingsfotos, Porträtaufnahme eines Häftlings, May 25, 1933.

40. See the files on Ernst in BArchB, BDC/RS, Ernst, Albert, 1.6.1910; BArchB, B 45 V 297.

41. See Raul Hilberg, *Perpetrators, Victims, Bystanders: The Jewish Catastrophe, 1933–1945* (London: Secker & Warburg, 1995); Mailänder, *Female SS Guards and Workaday Violence.*

42. KZ-N, B 45 V 297, Anzeige des ehemaligen Häftlings des KZ Neuengamme Hermann Struck gegen Albert Ernst, June 22, 1946.

43. KZ-N, TNA, WO 235/248, Eidesstattliche Erklärung von Albert Ernst vor dem britischen Ermittler Leutnant F. J. Kelley, June 25, 1946.

44. British National Archives, WO 235/248.

45. ABMA-B Statements Collection, account of Franciszek Hillmann, 95:118

46. ABMA-B Statements Collection, account of Anna Stefańska, 137:88.

47. ABMA-B Statements Collection, account of Henryk Porębski, 113:14.

48. Auschwitz Birkenau Museum, Memories, account of Wilhelm Brasse, http://23874-1-d9f733-01.services.oktawave.com/en/museum/about-the-available-data/memories/prisoners-photos-memories/.

49. Wachsmann, *KL,* 191–92.

50. Wachsmann, *KL,* 276.

51. Archives of the Association Française Buchenwald Dora, interview with Angéli. See also International Tracing Service Archive (ITS) 01010503.001.009.141, Häftlingspersonalkarte Georges Angéli, KL Buchenwald, 1943.

52. Brasse, *Wilhelm Brasse,* 33. See also ITS 01012603.023.302, Häftlingspersonalkarte Wilhelm Brasse, KL Auschwitz, 1940.

53. Testimony of Francisco Boix, in *Trial of the Major War Criminals before the International Military Tribunal,* 6:264.

54. See the file charging Roth under paragraph 175 in StAH 242-1 II_24896. The Nazis had stepped up their persecution of homosexual men in their

June 1935 revision of Paragraph 175, which both expanded the range of possible offenses and made the penalties for them more severe. See W. Jake Newsome, *Pink Triangle Legacies: Coming Out in the Shadow of the Holocaust* (Ithaca: Cornell University Press, 2022), especially chap. 1.

55. BArchB NS 3/1577, Karteikarte für Heinrich Roth aus dem SS-Wirtschaftsverwaltungshauptamt, KZ Gedenkstatte Neuengamme J5.1012, 1940, http://media.offenes-archiv.de/ha2_1_7_2_bio_1151.pdf.

56. See chapter 2 of this book.

57. LBI ME 880, Leo Baeck Memoir Collection, Inge Schlesinger memoirs, 1992, 4–5.

58. Elisabeth von Stengel's card (10339) is held at the Zentralarchiv zur Erforschung der Geschichte der Juden in Deutschland, Jüdische Gemeinde zu Berlin Bestand B. 1/9, Nr. 1 DP-Kartei 1945–1949 (ID: 20702).

59. Even as late as January 1944 the Auschwitz service was well stocked. See the inventory in USHMM RG-04.006M, reel 1, "Fotoabteilung-Bildstelle-Fotolabor," January 22, 1944, 4–5.

60. The men in SS and police guard units often told Jews that they were being relocated for work, a lie that was commonplace during the deportations to killing centers. See Christopher Browning, *Ordinary Men: Reserve Police Battalion 101 and the Final Solution in Poland* (New York: Harper Collins, 1992), especially chaps. 4 and 12.

61. See Brasse, *Wilhelm Brasse,* 124, 76.

62. Archives of the Association Française Buchenwald Dora, interview with Angéli.

63. Brasse, *Wilhelm Brasse,* 77.

64. Buchenwald Fotoarchiv, 003-01.027, Hermann Pister's album, 1943.

65. NARA Record Group 153, NWDNS-153-IK, Karl and Ilse Koch's private photo albums, 1938–1941.

66. Schulz was the head of the political department (Gestapo) at Mauthausen. See *Trial of the Major War Criminals before the International Military Tribunal,* 6:276.

67. Brasse, *Wilhelm Brasse,* 112.

68. Archives of the Association Française Buchenwald Dora, interview with Georges Angéli. See also ITS doc. 6747546, Häftlingspersonalkarte Rudolf Opitz, KL Buchenwald, 1939; and entry for Franz Rudolf Opitz in "Die Toten, 1937–1945," KZ Buchenwald Totenbuch, Buchenwald and Mittelbau-Dora Memorials Foundation, https://totenbuch.buchenwald.de/names/details/page/9/letter/o/person/1052/ref/names.

69. Archives of the Association Française Buchenwald Dora, interview with Angéli.

70. Brasse, *Wilhelm Brasse,* 62, 81–82.

71. LBI Memoir Collection ME 880, Inge Schlesinger memoirs, 8.

72. University of Chicago Library Special Collections Research Center, Edgar Kupfer-Koberwitz Dachau diaries, boxes 1–5, diaries 1–47. See also the portraits secretly made at Auschwitz by Jan Machnowski, Franciszek Jaźwiecki, Agnieszka Sieradzka, Gabriela Nikliborc, and Wiesława Zlot. Jan Machnowski and Franciszek Jaźwiecki, *Forbidden Art: Illegal Works by Concentration Camp Prisoners* (Oświęcim: Auschwitz-Birkenau State Museum, 2012).

73. Wachsmann, *KL,* 20. See also ITS, no. 8153700, folder 303, report by Emil Büge about his internment in KL Sachsenhausen from November 2, 1939, to April 20, 1943.

74. NARA Record Group 549, Records of United States Army, Europe, War Crimes Branch, War Crimes Case Files (Cases Tried), 1945–1959, case 000505, *U.S.A. v. Hans Altfuldisch et al.,* prosecution exhibit 153, folder 5, box 345, location 290/59/12/04. See also Dallas Michelbacher, "The Prisoner of War Camps of the Wehrmacht: Key Findings of the United States Holocaust Memorial Museum Encyclopedia of Camps and Ghettos, Volume IV," *Bulletin of the German Historical Institute,* no. 72 (2023): 59–68.

75. Archives of the Association Française Buchenwald Dora, interview with Georges Angéli.

76. USHMM 2010.511.1, letter of recommendation testifying to Maria Seidenberger's work in the Soennecken & Co. photo labs, November 4, 1944.

77. USHMM RG-50.486.0067 2, oral history interview with Maria Seidenberger by Wendy Lower, June 25, 2010. Kasak's flower photos would have been used as propaganda in Nazi coverage of the camps or as keepsakes for Dachau guards.

78. Nationalarchiv Prag, Kajak Karton 61, "Die heimlichen Tagebuchaufzeichnungen von Karel Kasak," notes from May 14, 1944.

79. USHMM 2010.511.1 (three folders).

80. USHMM, photograph 05063, ID 2154/11, courtesy of Jerzy Tomaszewski.

81. Archives of the Association Française Buchenwald Dora, interview with Georges Angéli.

82. Fotoarchiv Gedenkstätte Buchenwald 007-01.001–01.012.

83. See Dan Stone, "The Sonderkommando Photographs," *Jewish Social Studies* 7, no. 3 (2001): 132–48; Georges Didi-Huberman, *Images in Spite of All: Four Photographs from Auschwitz* (Chicago: University of Chicago Press, 2008).

84. Archives of the Auschwitz State Museum, materials of the camp resistance movement, declaration, cxiv, 57–58.

85. Fritz Bauer Institut Archiv, 4 Ks 2/63, Frankfurt Auschwitz trial interrogation of the witness Alfred Wóycicki, May 29, 1964.

86. Wachsmann, *KL,* 429.

87. USHMM, film courtesy of Anna Hassa Jarosky and Peter Hassa.

88. Germaine Tillion, *Ravensbrück* (Garden City, N.Y.: Anchor Press, 1975), xxi–xxii.

89. Clément Chéroux, Ilsen About, and Georges Angéli, Mémoire des Camps: Photographies des Camps de Concentration et d'Extermination Nazis (1933–1999)(Paris: Marval, 2001).

90. Nechama Tec, *Resistance: How Jews and Christians Fought Back against the Nazis* (Oxford: Oxford University Press, 2013), 4.

91. Archives of the Association Française Buchenwald Dora, interview with Georges Angéli.

92. Fotoarchiv Gedenkstätte Buchenwald, 007-01.012, "La dernière étape: Le crématoire (juin 44)."

93. Wachsmann, *KL,* 500.

94. Pike, *Spaniards in the Holocaust,* 204.

95. "Ivan's coming!," meaning that Soviet troops were arriving. Brasse, *Wilhelm Brasse*, 102.

96. Archives of the Association Française Buchenwald Dora, interview with Georges Angéli.

97. ABMA, Testimonies of Former Prisoners, testimony of Polish political prisoner Bronislaw Jureczek, xix, 31.

98. ABMA-B Statements Collection, account of Erwin Olszowka, 4:501, cited in Brasse, *Wilhelm Brasse*, 16.

4. Fabricating Innocence

1. William L Shirer, *"This Is Berlin": Radio Broadcasts, 1938–40* (Woodstock, N.Y.: Overlook Press, 1999), 368.

2. A point typically made about genres other than private wartime photography. See Ofer Ashkenazi, "Reading Private Photography," *American Historical Review* 127, no. 4 (December 2022): 1607.

3. Christopher Browning, *Ordinary Men: Reserve Police Battalion 101 and the Final Solution in Poland* (New York: HarperCollins, 1992). Jürgen Matthäus has also insightfully drawn a parallel between the banality of Eva Braun's wartime albums and the albums made by German soldiers. See Jürgen Matthäus, "Kriegsfotos auf dem Obersalzberg Anmerkungen zu Eva Brauns Albumsammlung," *Zeitschrift für Geschichtswissenschaft* (2021): 224–39; Jürgen Matthäus, "Opa im Osten: private deutsche Fotoalben zum Zweiten Weltkrieg," *Fotogeschichte* 165 (2022): 26–36. See also his forthcoming book, Jürgen Matthäus, *Gerahmte Gewalt: private Fotoalben von Deutschen im "Osteinsatz" und die kollektive Erinnerung an den Zweiten Weltkrieg* (Berlin: Metropol Verlag, 2025).

4. David A. Harrisville, *The Virtuous Wehrmacht: Crafting the Myth of the German Soldier on the Eastern Front, 1941–1944* (Ithaca: Cornell University Press, 2021), 205.

5. Nicholas Stargardt has raised the question of what Germans thought they were fighting for and how they carried on the war until the "bitter end," concluding that Germans' sense of patriotism, even if they were not themselves Nazis, as well as their personal relationships and their hopes for a German victory and a secure future helped them continue fighting. Identification with the fighting men kept the German population in turn energized, refusing to give up hope until the very end. Nicholas Stargardt, *The German War: A Nation under Arms* (New York: Basic, 2015). Thomas Kühne has also emphasized the importance of comradeship and the concept of the *Volksgemeinschaft* in bonding soldiers and their families together around war and genocide. See Thomas Kühne, *Belonging and Genocide: Hitler's Community, 1918–1945* (New Haven: Yale University Press, 2013), and *The Rise and Fall of Comradeship: Hitler's Soldiers, Male Bonding and Mass Violence in the Twentieth Century* (Cambridge: Cambridge University Press, 2017).

6. Their fear that the cycle of hunger, hardship, and turmoil afflicting German cities after World War I would repeat itself if living standards slipped too far governed the Nazis' pro-consumer impulse. See Jonathan Wiesen, *Creating the Nazi Marketplace: Commerce and Consumption in the Third Reich*

(Cambridge: Cambridge University Press, 2011). This revision challenges the argument made by Adam Tooze, who claimed in *The Wages of Destruction: The Making and Breaking of the Nazi Economy* (London: Allen Lane, 2006) that the regime recklessly pursued arms production without much concern for consumer needs.

7. Joseph Goebbels quoted in Willy Frerk, "Das Erlebnis des Einzelnen ist zu einem Volkserlebnis geworden und das durch die Kamera," *Photofreund* (1933): 417–18, cited in Timm Starl, *Knipser: Bildgeschichte der privaten Fotografie in Deutschland und Österreich von 1880 bis 1980* (Munich: Koehler & Amelang, 1995), 19.

8. Along with other American corporations like Standard Oil, ITT, IBM, and Ford, Kodak maintained active relations with the Nazi regime well into World War II to preserve its market position. Documents at the National Archives in Washington, D.C., have revealed that Kodak exploited Jewish slave labor in both German branches throughout the war. See Michael J. Bayzler, *Holocaust Justice: The Battle for Restitution in America's Courts* (New York: New York University Press, 2003), 304.

9. "Photographieren in der Militärzeit," *Photoblätter* 13, no. 6 (June 1936): 161.

10. *Die Wehrmacht*, no. 19 (August 1, 1937): 31.

11. *Die Wehrmacht*, no. 13 (May 7, 1937): 24.

12. StAH, 430-5 1165-09, Report from the Harburg Chamber of Crafts on the situation of the crafts industry in the period from July 1 to September 30, 1936.

13. StAH, 430-5 1165-09, Report from the Harburg Chamber of Crafts, 1936.

14. William Fagan, "Leica Cameras in the 1930s: A Decade of Progress," *Macfilos*, January 20, 2016. See also Hans-Michael Koetzle, *Eyes Wide Open! 100 Years of Leica* (Berlin: Kehrer, 2015).

15. "Soldaten photographieren," *Photoblätter*, no. 14 (January 1937): 188.

16. Hartmut Berghoff and Berti Kolbow, "Flourishing in a Dictatorship: Agfa's Marketing and the Nazi Regime," *Journal of Historical Research in Marketing* 5, no. 1 (2013): 77.

17. Those who did not own cameras when they began their military service borrowed them from one another or stole those they found in occupied cities and villages or from enemy troops. Outside military ranks, an estimated 7 million people owned cameras. See Starl, *Knipser*, 98.

18. *Die Wehrmacht* 4, no. 11 (May 22, 1940): 14.

19. See Nicholas Stargardt, "Legitimacy through War?," in *Beyond the Racial State: Rethinking Nazi Germany*, ed. Devin Pendas, Mark Roseman, and Richard Wetzell (Cambridge: Cambridge University Press, 2017), 402–28. This was particularly important during the crisis years of 1942 and 1943, when German soldiers and civilians responded to the firebombing of Hamburg and the German defeat at Stalingrad with an ever-increasing focus on their own personal futures rather than on matters of state loyalty or racial unity. See Nicholas Stargardt, "Beyond Consent and Coercion: Wartime Crises in Nazi Germany," *History Workshop Journal* 72, no. 1 (2011); 202. Letter-writing during

war acquired an importance that was not limited to the German case or even to World War II. See Veit Didczuneit, Jens Ebert, and Thomas Jander, *Schreiben im Krieg, Schreiben vom Krieg: Feldpost im Zeitalter der Weltkriege* (Essen: Klartext, 2011); Frank Schumann, *Was tun wir hier? Soldatenpost und Heimatbriefe aus zwei Weltkriegen* (Rheda-Wiedenbrück: RM-Buch-und-Medien-Vertrieb, 2013); Jörg Echternkamp, *Kriegsschauplatz Deutschland, 1945: Leben in Angst, Hoffnung auf Frieden; Feldpost aus der Heimat und von der Front* (Paderborn: Ferdinand Schöningh, 2006).

20. Alexander Hummel, "Fotografieren im Kriegssommer, 1940," *Photoblätter* 17, no. 7 (1940): 121–22.

21. *Die Wehrmacht* 4, no. 7 (March 27, 1940): 19.

22. *Die Wehrmacht* 4, no. 15 (June 17, 1940): 17.

23. A member of the Stahlhelm, the NSDAP, and then the SA, the chemist and manufacturer Carl Schleussner had begun making cameras after taking over the camera factory Kamerafabrik der Gebrüder Wirgin in Wiesbaden from its Jewish owners in 1938, acquiring their machines, tools, equipment, warehouses, and staff. Brothers Heinrich, Max, and Josef Wirgin all fled Germany for America that year, and after the war they would reestablish the Wirgin company in Wiesbaden. Sabine Hock, "Schleussner, Carl A," *Frankfurter Biographie* 2 (1996): 289–91.

24. *Die Wehrmacht* 4, no. 15 (June 17, 1940): 17.

25. *Die Wehrmacht* 5, no. 18 (August 28, 1940): 21.

26. *Die Wehrmacht* 4, no. 7 (March 27, 1940): 19.

27. *Berliner Illustrirte Zeitung*, August 15, 1940, also shown in *Die Wehrmacht* 4, no. 17 (August 14, 1940): 21.

28. *Berliner Illustrirte Zeitung*, September 4, 1941.

29. Wilhelm Reibert, *Der Dienstunterricht im Reichsheer: ein Handbuch für den deutschen Soldaten* (Berlin: Mittler, 1934), 142–43.

30. "Unsere Frauen- sollten mehr fotografieren!" *Photoblätter* 16, no. 11 (1939): 334. Also see "Mutter und Kind, eine photographische Lebensaufgabe," *Photoblätter* 5, no. 16 (May 1939): 129–39.

31. See chapters 1 and 2 of this book.

32. There is a rich literature on prescribed gender roles during the Third Reich. See, for example, Claudia Koonz, *Mothers in the Fatherland: Women, the Family and Nazi Politics* (London: Methuen, 1988); Jill Stephenson, *Women in Nazi Germany* (London: Routledge, 2015); Elizabeth D. Heineman, *What Difference Does a Husband Make? Women and Marital Status in Nazi and Postwar Germany* (Berkeley: University of California Press, 2003).

33. *Die Wehrmacht* 4, no. 12 (June 5, 1940): 16.

34. "Soldaten Weihnachten, 1940," *Die Fotografie mit Spiegelreflex-Kameras* 7, no. 42 (1940): 2.

35. BA MA W6/440, "Freizeitgestaltung der Truppe: Vorschläge und Anregungen," *Tournisterschrift des Oberkommandos der Wehrmacht* 63 (1942): 4–5, also cited in Shelley Baranowski, *Strength through Joy: Consumerism and Mass Tourism in the Third Reich* (Cambridge: Cambridge University Press, 2007), 226.

36. BA MA RW 4450, Fiche 123, no. 450/355, letter to Oberbefehlshaber der Luftwaffe Generalfeldmarschall Göring, April 2, 1940.

37. Some women also sent small albums to the front. See, for example, the reference to the album made for Hans Karl Schmidt by his parents in MfK-FA (3.2002.0251), Hans-Karl Schmidt to his parents, January 7, 1945. In other cases, soldiers made their own albums at the front or when they returned home either on leave or after the war. See, for example, BA MA RH 46/916, Foto-Kriegstagebuch der Major Lütze, 1941–42; and BA MA MSG 2, no. 19663.

38. Joseph Goebbels's New Year's speech of December 31, 1940, in *Die Zeit ohne Beispiel: Reden und Aufsätze aus den Jahren 1939/40/41* (Munich: Zentralverlag der NSDAP, 1941), 351–58.

39. F. H. Woweries, *Deutsche Fibel: Worte an Kameraden* (Berlin: Wilhelm Limpert-Verlag, 1940).

40. BA MA RH 37 / 2376, document Ia/351, Abschrift gez. v. Brauchtisch, Oberbefehlshaber des Heeres, April 13, 1938.

41. BA MA RW 5912 / 2, S. 12/525, Abschrift gez. Raeder an Flottenkommando Kiel, May 27, 1938.

42. BA MA RW 5912 / 2, S. 12/525, Raeder to Flottenkommando Kiel.

43. H. Erdmann, "Die Kamera während unserer Dienstzeit," *Photofreund* 19, no. 17 (September 1, 1939): 316.

44. "Fotografieren verboten," *Die Foto-Schau* 4, no. 5 (1940): 2.

45. Joseph Goebbels, "Was ist ein Opfer?," *Das Reich,* December 28, 1941.

46. Walter Tießler, *Nicht Phrasen sondern Klarheit* (Berlin: Franz Eher, 1942). For more on Tießler and his role in Nazi propaganda, see R. L. Bytwerk, "Grassroots Propaganda in the Third Reich: The Reich Ring for National Socialist Propaganda and Public Enlightenment," *German Studies Review* 33 (2010): 93–118.

47. BA MA, Oberste Befehlshaber der Wehrmacht, *Abwehr von Spionage, Sabotage und Zersetzung in der Wehrmacht, 1941/42* (Berlin, 1942), 48, 71.

48. Oberste Befehlshaber der Wehrmacht, *Abwehr von Spionage, Sabotage und Zersetzung in der Wehrmacht,* 70.

49. Der Reichsführer SS und Chef der Deutschen Polizei, *Was tue ich im Ernstfall? Eine Aufklärungsschrift für das deutsche Volk* (Berlin: Verlag Hermann Hilliger, 1940), 21–23.

50. BA MA, Order of General Chief of Staff Pemsel, RH 24-18/242.

51. BA MA, Postamt Königsberg to Luftgaukommando IC, 29.12.1941, Betr: Fotografieren von Exekutionen, RL 24/9.

52. See LOC IMT NOKW no. 2523, letter of July 22, 1941, from the 11th Army, signed by Chief of the General Staff Otto Woehler; order concerning executions by the SD issued by Walther von Reichenau, August 10, 1941, reproduced in *The German Army and Genocide: Crimes against War Prisoners, Jews, and Other Civilians in the East, 1939–1944,* ed. Paul Bradish and the Hamburg Institute for Social Research, trans. Scott Abbott (New York: New Press, 1999), 89. Also see BA MA, Oberste Befehlshaber der Wehrmacht, *Abwehr von Spionage, Sabotage und Zersetzung in der Wehrmacht,* 48; BA MA RH 26-285/44, Sicherung Division 285 IC no. 41 to Divisionskommando, Abschrift von Oberkommando des Heeres Betr: Photographieren der Vollstreckung von Urteilen durch standrechtliche Erschiessung, November 28, 1941.

53. These functioned similarly to the threats issued to soldiers should they stray out of line in other behaviors as well. See Robert Loeffel, "Sippenhaft, Terror and Fear in Nazi Germany: Examining One Facet of Terror in the Aftermath of the Plot of 20 July 1944," *Contemporary European History* 16, no. 1 (2007): 51–69.

54. BAL, B 162/2500 AR-Z 14/58, Heinrich Hippler Vernehmungsniederschrift, November 11, 1958, 1–4.

55. Soldiers who did take these kinds of pictures generally kept them to themselves or circulated them among the soldiers in their unit rather than sending them home to their families, a fact attested to by the number of incriminating photos found by Soviet soldiers on the bodies of dead Germans rather than in their letters home. See *Soviet Documents on Nazi Atrocities* (London: Soviet Embassy, 1942).

56. Christoph Dieckmann, *The Persecution and Mass Murder of Lithuanian Jews during Summer and Fall of 1941* (Vilnius: Margi Rastai, 2007), 129.

57. Statement of Wehrmacht Lance Corporal (Gefreiter) in Baker's Company from 8/7/1959: Zentrale Stelle der Landesjustizverwaltungen Ludwigsburg, 2 AR-Z 21/48, 3647. Also cited in Ernst Klee, Willi Dressen, and Volker Riess, *Schöne Zeiten: Judenmord aus der Sicht der Täter und Gaffer* (Frankfurt am Main: S. Fischer, 1989), 32.

58. "Die Massenhinrichtung in Zhitomir," in Bradish et al., *The German Army and Genocide*, 86.

59. "Fotografieren an der Front," *Die Fotografie mit Spiegelreflex Kameras* 7, no. 42 (1940): 18.

60. Albert Neuhaus to Agnes Neuhaus, in *Zwischen Front und Heimat: Der Briefwechsel des münsterischen Ehepaares Agnes und Albert Neuhaus, 1940–1944*, ed. Karl Reddemann (Münster: Regensberg, 1996), 541.

61. Agnes Neuhaus to Albert Neuhaus, August 25, 1940, in Reddemann, *Zwischen Front und Heimat*, 80.

62. MfK-FA (3.2002.7135), Elisabeth Spemann to her husband, September 3, 1939. Friedrich Spemann had fought in the First World War and became a university lecturer until reentering military service as a reserve lieutenant in August 1939, participating in the Polish and Ukrainian campaigns until his discharge in 1943 due to old age.

63. MfK-FA (3.2002.0349), Irene Guicking to Ernst Guicking, August 20, 1940.

64. USHMM, Archivalien des ehemaligen Heeresarchivs (Fond 1275), Records of the Former Military Archive, RG-11.001M.13, reel 397, folder 389, undated letter from an unknown soldier to an unknown person in Germany.

65. MfK-FA (3.2002.7139), Hellmuth H. to his family, October 18, 1939.

66. MfK-FA (3.2002.1283), Paul Strache to his wife, May 14, 1940.

67. MfK-FA (3.2002.1288), Hans Simon to his mother, March 18, 1941.

68. This chapter is based primarily on the loose photos and albums housed at the Bundesarchiv Militärchiv in Freiburg, Germany; the United States Holocaust Memorial Museum in Washington, D.C.; the Museum für Kommunikation Feldpost Archiv in Berlin; and the Houghton Special Collections Library at Harvard University in Cambridge, Mass. Additional albums can also be accessed

through the Deutsches Wehrkundearchiv, https://www.deutsches-wehrkun
dearchiv.de/bildarchiv/.

69. HOU MS Span 183, José María Castañé et al., *José María Castañé Collection of War-Related Photograph Albums, 1900–1970*, "Kriegserinnerungen, 1940–1941," vol. 56, no. 4219.

70. Janina Struk, *Private Pictures: Soldiers' Inside View of War* (London: I. B. Tauris, 2011), 120. Jewish-owned photography businesses in German-occupied Europe, in contrast, were taken over by the authorities. William Herskovic, for example, was born in Fišar (formerly Hungary, now Slovakia) and moved to Antwerp in 1929. His photography business was confiscated in the spring of 1942 "by order of the Military Commander in Chief in Belgium and the North of France on Economic Measures against Jews." USHMM 1991.211.3, requisition order for the photographic studio of William Herskovic, April 11, 1942.

71. MfK-FA (3.2008.1388), Karl Nünnighoff to his parents, July 9, 1942.

72. MfK-FA (3.2002.0904), Martin Meier to his wife, June 4, 1940.

73. One particularly noteworthy case of self-portraiture is a two-volume album series in which the soldier who compiled the albums is pictured in every single photograph. See BA MA MSG 2 no. 19663.

74. MfK-FA (3.2002.0257), Willi Betz to his girlfriend, September 17, 1940.

75. Individual labor service was made compulsory in the summer of 1938 following a phase beginning in 1935 of universal compulsory military and labor service. See Kiran K. Patel, *Soldiers of Labor: Labor Service in Nazi Germany and New Deal America, 1933–1945* (Washington, D.C.: German Historical Institute, 2010), 104.

76. Other collections in which comradeship is a prominent focus include BAM MSG 2 no. 19317, no. 18860; HOU MS Span 183, vol. 23, "Meine Kriegserinnerungen, 1942–1943"; vol. 61, "Aus großer Zeit, 1941–1942"; vol. 15, "Meine Dienstzeit, 1941–1942"; vol. 20, "Meine Dienstzeit," 1932–1937; vol. 80, "German Army Officer's Photograph Album, 1936–1937," MfK-FA 3.2002.0816, 3.2002.7532, 3.2002.2195, 3.2009.0853, 3.2002.7258, 3.2002.1219.

77. MfK-FA (3.2002.0224), Klaus Becker to his wife, January 13, 1941.

78. Trug und Schein 410416-2-1, Hilde to Roland, April 16, 1941. https://trugundschein.de/index.php?p=briefe

79. MfK-FA (3.2002.7504), Karl Schwegler to his girlfriend, October 27, 1939.

80. Similar canoeing scenes are pictured in StAH 424-88/50_136 vol. 2. Also see LAB A Rep 244-03 no. 1012 and A Rep 244-03 no. 647B.

81. For more on the presence of the natural world in photographs, see Maiken Umbach, "Selfhood, Place, and Ideology in German Photo Albums, 1933–1945," *Central European History* 48, no. 3 (2015): 343–48. On Nazi efforts to encourage Germans to get out of doors, particularly through the organization Strength through Joy, see Baranowski, *Strength through Joy*. On the longer twentieth-century history of naturist movements in Germany, see John A. Williams, *Turning to Nature in Germany: Hiking, Nudism, and Conservation, 1900–1940* (Stanford: Stanford University Press, 2007). Including animals in so many of these photos allowed soldiers to re-create their own family lives at the front with fellow soldiers and even pets as members. Animals appear routinely in

other photo collections, including, for example, BA MA MSG 2 H 4 EG; Franz Döring's collection at MfK-FA 3.2002.1325; and the album Inge Mundt compiled for her husband, Paul Mundt, while he was away at the front, MfK-FA 3.2002.937.0 and MfK-FA 3.2002.0816.

82. Williams, *Turning to Nature*, 58.

83. Nudity comes up often in soldiers' collections. See, e.g., BA MA MSG 2 19473, USHMM, 101st Police Battalion photo albums, 1999.99.1–3.

84. A similar scene can be found in an album belonging to Martin Söhner (May 5, 1908–July 1968) in an undated photograph showing three soldiers bathing with a nude fourth man in a lake. I am grateful to Jasmin Söhner for sharing this collection with me. Private photograph collection of Jasmin Söhner, prewar and wartime photographs of Martin Söhner, member of the 4th Gebirgsdivision "Enzian," Raum Balingen–Albstadt, 1944.

85. A similar canoeing scene with other soldiers participating is pictured in StAH 424-88/50_136, vol. 2. Other photo collections in which leisure scenes appear include LAB A Rep 244-03 no. 1012 and A Rep 244-03 no. 647 B.

86. HOU MS Span 183, vol. 42, "Meine Dienstzeit, 1938–1942."

87. This emphasis is all the more chilling considering that famine and starvation were used by the Germans as weapons of war. See Karel Berkhoff, *Harvest of Despair: Life and Death in Ukraine under Nazi Rule* (Cambridge: Harvard University Press, 2008).

88. Albert Neuhaus to Agnes, June 10, 1942, in Reddemann, *Zwischen Front und Heimat*, 539. Other collections in which food and eating with fellow soldiers is a prominent focus include BA MA MSG 2 19663, and HOU MS Span 183, vol. 24, "Kriegserinnerungen, 1939."

89. HOU MS Span 183, vol. 42, "Meine Dienstzeit, 1938–1942."

90. See MfK-FA 3.2002.7532, 3.2002.2937; BAM MSG 2 nos. 19317 and 19663; HOU MS Span 183, vol. 23.

91. Edward Westermann, *Drunk on Genocide: Alcohol and Mass Murder in Nazi Germany* (Ithaca: Cornell University Press, 2021).

92. Patel, *Soldiers of Labor*, 252.

93. Hester Vaizey, "Husbands and Wives: An Evaluation of the Emotional Impact of World War Two in Germany," *European History Quarterly* 40, no. 3 (2010): 389–411.

94. Pictures depicting outdoor shaving are also present in BAM MSG 2 nos. 19317 and 18860; "Meine Dienstzeit," nos. 19473 and 19663; StAH 424-88/50_136, vol. 1.

95. Eve Kosofsky Sedgwick, *Between Men: English Literature and Male Homosocial Desire* (New York: Columbia University Press, 2016).

96. See, for more examples, HOU MS Span 183, vol. 10, 23; BA MA MSG 2 19663; MfK-FA 3.2002.7532; LAB A Rep 244-03 no. 1012.

97. Photographs showing letters being opened are common in soldiers' albums and loose photos. See HOU MS Span 183, vol. 42, "Meine Dienstzeit, 1938–1942."

98. See BA MA RW 4450 Fiche 123 no. 450/355, letter to Oberbefelshaber der Luftwaffe Generalfeldmarschall Göring, April 2, 1940; "Unsere Frauen—sollten mehr fotografieren!," *Photoblätter* 16, no. 11 (1939): 334.

99. Other collections featuring captured or killed Soviet soldiers include BA MA MSG 2 no. 19317, "Photographisches Kriegstagebuch des Majors Lütze," RH 46/916 and 914; and MfK-FA 3.2002.1241. See also Martin Söhner, undated photograph, "Unser [Gebirgs?/Infanterie?] regiment hat Gefangene gemacht," private collection of Jasmin Söhner.

100. MfK-FA (3.2002.0889), Anton Böhrer to his parents and sister, December 25, 1941.

101. They also hinted at the excuses German generals would make following their defeat in the winter of 1941 that the weather had been responsible for their slow advance. See Gerhard L. Weinberg, *A World at Arms: A Global History of World War II* (New York: Cambridge University Press, 2010), 274. Language describing Russian roads as "paths" appears often in the German soldiers' letters from the front which the Nazi Party published as part of a massive propaganda effort to show Germans at home what conditions in the Soviet Union were like. See Wolfgang Diewerge, *Deutsche Soldaten sehen die Sowjet-Union: Feldpostbriefe aus dem Osten* (Berlin: Wilhelm Limpert-Verlag, 1941).

102. Julia S. Torrie, "Visible Trophies of War: German Occupiers' Photographic Perceptions of France, 1940–44," in *The Ethics of Seeing: Photography and Twentieth-Century German History,* ed. Jennifer Evans, Paul Betts, and Stefan-Ludwig Hoffmann (New York: Berghahn, 2018), 108–37.

103. Raffael Scheck, *French Colonial Soldiers in German Captivity during World War II* (New York: Cambridge University Press, 2014).

104. Raul Hilberg, *The Destruction of the European Jews* (New Haven: Yale University Press, 2003).

105. Among these were the notable collections created by Heinrich "Heinz" Jost, a German soldier who entered the Warsaw ghetto on September 9, 1941, and Joe Heydecker, a German soldier who photographed the ghetto in detail in early 1941. See Gunther Schwarberg, *Im Ghetto von Warschau: Heinrich Josts Photographien* (Göttingen: Steidl, 2001); Joe J. Heydecker, "Photographing behind the Warsaw Ghetto Wall, 1941," *Holocaust and Genocide Studies* 1, no. 1 (1986): 63–77; Heinz Jöst and Yitzhak Arad, *A Day in the Warsaw Ghetto* (Yad Vashem: Holocaust Martyrs' and Heroes Remembrance Authority, the Museum, 1988).

106. HOU MS Span 183, vol. 42, "Meine Dienstzeit, 1938–1942."

107. MfK-FA (3.2002.7130), Adalbert Huber to his wife, April 25, 1942.

108. MfK-FA (3.2009.0574), Franz Schmidt to his brother Reinhard, March 6, 1943.

109. MfK-FA (3.2013.355), Wolfgang Panzer to his wife, October 8, 1942.

110. MfK-FA (3.2002.1256), Georg Koch to "Verlobte Lyddi," December 21, 1943.

111. MfK-FA (3.2002.1214), Hans-Joachim S. to his wife, July 9, 1944.

112. MfK-FA (3.2002.0822) AK 39, Gefrieter Ludwig Kerstiens, "Bilder aus meiner Frontzeit," 48.

113. MfK-FA, Gerd Schneider, "Der Soldat mit dem Bildwerk," in *Doch ich lieb Dich hoch über den Dingen: ein Kriegstagebuch* (Stuttgart: Strecker und Schröder, 1943), 23.

114. *Berliner Illustrirte Zeitung,* November 9, 1944.

115. MfK-FA (3.2002.1246), Walter Kappmeier to his wife, December 30, 1944.

116. MfK-FA (3.2002.0315), Michael Wutz to his wife and daughter, March 26, 1945.

117. Richard J. Evans, *The Third Reich at War, 1939–1945* (New York: Penguin, 2010), 656.

118. MfK-FA (3.2002.0302), Horst Feldbusch to his father, April 2, 1944.

119. MfK-FA (3.2002.0251), Hans-Karl Schmidt to his parents, January 7, 1945.

5. Concocting Decency

1. Stephen Fritz, *Frontsoldaten: The German Soldier in World War II* (Lexington: University Press of Kentucky, 1995), 13; Rolf-Dieter Müller, *Hitler's Wehrmacht, 1935–1945* (Lexington: University Press of Kentucky, 2016).

2. Peter Longerich, *Heinrich Himmler* (Oxford: Oxford University Press, 2013). The SD was the Sicherheitsdienst, the Nazi intelligence agency.

3. "The many thousand prisoners who are secured in the concentration camps are, partly as individuals and partly by virtue of their collective character, the same enemies of the state who wore down and destroyed Germany's domestic front during the [First] World War. . . . Thus the concentration camps represent island-like sites of battle on the domestic front, theater[s] of war in each of which a handful of men protect Germany from its internal enemies." "Kriegsgebiet KZ," *Das Schwarze Korps*, no. 5, December 21, 1939.

4. USHMM RG-11.001 M.20, reel 91, Fond 1367, Opis 2, folder 19, Eicke order to the Camp SS, summer 1934. See also BArchB SS File, Theodor Eicke, Kommandanturbefehl Eicke, June 2, 1934.

5. Marianne Hirsch has argued that enshrining certain ideals of family life is endemic to the practice of photography. Marianne Hirsch, *Family Frames: Photography, Narrative, and Postmemory* (Cambridge: Harvard University Press, 1997), 5.

6. See USHMM 2013.455.1, Gerd Pleiss, photo album, "Zur Erinnerung an meine Dienstzeit bei der Leibstandarte SS Adolf Hitler," 1936–37; Weiner Library, London, no. 31, photo album titled "SS Erinnerungen an meine Dienstzeit," 1925–1945.

7. BA MA RS 24/20 SS Gren. Rgt. 20 "Hohenstaufen" betr: Fotografieren und Bilder für Regiments Tätigskeitsbericht bezw. Kriegstagebuch, March 1, 1944, 145–52.

8. BA MA RS 24/20 S. 156, "Fotografieren und Besitz von Fotoapparaten," SS Pz. Gren. Rgt 20 Hohenstaufen Abteilung 1aWk, March 3, 1944.

9. BA MA RS 24/20 S. 147, "Fotoapparate in der Kompanie," March 1, 1944.

10. BA MA RS 24/20 S. 151, "Bescheinigung!," 1944.

11. BA MA RS 24/20 S. 156, "Fotografieren und Besitz von Fotoapparaten." Sennheim was a camp established in France in 1942 for the training of non-German SS members from France, Norway, the Netherlands, Croatia, and Ireland. The camp also housed male prisoners from Italy, the Soviet Union, and

Poland. The camp was evacuated in September 1944 and all remaining inmates were sent to Dachau. See "Gruppe 'Wüsste' Complex," in *The United States Holocaust Memorial Museum Encyclopedia of Camps and Ghettos, 1933–1945*, ed. Geoffrey P. Megargee (Bloomington: Indiana University Press, 2009), 1061.

12. BA MA RS 24/20 S. 159, "Zur Prüfung eingesandte Bilder fur Februar 1944," March 20, 1944.

13. BA MA RS 24/20, "Fotografieren und Besitz von Fotoapparaten," 156.

14. BArchB NS19/1796 fol. N334, Befehl von Heinrich Himmler, July 15, 1942; BArchB NS19/1796 fols. 12–13, June 1944.

15. Reinhard Heydrich to SS-Führungshauptamt, SS- und Polizeiführer, Ordnungspolizei, SD, Sicherheitspolizei, Staatspolizei, Kriminalpolizei, über Photographieren von Exekutionen, April 16, 1942; BArchB NS19/1796 fol. 14 no. 250/4. Also see the orders reproduced for Waffen-SS units, Auszug aus dem Verordnungsblatt der Waffen-SS (V. Bl. D. W. SS), July 15, 1944, Nr. 14 5 Jahrg. 379: Fotografieren von Exekutionen.

16. The court hoped to make an example of Täubner in order to discourage other SS men from engaging in such behavior. He received a five-year prison sentence for initiating unauthorized executions and a three-year sentence for photographing them, according to Sections 147 and 92 of the German Military Penal Code. Himmler later overturned this verdict and sent Täubner back to the front. See Bundesarchiv Außenstelle Ludwigsburg (BAL) B 162/21020 AR 330/59 document 29/42, Fedurteil gegen den SS-Max Täubner, May 24, 1943; BAL B 162/21020 AR 330/59 document 207/42, Niederschrift über die Vernichtung von 69 Lichtbildern gegen den SS-Untersturmführer Max Täubner, November 3, 1943.

17. BAL, B162/21020 AR 330/59 document 29/42, Feldurteil, Oberstes SS- und Polizeigericht gegen den SS-Max Täubner, May 24, 1943. Although the Täubner case is often portrayed as a trial for the murders of Jews, it was dubbed "The Case of the Photographs" in SS records. See, e.g., Yehoshua Büchler, "Unworthy Behavior": The Case of SS Officer Max Täubner," *Holocaust and Genocide Studies* 17 (2003): 409–29; Dick de Mildt, "Getting Away with Murder: The Täubner Case," in *Nazi Crimes and the Law*, ed. Henry Friedlander and Nathan Stoltzfus (Cambridge: Cambridge University Press, 2016), 101–12.

18. Feldurteil, Oberstes SS- und Polizeigericht gegen den SS-Max Täubner.

19. BAL, B162/21020 AR330/59 document 207/42, Niederschrift über die Vernichtung von 69 Lichtbildern gegen den SS-Untersturmführer Max Täubner, November 3, 1943.

20. Private collection, photo album of SS-Sturmmann Adolf Fritz, 1940–1949. See also the album compiled by an unidentified Waffen-SS soldier, USHMM 1992.227, box 1, folder 1, "Waffen-SS Photograph Album," 1933–1945.

21. For an overview of the Hiwis, see Karel Berkhoff, *Harvest of Despair: Life and Death in Ukraine under Nazi Rule* (Cambridge: Harvard University Press, 2008), 107.

22. On wartime burial of German soldiers, see Doris Bergen, *Between God and Hitler: Military Chaplains in Nazi Germany* (Cambridge: Cambridge University Press, 2023).

23. USHMM RG-04.006M reel 1, Kommandanturbefehl Nr. 4/43, signed Hoess, February 2, 1943.

24. USHMM RG-04.006M reel 1, Kommandanturbefehl Nr. 20/44, signed Hoess, July 29, 1944.

25. USHMM Zentralbauleitung der Waffen-SS und Polizei Auschwitz (Fond 502), reel 20, folder 32, Kommandanturbefehl Nr. 13/42, August 4, 1942.

26. Men of the Order Police battalions also used photography in this way. On the use of photography by a member of Reserve Police Battalion 131, see Julie R. Keresztes, "Photography as a Wartime Service to Family and Nation in Nazi-Occupied Europe," *German History* 40, no. 2 (June 2022): 197–219.

27. KZ-Gedenkstätte Neuengamme, Ng. 7.6, Hugo Behncke to his wife, January 28, 1944.

28. Elissa Mailänder, *Female SS Guards and Workaday Violence: The Majdanek Concentration Camp* (East Lansing: Michigan State University Press, 2015), 98.

29. Thüringisches Hauptstaatsarchiv Weimar NS-Archiv des MfS ZO 43 Akte 13, Bl. 95r, "Zur Erinnerung an Dini und Werner Fricke. Weimar, den 30.3.41," 1941.

30. Thüringisches Hauptstaatsarchiv Weimar NS-Archiv des MfS ZO 43 Akte 13, Bl. 206, "Blick auf die Terrasse des Hauses von SS-Hauptscharführer Werner Fricke in der SS-Siedlung in Kleinobringen," 1941, Also found in Foto-archiv Buchenwald, 061-05.019.

31. Fotoarchiv Gedenkstätten Buchenwald und Mittelbau-Dora 360-01 Georg Brendle Fotoalbum "Erinnerungen an meine Dienstzeit," 1939–40.

32. Gedenkstätte Buchenwald 100-12.017, Ein Angehöriger der SS-Kraftfahr-Ausbildungs- und Ersatz-Abteilung fährt stehend auf seinem Motor-rad vor den Kommandanturgaragen entlang, 1943.

33. Nikolaus Wachsmann, *KL: A History of the Nazi Concentration Camps* (London: Little, Brown Book Group, 2015), 102. See also Niels Weise, *Eicke: Eine SS-Karriere zwischen Nervenklinik, KZ-System und Waffen-SS* (Paderborn: Ferdinand Schöningh, 2013).

34. USHMM Zentralbauleitung der Waffen-SS und Polizei Auschwitz (Fond 502), reel 20, folder 32, Kommandanturbefehl Nr. 13/42, August 4, 1942.

35. This challenges the tendency among scholars to suggest that only SS personnel staffing Nazi concentration and transit camps practiced photogra-phy. See chapter 5 in Janina Struk, *Photographing the Holocaust: Interpretations of the Evidence* (London: I. B. Tauris, 2004).

36. The Sonderkommandos consisted mainly of Jewish prisoners whom the SS forced to dispose of bodies in the gas chambers and crematoria at Auschwitz and other killing centers including Sobibor and Treblinka. They were typically shot after several weeks or months and replaced with new arrivals. See Yitzhak Arad, *The Operation Reinhard Death Camps: Belzec, Sobibor, Treblinka* (Bloomington: Indiana University Press, 2018), chap. 15.

37. When Johann Niemann's collection was made public, for example, schol-ars and correspondents fixed their attention on whether the pictures might show John Demjanjuk, a Ukrainian-born guard at Sobibor who in 2011 was convicted by a Munich court of being an accessory to the murder of 27,900 Jews

there. See Kerstin Sopke and Geir Moulson, "Historians: Sobibor Death Camp Photos May Feature Demjanjuk," AP News, January 31, 2020.

38. USHMM, 2020.8.1, ser. 1, file 14, album 1, "2. SS-T.V. Totenkopfverband Brandenburg" [original order], ca. 1934–1941.

39. For an overview of Niemann's life and career and an excellent discussion of his photographs, see Martin Cuppers, Anne Lepper, and Jürgen Matthäus, eds., *From "Euthanasia" to Sobibor: An SS Officer's Photo Collection* (Bloomington: Indiana University Press, 2022).

40. See chap. 39 in Yitzhak Arad, *The Operation Reinhard Death Camps: Belzec, Sobibor, Treblinka* (Bloomington: Indiana University Press, 2018).

41. It was also an important opportunity to showcase their masculinity. See Thomas Kühne, "Protean Masculinity, Hegemonic Masculinity: Soldiers in the Third Reich," *Central European History* 51, no. 3 (2018): 390–418.

42. Cuppers, Lepper, and Matthäus, *From "Euthanasia" to Sobibor*, 20–21.

43. Geoffrey P. Megargee, ed., *The United States Holocaust Memorial Museum Encyclopedia of Camps and Ghettos, 1933–1945*, vol. 1 (Bloomington: Indiana University Press in association with the United States Holocaust Memorial Museum, 2008), 72.

44. This subject also dominates the photograph album made by Karl Hoecker while he was adjutant to Richard Baer at Auschwitz between May and December 1944. It contains over 120 pictures showing himself, his dog, day trips with fellow camp SS personnel, and meals with high-ranking officers. See USHMM 2007.24 box 1, folder 1, "SS Auschwitz Album," May–December 1944.

45. Cuppers, Lepper, and Matthäus, *From "Euthanasia" to Sobibor*, 159–66.

46. USHMM 2020.8.1, box 3, folder 1, album 2, Sobibor personnel official trip to Berlin and Potsdam, 1943.

47. See the envelopes from Ehrlich's studio in USHMM 2020.8.1, series 1, file 11, photograph 4, undated.

48. Such content appears in many other collections as well. The loose photographs compiled by SS-Standortarzt Dr. Eduard Wirths (1909–1945), for example, likewise show his family and colleagues while he was stationed at the Auschwitz-Birkenau concentration camp. Several photographs depict Wirths posed with his wife and three children on the hills of Solahütte. See USHMM 2015.66.1 Eduard Wirths collection, 1942–1944.

49. Niemann's photographs and albums testify to the broader participation of women in the world of the SS in the Holocaust as accomplices, bystanders, and perpetrators. See Wendy Lower, *Hitler's Furies: German Women in the Nazi Killing Fields* (Boston: Houghton Mifflin Harcourt, 2013).

50. This is an emphasis that appears in other collections as well, such as the album made by Kurt Franz while he was commandant of Treblinka. YVA 1448 ID 7316698, "A Private Album of Kurt Franz from the Time He Served in the Treblinka Extermination Camp," 1941–1943.

Epilogue

1. Deutscher Bundestag, *Plenarprotokoll 13/163, Bonn, 13. März 1997*, 14708–30, quotation at 14711.

2. David A. Harrisville, *The Virtuous Wehrmacht: Crafting the Myth of the German Soldier on the Eastern Front, 1941–1944* (Ithaca: Cornell University Press, 2021).

3. Harald Jähner, *Aftermath: Life in the Fallout of the Third Reich, 1945–1955* (New York: Alfred A. Knopf, 2022); Wolfram Wette, *The Wehrmacht: History, Myth, Reality* (Cambridge: Harvard University Press, 2007); Manfred Messerschmidt and Fritz Wüllner, *Die Wehrmachtjustiz im Dienste des Nationalsozialismus: Zerstörung einer Legende* (Baden-Baden: Nomos, 1987).

4. The investigation concluded that no other corrections were necessary beyond the ten incorrectly identified photographs. See Walter Manoschek, "Vernichtungskrieg: Verbrechen der Wehrmacht, 1941–1944: Innenansichten einer Ausstellung," *Zeitgeschichte* 2, no. 2 (2002): 67–75.

5. Interview with Hannes Heer by Lucy Burns, BBC World Service, *Witness History*, May 4, 2020. See also Hannes Heer and Klaus Naumann, eds., *War of Extermination: The German Military in World War II, 1941–1944,* trans. Roy Shelton (New York: Berghahn, 2009).

6. Christine R. Nugent, "The Voice of the Visitor: Popular Reactions to the Exhibition 'Vernichtungskrieg: Verbrechen der Wehrmacht, 1941–1944,'" *Journal of European Studies* 44, no. 3 (2014): 249–62; Bernd Ulrich, *Besucher einer Ausstellung: die Ausstellung "Vernichtungskrieg: Verbrechen der Wehrmacht 1941 bis 1944" in Interview und Gespräch* (Hamburg: Stiftung Hamburger Institut für Sozialforschung, 1998). A journalist who visited the exhibition recognized her father in one of the photos. *Suddeutsche Zeitung,* April 6, 1997.

7. Ruth Beckermann, dir., *Jenseits des Krieges* (Vienna: Aichholzer Filmproduktion, 1997).

8. Nugent, "Voice of the Visitor," 256.

9. Karl-Otto Sattler, "Polizei vermutet rechtsextremistischen Hintergrund," *Berliner Zeitung,* March 10, 1999.

10. Guest book, "Vernichtungskrieg: Verbrechen der Wehrmacht, 1941–1944," vol. 1, June 1–30, 1999, Hamburger Institut für Sozialforschung.

11. See Christopher R. Browning, *Ordinary Men: Reserve Police Battalion 101 and the Final Solution in Poland* (New York: HarperCollins, 1992); Daniel Jonah Goldhagen, *Hitler's Willing Executioners: Ordinary Germans and the Holocaust* (New York: Knopf, 1996).

12. Harald Welzer et al., *"Opa war kein Nazi": Nationalsozialismus und Holocaust im Familiengedächtnis* (Frankfurt: Fischer Taschenbuch Verlag, 2002). See also Harald Welzer, *Das kommunikative Gedächtnis: Eine Theorie der Erinnerung* (Munich: C. H. Beck, 2017).

13. Marianne Hirsch, *Family Frames: Photography Narrative and Postmemory* (Cambridge: Harvard University Press, 2016). See also Martha Langford, *Suspended Conversations: The Afterlife of Memory in Photographic Albums* (Montreal/Kingston: McGill-Queens University Press, 2001).

14. Martin P. Davidson, *The Perfect Nazi: Unmasking My SS Grandfather* (London: Penguin, 2011).

15. Alexandra Senfft, *Der lange Schatten der Täter: Nachkommen stellen sich ihrer NS-Familiengeschichte* (Munich: Piper, 2018).

16. Roger Frie, *Not in My Family: German Memory and Responsibility after the Holocaust* (Oxford: Oxford University Press, 2017).

17. Ruth Beckermann, *Jenseits des Krieges* shooting journal, entry for November 8, 1995, accessed December 13, 2017, http://www.ruthbeckermann.com/home.php?il=53.

18. Frie, *Not in My Family,* 225. The banality of other photo albums prompted many to send their own albums to the exhibition organizers, hopeful that they could assist them in identifying relatives in the more incriminating photos from the exhibition by using their "ordinary" family photograph albums. See Jane Caplan and Hannes Heer, "The Difficulty of Ending a War: Reactions to the Exhibition 'War of Extermination: Crimes of the Wehrmacht 1941 to 1944,'" *History Workshop Journal,* no. 46, (1998): 193.

19. A number of sequences in the film show descendants of Nazi perpetrators handling family photos that are completely at odds with the gruesome stories of guilt and violence they had uncovered. See Chanoch Zeevi, dir., *Hitler's Children* (Jerusalem: Maya Productions, 2011).

20. Some soldiers made sure that their loved ones back home destroyed any potentially incriminating photos. See Walter Kempowski, *Das Echolot: Fuga furiosa, ein kollektives Tagebuch Winter 1945,* 4 vols. (Munich: Knaus, 1999), 2:650, cited in Peter Fritzsche, "The Archive," *History & Memory* 17 (2005): 32. Also see correspondence between Kurt Miethke and his wife, MfK-FA, 3.2002.0912, Kurt Miethke to his wife, July 12, 1944.

21. See Elissa Mailänder, "Making Sense of a Rape Photograph: Sexual Violence as Social Performance on the Eastern Front, 1939–1944," *Journal of the History of Sexuality* 26, no. 3 (2017): 489–520; Julia S. Torrie, "Visible Trophies of War: German Occupiers' Photographic Perceptions of France, 1940–44," in *The Ethics of Seeing: Photography in Twentieth-Century German History,* ed. Jennifer Evans, Paul Betts, and Stefan Hoffman (New York: Berghahn, 2018), 108–37; Alexander B. Rossino, "Eastern Europe through German Eyes: Soldiers' Photographs, 1939–42," *History of Photography* 23, no. 4 (2015): 313–21; Petra Bopp and Andreas Koch, *Fremde im Visier: Fotoalben aus dem Zweiten Weltkrieg* (Bielefeld: Kerber, 2009); Petra Bopp, "Images of Violence in Wehrmacht Soldiers' Private Photo Albums," in *Violence and Visibility in Modern History,* ed. Jürgen Martschukat and Silvan Niedermeier (New York: Palgrave Macmillan, 2013), 181–97; Wendy Lower, *The Ravine: A Family, a Photograph, a Holocaust Massacre Revealed* (London: Head of Zeus, 2021).

22. The wartime albums of British, American, and Italian soldiers contain images showing similar themes, such as family, fellow soldiers, prisoners of war, and destruction. HOU MS Span 183, José María Castañé collection of war-related photograph albums, 1920–1950.

23. Christina Morina and Krijn Thijs, eds., *Probing the Limits of Categorization: The Bystander in Holocaust History* (New York: Berghahn, 2018); Jeffrey Herf, *Divided Memory: The Nazi Past in the Two Germanys* (Cambridge: Harvard University Press, 1997); Robert Moeller, *War Stories: The Search for a Usable Past in the Federal Republic of Germany* (Berkeley: University of California Press, 2001).

24. Mary Fulbrook, "Reframing the Past: Justice, Guilt, and Consolidation in East and West Germany after Nazism," *Central European History* 53, no. 2 (2020): 294–313. See also Mary Fulbrook, *Reckonings: Legacies of Nazi Persecution and the Quest for Justice* (Oxford: Oxford University Press, 2020).

25. Frank Biess, *Homecomings: Returning POWs and the Legacies of Defeat in Postwar Germany* (Princeton: Princeton University Press, 2009), 102. See also Jonathan R. Zatlin, "Repetition and Loss: Jewish Refugees and German Communists after the Holocaust, 1945–1951," *Leo Baeck Institute Year Book* 59, no. 1 (2014): 197–230.

26. Beckermann, *Jenseits des Krieges.* The survival of the *Volksgemeinschaft* concept into the postwar years has been addressed by, among others, Max Horkheimer, "Wir Nazis," in vol. 6 of his *Gesammelte Schriften* (Frankfurt am Main: Fischer, 1991), 404; and by Norbert Frei, *Vergangenheitspolitik: die Anfänge der Bundesrepublik und die NS-Vergangenheit* (Munich: Beck, 2012).

Bibliography

Archives

ABMA	Auschwitz-Birkenau State Museum Archives, Oświęcim, Poland
BA MA	Bundesarchiv Militärchiv, Freiburg, Germany
BArchB	Bundesarchiv, Berlin
BAL	Bundesarchiv Außenstelle Ludwigsburg, Germany
CCP	Center for Creative Photography Archives, Tucson
HOU	Harvard University Houghton Library and Archive, Cambridge, Mass.
ITS	International Tracing Service/Arolsen Archive, Bad Arolsen, Germany
KZ-B	KZ-Gedenkstätte Buchenwald, Weimar, Germany
KZ-N	KZ-Gedenkstätte Neuengamme, Hamburg
LAB	Landesarchiv Berlin
LBI	Leo Baeck Institute Archive, New York
LOC	Library of Congress, Washington, D.C.
MfK-FA	Berlin Museum für Kommunikation, Feldpost Archiv, Berlin
NARA	National Archives at College Park, Md.
StAH	Staatsarchiv Hamburg
StBB	Staatsbibliothek zu Berlin
UNH-MI	University of New Hampshire Milne Special Collections Library and Archive, Durham
USHMM	United States Holocaust Memorial Museum, Washington, D.C.
YIVO	Institute for Jewish Research, New York
YVA	Yad Vashem Archive, Jerusalem

Periodicals

Agfa Photoblätter
American Photography

Arbeitertum
Berliner Illustrirte Zeitung
Die Dame
Deutsche Nachrichten
Die Fotografie mit Spiegelreflex Kameras
Die Foto-Schau
Frankfurter Zeitung
Illustrierter Beobachter
Modern Photography
Münchner Illustrierte Presse
New York Times
Photofreund
Photographie für Alle: Zeitschrift für alle Zweige der Photographie
Photographische Chronik
Photographische Mitteilungen
Popular Photography
Pravda
Das Reich
Revue des Monats
Das Schwarze Korps
Uhu
Völkischer Beobachter
Die Wehrmacht
Zeitschrift fur das gesamte Polizei- und Kriminalwesen
Zeitwende

Books and Articles

Adorno, Theodor W., and Max Horkheimer. *Dialectic of Enlightenment.* New York: Continuum, 1972.

Allen, William S. *The Nazi Seizure of Power: The Experience of a Single German Town, 1930–1935.* New York: New Viewpoints, 1973.

Aly, Götz. *Hitler's Beneficiaries: How the Nazis Bought the German People.* London: Verso, 2007.

Angress, Werner T. *Witness to the Storm: A Jewish Journey from Nazi Berlin to the 82nd Airborne, 1920-1945.* Bloomington: Indiana University Press, 2019.

Anthony, Elizabeth. *The Compromise of Return: Viennese Jews after the Holocaust.* Detroit: Wayne State University Press, 2021.

Applegate, Celia, and Pamela Potter. "Cultural History: Where It Has Been and Where It Is Going." *Central European History* 51, no. 1 (2018): 75–82.

Arad, Yitzhak. *The Operation Reinhard Death Camps: Belzec, Sobibor, Treblinka.* Bloomington: Indiana University Press, 2018.

Arad, Yitzhak, Yisrael Gutman, and Abraham Margaliot, eds. *Documents on the Holocaust: Selected Sources on the Destruction of the Jews of Germany and Austria, Poland, and the Soviet Union.* Translated by Lea Ben Dor. Lincoln: University of Nebraska Press, 2004.

Ashkenazi, Ofer. "Exile at Home: Jewish Amateur Photography under National Socialism, 1933–1939." *Leo Baeck Institute Year Book* (2019): 115–40.

Ashkenazi, Ofer. "Reading Private Photography." *American Historical Review* 127, no. 4 (December 2022): 1606–34.

Ashton, Bodie A. "The Parallel Lives of Liddy Bacroff: Transgender (Pre)History and the Tyranny of the Archive in Twentieth-Century Germany." *German History* 42, no. 1 (March 2024): 79–100.

Bajohr, Frank, and Michael Wildt, eds. *Volksgemeinschaft: Neue Forschungen zur Gesellschaft des Nationalsozialismus.* Frankfurt am Main: Fischer Taschenbuch, 2009.

Bambi, Andrea, and Axel Drecoll. *Alfred Flechtheim: Raubkunst und Restitution.* Berlin: De Gruyter, 2015.

Baranowski, Shelley. "Family Vacation for Workers: The Strength through Joy Resort at Prora." *German History* 25, no. 4 (October 2007): 539–59.

Baranowski, Shelley. *Strength through Joy: Consumerism and Mass Tourism in the Third Reich.* Cambridge: Cambridge University Press, 2007.

Barkai, Avraham. *From Boycott to Annihilation: The Economic Struggle of German Jews, 1933–1943.* Hanover: University Press of New England, 1989.

Barkai, Avraham. *Nazi Economics: Ideology, Theory, and Policy.* New Haven: Yale University Press, 1990.

Barron, Stephanie, ed. *"Degenerate Art": The Fate of the Avant-Garde in Nazi Germany.* Los Angeles: Los Angeles County Museum of Art, 1991.

Bartov, Omer. *The Eastern Front, 1941–45: German Troops and the Barbarisation of Warfare.* Basingstoke: Palgrave, 2007.

Bartov, Omer. *Hitler's Army: Soldiers, Nazis, and War in the Third Reich.* New York: Oxford University Press, 1994.

Bayzler, Michael J. *Holocaust Justice: The Battle for Restitution in America's Courts.* New York: New York University Press, 2003.

Beckers, Marion, Hannelore Fischer, and Elisabeth Moortgat, eds. *Lotte Jacobi: Photographien.* Cologne: Wienand, 2012.

Beckers, Marion, and Elisabeth Moortgat. *Atelier Lotte Jacobi, Berlin, New York.* Berlin: Das Verborgene Museum, 1997.

Beckers, Marion, and Elisabeth Moortgat. *Yva: Photographien, 1925–1938 = Yva: Photographies, 1925–1938.* Tübingen: Wasmuth, 2001.

Beimler, Hans. *Im Mörderlager Dachau.* Moscow: Verlagsgenossenschaft Ausländischer Arbeiter in der UdSSR, 1933.

Benjamin, Walter. *Selected Writings.* Edited by Howard Eiland and Michael W. Jennings. Cambridge: Belknap Press of Harvard University Press, 2006.

Bergen, Doris. *Between God and Hitler: Military Chaplains in Nazi Germany.* Cambridge: Cambridge University Press, 2023.

Berghoff, Hartmut, and Berti Kolbow. "Flourishing in a Dictatorship: Agfa's Marketing and the Nazi Regime." *Journal of Historical Research in Marketing* 5, no. 1 (2013): 71–96.

Berghoff, Hartmut, and Uwe Spiekermann. *Decoding Modern Consumer Societies.* New York: Palgrave Macmillan, 2012.

Berkhoff, Karel. *Harvest of Despair: Life and Death in Ukraine under Nazi Rule.* Cambridge: Harvard University Press, 2008.

Berkowitz, Michael. *Jews and Photography in Britain.* Austin: University of Texas Press, 2015.

Berkowitz, Michael. "Photography as a Jewish Business: From High Theory, to Studio, to Snapshot." *East European Jewish Affairs* 39, no. 3 (2009): 389–400.

Bertillon, Alphonse. *La Photographie Judiciaire: Avec un Appendice sur la Classification et l'Identification Anthropométriques.* Paris: Gauthier-Villars, 1890.

Biess, Frank. *Homecomings: Returning POWs and the Legacies of Defeat in Postwar Germany.* Princeton: Princeton University Press, 2009.

Biess, Frank, and Robert Moeller, eds. *Histories of the Aftermath: The Legacies of the Second World War in Europe.* New York: Berghahn, 2010.

Blank, Ralf, Jörg Echternkamp, Karola Fings et al., eds. *Germany and the Second World War.* Vol. 9, part 1. *German Wartime Society, 1939–1945: Politicization, Disintegration, and the Struggle for Survival.* New York: Clarendon Press, 2008.

Blattner, Evamarie, and Nils Büttner. *Der fotografierte Krieg: Der Erste Weltkrieg zwischen Dokumentation und Propaganda.* Tübingen: Universitätsstadt Tübingen, 2014.

Böhler, Jochen, and Robert Gerwarth, eds. *The Waffen SS: A European History.* Oxford: Oxford University Press, 2017.

Bopp, Petra, and Andreas Koch. *Fremde im Visier: Fotoalben aus dem Zweiten Weltkrieg.* Bielefeld: Kerber, 2009.

Bradish, Paul, and the Hamburg Institute for Social Research, eds. *The German Army and Genocide: Crimes against War Prisoners, Jews, and Other Civilians in the East, 1939–1944.* Translated by Scott Abbott. New York: New Press, 1999.

Brasse, Wilhelm. *Wilhelm Brasse: Photographer 3444, Auschwitz, 1940–1945.* Eastbourne: Sussex Academic Press, 2012.

Broszat, Martin. *Der Staat Hitlers: Grundlegung und Entwicklung seiner inneren Verfassung.* Munich: Deutscher Taschenbuch-Verlag, 1969.

Browning, Christopher R. *Ordinary Men: Reserve Police Battalion 101 and the Final Solution in Poland.* New York: Harper Collins, 1992.

Browning, Christopher R. *The Origins of the Final Solution: The Evolution of Nazi Jewish Policy, September 1939–March 1942.* London: Arrow Books, 2005.

Bruttmann, Tal, Stefan Hördler, and Christoph Kreutzmüller. *Die fotografische Inszenierung des Verbrechens: Ein Album aus Auschwitz.* Darmstadt Academic, 2019.

Büchler, Yehoshua. "'Unworthy Behavior': The Case of SS Officer Max Taubner." *Holocaust and Genocide Studies* 17 (2003): 409–29.

Burke, Peter. *Eyewitnessing: The Uses of Images as Historical Evidence.* Ithaca: Cornell University Press, 2008.

Burleigh, Michael, and Wolfgang Wippermann. *The Racial State: Germany, 1933–1945.* Cambridge: Cambridge University Press, 2011.

Bytwerk, R. L. "Grassroots Propaganda in the Third Reich: The Reich Ring for National Socialist Propaganda and Public Enlightenment." *German Studies Review* 33 (2010): 93–118.

Caplan, Jane, ed. *Concentration Camps in Nazi Germany: The New Histories.* London: Routledge, 2010.

Caplan, Jane, and Hannes Heer. "The Difficulty of Ending a War: Reactions to the Exhibition 'War of Extermination: Crimes of the Wehrmacht, 1941 to 1944.'" *History Workshop Journal,* no. 46 (1998): 187–203.

Century, Rachel. *Female Administrators of the Third Reich.* London: Palgrave Macmillan, 2017.

Chaves, Ruth P., et al. *Fotografien aus den Lagern des NS-Regimes: Beweissicherung und asthetische Praxis.* Göttingen: Vandenhoeck & Ruprecht, 2018.

Chéroux, Clément, Ilsen About, and Georges Angéli. *Mémoire des Camps: Photographies des Camps de Concentration et d'Extermination Nazis (1933–1999).* Paris: Marval, 2001.

Court, Justin. "Picturing History, Remembering Soldiers: World War I Photography between the Public and the Private." *History and Memory* 29, no. 1 (2017): 72–103.

Cronin, Elizabeth. *Heimat Photography in Austria: A Politicized Vision of Peasants and Skiers.* Vienna: Photoinstitut Bonartes; Salzburg: Fotohof Edition, 2015.

Cüppers, Martin, Anne Lepper, and Jürgen Matthäus, eds. *From "Euthanasia" to Sobibor: An SS Officer's Photo Collection.* Bloomington: Indiana University Press, 2022.

Cuomo, Glenn, ed. *National Socialist Cultural Policy.* New York: St. Martin's Press, 1995.

Czech, Danuta, and Jadwiga Bezwińska, eds. *Kl Auschwitz Seen by the SS.* Oświeçim: Auschwitz-Birkenau State Museum, 2003.

Darré, Richard W. *Neuadel aus Blut und Boden.* Munich: J. F. Lehmann, 1930.

Davidson, Martin P. *The Perfect Nazi: Unmasking My SS Grandfather.* London: Penguin, 2011.

Dean, Martin. *Robbing the Jews: The Confiscation of Jewish Property in the Holocaust, 1933–1945.* Cambridge: Cambridge University Press, 2011.

de Grazia, Victoria. *The Culture of Consent: Mass Organization of Leisure in Fascist Italy.* Cambridge: Cambridge University Press, 1981.

Dewitz, Bodo von. *So wird bei uns der Krieg geführt: Amateurfotografie im Ersten Weltkrieg.* Munich: Tuduv-Verlagsgesellschaft, 1989.

Didczuneit, Veit, Jens Ebert, and Thomas Jander. *Schreiben im Krieg, Schreiben vom Krieg: Feldpost im Zeitalter der Weltkriege.* Essen: Klartext, 2011.

Didi-Huberman, Georges. *Images in Spite of All: Four Photographs from Auschwitz.* Chicago: University of Chicago Press, 2008.

Dieckmann, Christoph. *The Persecution and Mass Murder of Lithuanian Jews during Summer and Fall of 1941.* Vilnius: Margi Rastai, 2007.

Diewerge, Wolfgang. *Deutsche Soldaten sehen die Sowjet-Union: Feldpostbriefe aus dem Osten.* Berlin: Wilhelm Limpert-Verlag, 1941.

Douglas, Lawrence. *The Right Wrong Man: John Demjanjuk and the Last Great Nazi War Crimes Trial.* Princeton: Princeton University Press, 2018.

Dresdner, Albert. "German Commercial Photography." *Commercial Art* 4 (April 1928): 173–76.

Dressler, Horst Andress. *Three Years of the National-Socialist Community "Kraft durch Freude": Aims and Achievements.* Berlin: Verlag der deutschen Arbeitsfront, 1937.

Dressler, Oskar, ed. *Grosse Polizei-Ausstellung Berlin in Wort und Bild: Internationaler Polizeikongress in Berlin.* Vienna: Internationale öffentliche Sicherheit, 1927.

Echternkamp, Jörg. *Kriegsschauplatz Deutschland, 1945: Leben in Angst—Hoffnung und Frieden. Feldpost aus der Heimat und von der Front.* Paderborn: Ferdinand Schöningh, 2006.

Epstein, Catherine. *Model Nazi: Arthur Greiser and the Occupation of Western Poland.* Oxford: Oxford University Press, 2012.

Eskildsen, Ute, ed. *Fotografieren hieß teilnehmen: Fotografinnen der Weimarer Republik.* Dusseldorf: Richter, 1994.

Evans, Emily. "Soviet Photo and the Search for Proletarian Photography, 1926–1937." PhD dissertation, University of Illinois at Urbana-Champaign, 2014.

Evans, Jennifer, Paul Betts, and Stefan Hoffman, eds. *The Ethics of Seeing: Photography in Twentieth-Century German History.* New York: Berghahn, 2018.

Evans, Richard J. *The Third Reich in Power, 1933–1939.* London: Penguin, 2006.

Evans, Richard J. *The Third Reich at War, 1939–1945.* New York: Penguin, 2010.

Fitzpatrick, Sheila. *Everyday Stalinism: Ordinary Life in Extraordinary Times; Soviet Russia in the 1930s.* Oxford: Oxford University Press, 1999.

Frei, Norbert. *1945 und wir: Das dritte Reich im Bewußtsein der Deutschen.* Munich: Deutscher Taschenbuch Verlag, 2005.

Frei, Norbert. *Vergangenheitspolitik: Die Anfänge der Bundesrepublik und die NS-Vergangenheit.* Munich: Beck, 2012.

Frie, Roger. *Not in My Family: German Memory and Responsibility after the Holocaust.* Oxford: Oxford University Press, 2017.

Friedlander, Henry, and Nathan Stoltzfus, eds. *Nazi Crimes and the Law.* Cambridge: Cambridge University Press, 2016.

Friedländer, Saul. *Nazi Germany and the Jews.* Vols. 1–2. London: Phoenix, 2008.

Fritz, Stephen. *Frontsoldaten: The German Soldier in World War II.* Lexington: University Press of Kentucky, 1995.

Fritz, Stephen G., and Klaus Kochmann. *Hitlers Frontsoldaten: der erzählte Krieg.* Berlin: Henschel, 1998.

Fritzsche, Peter. "The Archive." *History & Memory* 17 (2005): 15–44.

Fritzsche, Peter. *Germans into Nazis.* Cambridge: Harvard University Press, 2003.

Frübis, Hildegard, Clara M. Oberle, and Agnieszka Pufelska. *Fotografien aus den Lagern des NS-Regimes: Beweissicherung und Ästhetische Praxis.* Vienna: Böhlau Verlag, 2019.

Fuchs, Karl. *Your Loyal and Loving Son: The Letters of Tank Gunner Karl Fuchs, 1937–41.* Edited by Horst F. Richardson. Washington, D.C.: Brassey's, 2003.

Fulbrook, Mary. *Reckonings: Legacies of Nazi Persecution and the Quest for Justice.* Oxford: Oxford University Press, 2020.

Fulbrook, Mary. "Reframing the Past: Justice, Guilt, and Consolidation in East and West Germany after Nazism." *Central European History* 53, no. 2 (2020): 294–313.

Gay, Peter. *Weimar Culture: The Outsider as Insider.* New York: Norton, 2001.

Gellately, Robert. *Backing Hitler: Consent and Coercion in Nazi Germany.* Oxford: Oxford University Press, 2013.

Gellately, Robert. *The Gestapo and German Society: Enforcing Racial Policy, 1933–1945.* Oxford: Clarendon Press, 1990.

Georg, Willy. Rafael F. Scharf, comp. *In the Warsaw Ghetto, Summer 1941.* New York: Aperture, 1993.

Gerwarth, Robert. *Hitler's Hangman: The Life of Heydrich.* New Haven: Yale University Press, 2012.

Geyer, Michael, and Sheila Fitzpatrick. *Beyond Totalitarianism: Stalinism and Nazism Compared.* Cambridge: Cambridge University Press, 2009.

Gidal, Nachum Tim. *Jews in Photography.* New York: Leo Baeck Institute, 1987.

Giloi, Eva. *Monarchy, Myth and Material Culture in Germany, 1750–1950.* Cambridge: Cambridge University Press, 2011.

Goebbels, Joseph. *Revolution der Deutschen: 14 Jahre Nationalsozialismus.* Oldenburg: Gerhard Stalling, 1933.

Goeschel, Christian. "Suicide in Nazi Concentration Camps, 1933–1939." *Journal of Contemporary History* 45, no. 3 (2010): 628–48.

Goldhagen, Daniel Jonah. *Hitler's Willing Executioners: Ordinary Germans and the Holocaust.* New York: Knopf, 1996.

Gosselk, Detlef, ed., *Liselotte Strelow (1908–1981): Erinnerungen.* Bad Bevensen: Herz-Kreislauf-Klinik, 1989.

Grube, Eric. "Borderland Brothers: Austrofascist Competition and Cooperation with National Socialists, 1936–1938." *Journal of Austrian Studies* 56, no. 1 (2023): 1–24.

Gruner, Wolf. *Resisters: How Ordinary Jews Fought Persecution in Hitler's Germany.* New Haven: Yale University Press, 2023.

Guerin, Frances. *Through Amateur Eyes: Film and Photography in Nazi Germany.* Minneapolis: University of Minnesota Press, 2011.

Hannavy, John. *Encyclopedia of Nineteenth-Century Photography.* New York: Routledge, 2008.

Harrisville, David A. *The Virtuous Wehrmacht: Crafting the Myth of the German Soldier on the Eastern Front, 1941–1944.* Ithaca: Cornell University Press, 2021.

Harvey, Elizabeth, Johannes Hürter, Maiken Umbach, and Andreas Wirsching, eds. *Private Life and Privacy in Nazi Germany.* Cambridge: Cambridge University Press, 2019.

Hébert, Valerie, ed. *Framing the Holocaust: Photographs of a Mass Shooting in Latvia, 1941.* Madison: University of Wisconsin Press, Published in Association with the United States Holocaust Memorial Museum, 2023.

Heer, Hannes. *The Discursive Construction of History: Remembering the Wehrmacht's War of Annihilation.* Basingstoke: Palgrave Macmillan, 2008.

Heer, Hannes. *Vernichtungskrieg: Verbrechen der Wehrmacht, 1941–1944.* Frankfurt am Main: Zweitausendeins, 1999.

Heer, Hannes, and Klaus Naumann, eds. *War of Extermination: The German Military in World War II, 1941–1944.* Translated by Roy Shelton. New York: Berghahn, 2009.

Heiber, Helmut, ed. *Goebbels-Reden.* Vol. 1. *1931–1939.* Düsseldorf: Droste Verlag, 1970.

Heindl, Robert. "The Technique of Criminal Investigation in Germany." *Annals of the American Academy of Political and Social Science* 146 (November 1929): 223–36.

Heineman, Elizabeth D. *What Difference Does a Husband Make? Women and Marital Status in Nazi and Postwar Germany.* Berkeley: University of California Press, 2003.

Henderson, Bruce. *Sons and Soldiers: The Untold Story of the Jews Who Escaped the Nazis and Returned with the U.S. Army to Fight Hitler.* New York: HarperCollins, 2017.

Henry, Patrick. *Jewish Resistance to the Nazis.* Washington, D.C.: Catholic University of America Press, 2014.

Herf, Jeffrey. *Divided Memory: The Nazi Past in the Two Germanys.* Cambridge: Harvard University Press, 1999.

Herf, Jeffrey. *Reactionary Modernism: Technology, Culture, and Politics in Weimar and the Third Reich.* Cambridge: Cambridge University Press, 1984.

Hermand, Jost. *Kultur in finsteren Zeiten: Nazifaschismus, Innere Emigration, Exil.* Cologne: Böhlau, 2010.

Hermand, Jost, and James D. Steakley, eds. *Heimat, Nation, Fatherland: The German Sense of Belonging.* New York: P. Lang, 1997.

Herz, Rudolf. *Hoffmann & Hitler: Fotografie als Medium des Führer-Mythos.* Munich: Klinkhardt & Biermann, 1994.

Herz, Rudolf, and Brigitte Bruns. *Hof-Atelier Elvira, 1887–1928: Astheten, Emanzen, Aristokraten.* Munich: Münchner Stadtmuseum, 1985.

Herzog, Dagmar. *Sexuality and German Fascism.* New York: Berghahn, 2005.

Herzog, Eugen, and Helga Herzog Godfrey. *WWII Diary of a German Soldier.* Bloomington: AuthorHouse, 2006.

Heydecker, Joe J. "Photographing behind the Warsaw Ghetto Wall, 1941." *Holocaust and Genocide Studies* 1, no. 1 (1986): 63–77.

Hilberg, Raul. *The Destruction of the European Jews.* New Haven: Yale University Press, 2003.

Hilberg, Raul. *Perpetrators, Victims, Bystanders: The Jewish Catastrophe, 1933–1945.* London: Secker & Warburg, 1995.

Hirsch, Marianne. *Family Frames: Photography, Narrative, and Postmemory.* Cambridge: Harvard University Press, 2016.

Hoffmann, Heinrich. *Hitler Was My Friend.* London: Burke, 1955.

Honnef, Klaus, et al. *Liselotte Strelow: Retrospektive, 1908–1981.* Ostfildern: Hatje Cantz, 2008.

Horkheimer, Max. *Gesammelte Schriften.* Vol. 6. Frankfurt am Main: Fischer, 1991.

Huener, Jonathan, and Francis R. Nicosia, eds. *The Arts in Nazi Germany: Continuity, Conformity, Change.* Vermont Studies on Nazi Germany and the Holocaust. New York: Berghahn, 2006.

Hull, Isabel V. *Absolute Destruction: Military Culture and the Practices of War in Imperial Germany.* Ithaca: Cornell University Press, 2013.

Irrgang, Christina. *Hitlers Fotograf: Heinrich Hoffmann und die nationalsozialistische Bildpolitik.* Bielefeld: Transcript Verlag, 2020.

Jäger, Jens. *Gesellschaft und Photographie: Formen und Funktionen der Photographie in England und Deutschland, 1839–1860.* Wiesbaden: VS Verlag für Sozialwissenschaften, 1995.

Jäger, Jens. "Photography: A Means of Surveillance? Judicial Photography, 1850 to 1900." *Crime, Histoire & Sociétés* 5, no. 1 (2001): 27–51.

Jahn, Peter, and Ulrike Schmiegelt. *Foto-feldpost: Geknipste Kriegserlebnisse, 1939–1945.* Berlin: Elefanten Press, 2000.

Jähner, Harald. *Aftermath: Life in the Fallout of the Third Reich, 1945–1955.* New York: Alfred A. Knopf, 2022.

James, Harold. *Deutschland in der Weltwirtschaftskrise, 1924–1936.* Stuttgart: Deutsche Verlags-Anstalt, 1988.

Jarausch, Konrad. *Reluctant Accomplice: A Wehrmacht Soldier's Letters from the Eastern Front.* Princeton: Princeton University Press, 2011.

Jarausch, Konrad H., and Michael Geyer. *Shattered Past: Reconstructing German Histories.* Princeton: Princeton University Press, 2003.

Jefferies, Matthew. "Die Schöne Heimat? Depictions of Germany in a Popular Photobook from the Second Empire to the Federal Republic." *New German Critique* 46 (2019): 35–63.

Jennings, Eric T. *Last Exit from Vichy France: The Martinique Escape Route and the Ambiguities of Emigration.* Chicago: University of Chicago, 2002.

Johnson, Eric A. *The Nazi Terror: The Gestapo, Jews and Ordinary Germans.* London: Murray, 2002.

Johnson, Eric A., and Karl-Heinz Reuband. *What We Knew: Terror, Mass Murder, and Everyday Life in Nazi Germany.* New York: Basic Books, 2005.

Jöst, Heinz, and Yitzhak Arad. *A Day in the Warsaw Ghetto.* Yad Vashem: Holocaust Martyrs' and Heroes' Remembrance Authority, the Museum, 1988.

Jungius, Martin, and Wolfgang Seibel. "The Citizen as Perpetrator: Kurt Blanke and Aryanization in France, 1940–1944." *Holocaust and Genocide Studies* 22, no. 3 (2008): 441–74.

Die Kamera: Ausstellung für Fotografie, Druck und Reproduktion, amtlicher Katalog und Führer, Berlin 1933, 4. bis 19. November. Berlin, 1933.

Kempowski, Walter. *Das Echolot: Fuga furiosa, ein kollektives Tagebuch, Winter 1945.* 4 vols. Munich, 1999.

Kennedy, David M. *Freedom from Fear: The American People in Depression and War, 1929–1945.* New York: Oxford University Press, 2005.

Kerbs, Diethart. *Auf den Straßen von Berlin: Der Fotograf Willy Römer, 1887–1979.* Bönen: Deutsches Historisches Museum, 2004.

Kerbs, Diethart. "Kalte Zeit: Über die zweite Lebenshälfte (1933–1979) des Berliner Pressefotografen Willy Römer." *Fotogeschichte* 24, no. 94 (2004): 68–70.

Kerbs, Diethart, Walter Uka, and Brigitte Walz-Richter, eds. *Zur Geschichte der Pressefotografie, 1930–36: Die Gleichschaltung der Bilder.* Berlin: Frölich & Kaufmann, 1983.

Keresztes, Julie R. "Photography as a Wartime Service to Family and Nation in Nazi-Occupied Europe." *German History* 40, no. 2 (June 2022): 197–219.

Keresztes, Julie R. "Shaming through Photographic Denunciation in Nazi Germany, 1933–1938." *Contemporary European History* (2023): 1–12.

Kershaw, Ian. *Hitler.* Hoboken: Taylor and Francis, 2014.

Kershaw, Ian. *Popular Opinion and Political Dissent in the Third Reich: Bavaria, 1933–1945.* Oxford: Clarendon Press, 2005.

Klee, Ernst, Willi Dressen, and Volker Riess. *Schöne Zeiten: Judenmord aus der Sicht der Täter und Gaffer.* Frankfurt am Main: S. Fischer, 1989.

Klemperer, Victor. *I Shall Bear Witness: The Diaries of Victor Klemperer, 1933–1941.* London: Folio Society, 2006.

Koetzle, Hans-Michael. *Eyes Wide Open! 100 Years of Leica.* Berlin: Kehrer, 2015.

Kogon, Eugen. *The Theory and Practice of Hell: The German Concentration Camps and the System behind Them.* New York: Berkeley, 1980.

König, Wolfgang. "Der Volksempfänger und die Radioindustrie: ein Beitrag zum Verhältnis von Wirtschaft und Politik im Nationalsozialismus." *Vierteljahrschrift für Sozial und Wirtschaftsgeschichte* 90 (2003): 269–89.

Koonz, Claudia. *Mothers in the Fatherland: Women, the Family, and Nazi Politics.* London: Routledge, 2014.

Koonz, Claudia. *The Nazi Conscience.* Cambridge: Belknap Press of Harvard University Press, 2003.

Kracauer, Siegfried. "Die Photographie." *Frankfurter Zeitung,* October 28, 1927.

Kreutzmüller, Christoph. *Final Sale in Berlin: The Destruction of Jewish Commercial Activity, 1930–1945.* New York: Berghahn, 2017.

Kreutzmüller, Christoph. *Ein Pogrom im Juni: Fotos antisemitischer Schmierereien in Berlin, 1938.* Berlin: Hentrich & Hentrich, 2013.

Kreutzmüller, Christoph. "Staging a Boycott: Photographs of the Nazi Attack on Jewish-Owned Businesses in April 1933." *Holocaust and Genocide Studies* 38, no. 1 (Spring 2024): 1–17.

Kreutzmüller, Christoph, Michael Wildt, and Mosche Zimmermann, eds. *National Economies: Volkswirtschaft, Racism and Economy in Europe between the Wars (1918–1939/45).* Newcastle upon Tyne: Cambridge Scholars Publishing, 2015.

Kreutzmüller, Christoph, and Theresia Ziehe. "Crossing Borders in the Summer of 1935: Fritz Fürstenberg's Photographs of Persecution in National Socialist Germany." *Leo Baeck Institute Year Book* (2019): 73–89.

Kroener, Bernhard, Rolf-Dieter Müller, and Hans Umbreit, eds. *Germany and the Second World War.* Vol. 2. *Organization and Mobilization of the German Sphere of Power.* New York: Clarendon Press, 2003.

Krohn, Claus-Dieter. *Handbuch der deutschsprachigen Emigration, 1933–1945.* Darmstadt: Wissenschaftliche Buchgesellschaft, 2008.

Krylova, Anna. *Soviet Women in Combat: A History of Violence on the Eastern Front.* Cambridge: Cambridge University Press, 2014.

Kühne, Thomas. *Belonging and Genocide: Hitler's Community, 1918–1945.* New Haven: Yale University Press, 2013.

Kühne, Thomas. "Protean Masculinity, Hegemonic Masculinity: Soldiers in the Third Reich." *Central European History* 51, no. 3 (2018): 390–418.

Kühne, Thomas. *The Rise and Fall of Comradeship: Hitler's Soldiers, Male Bonding and Mass Violence in the Twentieth Century.* Cambridge: Cambridge University Press, 2017.

Langford, Martha. *Suspended Conversations: The Afterlife of Memory in Photographic Albums.* Montreal: McGill-Queens University Press, 2001.

Laqueur, Walter. *Weimar: A Cultural History, 1918–1933.* London: Phoenix Press, 2000.

Lässig, Simone, and Miriam Rürup, eds. *Space and Spatiality in Modern German-Jewish History.* New York: Berghahn, 2019.

Lendvai-Dircksen, Erna. *Das deutsche Volksgesicht*. Berlin: Kulturelle Verlagsgesellschaft, 1932.

Loeffel, Robert. "Sippenhaft, Terror and Fear in Nazi Germany: Examining One Facet of Terror in the Aftermath of the Plot of 20 July 1944." *Contemporary European History* 16, no. 1 (2007): 51–69.

Longerich, Peter. *Heinrich Himmler*. Oxford: Oxford University Press, 2013.

Longerich, Peter. *Hitler: A Biography*. Oxford: Oxford University Press, 2019.

Lower, Wendy. *Hitler's Furies: German Women in the Nazi Killing Fields*. Boston: Houghton Mifflin Harcourt, 2013.

Lower, Wendy. *Nazi Empire-Building and the Holocaust in Ukraine*. Chapel Hill: University of North Carolina Press, 2007.

Lower, Wendy. *The Ravine: A Family, a Photograph, a Holocaust Massacre Revealed*. London: Head of Zeus, 2021.

Machnowski, Jan, and Franciszek Jaźwiecki. *Forbidden Art: Illegal Works by Concentration Camp Prisoners*. Oświęcim: Auschwitz-Birkenau State Museum, 2012.

Magilow, Daniel H., ed. *The Absolute Realist: Collected Writings of Albert Renger-Patzsch, 1923–1967*. Los Angeles: Getty Research Institute, 2023.

Magilow, Daniel H. *The Photography of Crisis: The Photo Essays of Weimar Germany*. University Park: Pennsylvania State University Press, 2012.

Mailänder, Elissa. *Female SS Guards and Workaday Violence: The Majdanek Concentration Camp, 1942–1944*. East Lansing: Michigan State University Press, 2015.

Mailänder, Elissa. "Making Sense of a Rape Photograph: Sexual Violence as Social Performance on the Eastern Front, 1939–1944." *Journal of the History of Sexuality* 26, no. 3 (2017): 489–520.

Manoschek, Walter. "Vernichtungskrieg: Verbrechen der Wehrmacht, 1941–1944. Innenansichten einer Ausstellung." *Zeitgeschichte* 29 (2002): 67–75.

Martschukat, Jürgen, and Silvan Niedermeier, eds. *Violence and Visibility in Modern History*. New York: Palgrave Macmillan, 2013.

Mason, Timothy. "Labour in the Third Reich, 1933–1939." *Past & Present* 33 (1966): 112–41.

Mason, Timothy. "Women in Germany, 1925–1940: Family Welfare and Work." *History Workshop* 2 (1976): 5–32.

Mason, Timothy, and Jane Caplan. *Nazism, Fascism, and the Working Class*. Cambridge: Cambridge University Press, 2003.

Matthäus, Jürgen. *Gerahmte Gewalt: Private Fotoalben von Deutschen im "Osteinsatz" und die kollektive Erinnerung an den Zweiten Weltkrieg*. Berlin: Metropol Verlag, 2025.

Matthäus, Jürgen. "Kriegsfotos auf dem Obersalzberg Anmerkungen zu Eva Brauns Albumsammlung," *Zeitschrift für Geschichtswissenschaft* (2021): 224–39.

Matthäus, Jürgen. "Opa im Osten: Private deutsche Fotoalben zum Zweiten Weltkrieg," *Fotogeschichte* 165 (2022): 26–36.

Maxwell, Anne. *Picture Imperfect: Photography and Eugenics, 1870–1940*. London: Eastbourne Sussex Press, 2010.

Mazower, Mark. "Military Violence and National Socialist Values: The Wehrmacht in Greece, 1941–1944." *Past & Present* 134 (1992): 129–58.

McElligott, Anthony, and Tim Kirk, eds. *Working towards the Führer: Essays in Honour of Sir Ian Kershaw.* Manchester: Manchester University Press, 2004.

McKitrick, Frederick L. *From Craftsmen to Capitalists: German Artisans from the Third Reich to the Federal Republic, 1939–1953.* New York: Berghahn, 2016.

Megargee, Geoffrey P. *The United States Holocaust Memorial Museum Encyclopedia of Camps and Ghettos, 1933–1945.* Vols. 1–3. Bloomington: Indiana University Press, Published in Association with the United States Holocaust Memorial Museum, 2012.

Messerschmidt, Manfred, and Fritz Wüllner. *Die Wehrmachtjustiz im Dienste des Nationalsozialismus: Zerstörung einer Legende.* Baden-Baden: Nomos, 1987.

Michaelson, Mark, and Steven Kasher. *Least Wanted: A Century of American Mugshots.* New York: Galerie Steven Kasher, 2006.

Michaud, Eric, and Janet Lloyd. *The Cult of Art in Nazi Germany.* Stanford: Stanford University Press, 2004.

Michelbacher, Dallas. "The Prisoner of War Camps of the Wehrmacht: Key Findings of the United States Holocaust Memorial Museum Encyclopedia of Camps and Ghettos, Volume IV." *Bulletin of the German Historical Institute,* no. 72 (2023): 59–68.

Milton, Sybil. "The Camera as Weapon: Documentary Photography and the Holocaust." *Simon Wiesenthal Center Annual* 1 (1984): 45–68.

Milton, Sybil. "Photography as Evidence of the Holocaust." *History of Photography* 23 (1999): 303–12.

Moeller, Robert G. *War Stories: The Search for a Usable Past in the Federal Republic of Germany.* Berkeley: University of California Press, 2003.

Morina, Christina, and Krijn Thijs, eds. *Probing the Limits of Categorization: The Bystander in Holocaust History.* New York: Berghahn, 2018.

Morsch, Günter. *Von der Sachsenburg nach Sachsenhausen: Bilder aus dem Fotoalbum eines KZ-Kommandanten.* Berlin: Metropol, 2007.

Mühlhäuser Regina. *Eroberungen: Sexuelle Gewalttaten und intime Beziehungen deutscher Soldaten in der Sowjetunion, 1941–1945.* Hamburg: Hamburger Edition, 2010.

Müller, Melissa, and Monika Tatzkow. *Lost Lives, Lost Art: Jewish Collectors, Nazi Art Theft, and the Quest for Justice.* New York: Vendome Press, 2010.

Müller, Rolf-Dieter. *Hitler's Wehrmacht, 1935–1945.* Lexington: University Press of Kentucky, 2016.

Neitzel, Sönke, Harald Welzer, and Jefferson S. Chase. *Soldaten: On Fighting, Killing, and Dying; The Secret World War II Tapes of German POWs.* London: Simon & Schuster, 2013.

Newsome, W. Jake. *Pink Triangle Legacies: Coming Out in the Shadow of the Holocaust.* Ithaca: Cornell University Press, 2022.

Niemann, Friedrich R. *Feldpost: The War Letters of Friedrich Reiner Niemann, a German Soldier on the Eastern Front.* Edited and translated by Denis Havel. Charleston: Fonthill, 2016.

Nugent, Christine R. "The Voice of the Visitor: Popular Reactions to the Exhibition 'Vernichtungskrieg. Verbrechen Der Wehrmacht 1941–1944.'" *Journal of European Studies* 44, no. 3 (2014): 249–62.

Patel, Kiran K. *Soldiers of Labor: Labor Service in Nazi Germany and New Deal America, 1933–1945.* Washington, D.C.: German Historical Institute, 2010.

Paul, Friedrich. *Handbuch der kriminalistischen Photographie für Beamte der Gerichte, der Staatsanwaltschaften und der Sicherheitsbehörden.* Berlin: J. Guttentag, 1900.

Paul, Gerhard, and Klaus-Michael Mallmann. *Die Gestapo: Mythos und Realität.* Darmstadt: Primus, 2003.

Pegelow, Thomas, Jürgen Matthäus, and Mark W. Hornburg, eds. *Beyond "Ordinary Men": Christopher R. Browning and Holocaust Historiography.* Paderborn: Ferdinand Schöningh, 2019.

Pehle, Walter H. *November 1938: From "Reichskristallnacht" to Genocide.* New York: Berg, 1991.

Pelizzari, Maria A. *Photography and Italy.* London: Reaktion Books, 2011.

Pendas, Devin O. *The Frankfurt Auschwitz Trial, 1963–1965: Genocide, History and the Limits of the Law.* Cambridge: Cambridge University Press, 2011.

Pendas, Devin O., Mark Roseman, and Richard F. Wetzell, eds. *Beyond the Racial State: Rethinking Nazi Germany.* Washington, D.C.: German Historical Institute, 2017.

Petropoulos, Jonathan. *Art as Politics in the Third Reich.* Chapel Hill: University of North Carolina Press, 1999.

Petropoulos, Jonathan. *Artists under Hitler: Collaboration and Survival in Nazi Germany.* New Haven: Yale University Press, 2015.

Peukert, Detlev. *The Weimar Republic: The Crisis of Classical Modernity.* New York: Hill and Wang, 2008.

Pike, David W. *Spaniards in the Holocaust: Mauthausen, the Horror on the Danube.* London: Routledge, 2000.

Pilecki, Witold. *Freiwillig nach Auschwitz: die geheimen Aufzeichnungen des Häftlings Witold Pilecki.* Translated by Dagmar Mallett. Zurich: Orell Füssli, 2013.

Pine, Lisa. *Hitler's "National Community": Society and Culture in Nazi Germany.* London: Bloomsbury Academic, 2017.

Pohl, Dieter. *Die Ermordung der europäischen Juden: Eine Umfassende Dokumentation des Holocaust, 1941–1945.* Munich: Piper, 1990.

Reddemann, Karl, ed. *Zwischen Front und Heimat: Der Briefwechsel des münsterischen Ehepaares Agnes und Albert Neuhaus, 1940–1944.* Münster: Regensberg, 1996.

Reich, Amos Morris. *Racial Photography as Scientific Evidence, 1876–1980.* Chicago: University of Chicago Press, 2016.

Reichskulturkammer. *Handbuch der Reichskulturkammer.* Berlin: Deutscher Verlag für Politik und Wirtschaft, 1937.

Reisen, Andreas. *Der Passexpedient: Geschichte der Reisepässe und Ausweisdokumente—vom Mittelalter bis zum Personalausweis im Scheckkartenformat.* Baden-Baden: Nomos, 2012.

Rizzo, Lorena. *Photography and History in Colonial Southern Africa: Shades of Empire.* Abingdon: Routledge, 2020.

Ross, Kerry. *Photography for Everyone: The Cultural Lives of Cameras and Consumers in Early Twentieth-Century Japan.* Stanford: Stanford University Press, 2015.

Rossino, Alexander B. "Eastern Europe through German Eyes: Soldiers' Photographs, 1939–42." *History of Photography* 23, no. 4 (2015): 313–21.

Sachsse, Rolf. *Die Erziehung zum Wegsehen: Fotografie im NS-Staat.* Dresden: Philo Fine Arts, 2003.

Sait, Bryce. *The Indoctrination of the Wehrmacht: Nazi Ideology and the War Crimes of the German Military*. New York: Berghahn, 2019.

Samols, Steven. "Capturing Difference: The *Wurstelprater* Photobook in Turn-of-the-Century Vienna." *Leo Baeck Institute Year Book* 67, no. 1 (2022): 55–76.

Samuel, Raphael. *Theatres of Memory*. Vol. 1. London: Verso, 1994.

Scheck, Raffael. *French Colonial Soldiers in German Captivity during World War II*. New York: Cambridge University Press, 2014.

Schlenker, Ines. *Hitler's Salon: The Grosse Deutsche Kunstausstellung at the Haus der Deutschen Kunst in Munich, 1937–1944*. Bern: P. Lang, 2007.

Schneider, Gerd. *Doch ich lieb Dich hoch über den Dingen: Ein Kriegstagebuch*. Stuttgart: Strecker und Schröder, 1943.

Schönfeld, Christiane, and Carmel Finnan, eds. *Practicing Modernity: Female Creativity in the Weimar Republic*. Würzburg: Königshausen und Neumann, 2006.

Schumann, Frank. *Was tun wir hier? Soldatenpost und Heimatbriefe aus Zwei Weltkriegen*. Rheda-Wiedenbrück: RM-Buch-und-Medien-Vertrieb, 2013.

Schutts, Jeff R. "Coca-Colonization, 'Refreshing' Americanization, or Nazi Volksgetränk? The History of Coca-Cola in Germany, 1929–1961." PhD dissertation, Georgetown University, 2003.

Schwarberg, Gunther. *Im Ghetto von Warschau: Heinrich Josts Photographien*. Göttingen: Steidl, 2001.

Sedgwick, Eve Kosofsky. *Between Men: English Literature and Male Homosocial Desire*. New York: Columbia University Press, 2016.

Senfft, Alexandra. *Der lange Schatten der Täter: Nachkommen stellen sich ihrer NS-Familiengeschichte*. Munich: Piper, 2018.

Shirer, William L. *"This Is Berlin": Radio Broadcasts, 1938–40*. Woodstock, N.Y.: Overlook Press, 1999.

Shneer, David. "Picturing Grief: Soviet Holocaust Photography at the Intersection of History and Memory." *American Historical Review* 115, no. 1 (2010): 28–52.

Shneer, David. *Through Soviet Jewish Eyes: Photography, War, and the Holocaust*. New Brunswick: Rutgers University Press, 2012.

Siegel, Steffen. *First Exposures: Writings from the Beginnings of Photography*. Los Angeles: J. Paul Getty Museum, 2017.

Sontag, Susan. *On Photography*. London: Allen Lane, 1978.

Stahel, David, ed. *Mass Violence in Nazi-Occupied Europe*. Bloomington: Indiana University Press, 2018.

Stahel, David. *Operation Barbarossa and Germany's Defeat in the East*. Cambridge: Cambridge University Press, 2012.

Stargardt, Nicholas. "Beyond Consent and Coercion: Wartime Crises in Nazi Germany." *History Workshop Journal* 72, no. 1 (2011): 190–204.

Stargardt, Nicholas. *The German War: A Nation Under Arms*. New York: Basic, 2015.

Stargardt, Nicholas. "The Troubled Patriot: German *Innerlichkeit* in World War II." *German History* 28, no. 3 (2010): 326–42.

Starl, Tim. *Knipser: Die Bildgeschichte der privaten Fotografie in Deutschland und Österreich von 1880 bis 1980*. Munich: Koehler & Amelang, 1995.

Steber, Martina, and Bernhard Gotto, eds. *Visions of Community in Nazi Germany: Social Engineering and Private Lives.* Oxford: Oxford University Press, 2018.

Steinbacher, Sybille. *Volksgenossinnen: Frauen in der NS-Volksgemeinschaft.* Göttingen: Wallstein, 2007.

Steinweis, Alan. *Art, Ideology, and Economics in Nazi Germany: The Reich Chambers of Music, Theater, and the Visual Arts.* Chapel Hill: University of North Carolina Press, 1993.

Steinweis, Alan E. "Weimar Culture and the Rise of National Socialism: The Kampfbund für Deutsche Kultur." *Central European History* 24, no. 4 (1991): 402–23.

Stephenson, Jill. *Women in Nazi Germany.* London: Routledge, 2015.

Stiewe, Willy, and Heiner Kurzbein. *Foto und Volk.* Halle: Wilhelm Knapp, 1933.

Stone, Dan. "The Sonderkommando Photographs." *Jewish Social Studies* 7, no. 3 (2001): 132–48.

Struk, Janina. *Photographing the Holocaust: Interpretations of the Evidence.* London: I. B. Tauris, 2004.

Struk, Janina. *Private Pictures: Soldiers' Inside View of War.* London: I. B. Tauris, 2011.

Süß, Dietmar. *Tod aus der Luft: Kriegsgesellschaft und Luftkrieg in Deutschland und England.* Munich: Siedler Verlag, 2011.

Sydnor, Charles W. *Soldiers of Destruction: The SS Death's Head Division, 1933–1945.* Princeton: Princeton University Press, 1990.

Tagg, John. *The Burden of Representation.* Minneapolis: University of Minnesota Press, 1988.

Tec, Nechama. *Resistance: How Jews and Christians Fought Back against the Nazis.* Oxford: Oxford University Press, 2013.

Thamer, Hans-Ulrich. "Geschichte und Propaganda: Kulturhistorische Ausstellungen in der NS-Zeit." *Geschichte und Gesellschaft* 24, no. 3 (1998): 349–81.

Tießler, Walter. *Nicht Phrasen sondern Klarheit.* Berlin: Franz Eher, 1942.

Tillion, Germaine. *Ravensbrück.* Garden City, N.Y.: Anchor Press, 1975

Tooze, Adam. *The Wages of Destruction: The Making and Breaking of the Nazi Economy.* London: Allen Lane, 2006.

Torrie, Julia. *German Soldiers and the Occupation of France, 1940–1944.* Cambridge: Cambridge University Press, 2019.

Trachtenberg, Alan, ed., comp. Amy W. Meyers. *Classic Essays on Photography.* New Haven: Leete's Island Books, 2005.

Ullstein, Herman. *The Rise and Fall of the House of Ullstein.* New York: Simon and Schuster, 1943.

Ulrich, Bernd. *Besucher einer Ausstellung: Die Ausstellung "Vernichtungskrieg. Verbrechen der Wehrmacht 1941 bis 1944" in Interview und Gespräch.* Hamburg: Stiftung Hamburger Institut für Sozialforschung Hamburg, 1998.

Umbach, Maiken. "Selfhood, Place, and Ideology in German Photo Albums, 1933–1945." *Central European History* 48, no. 3 (2015): 335–65.

Vaizey, Hester. *Family Life in Germany, 1939–48.* Basingstoke: Palgrave Macmillan, 2010.

Vaizey, Hester. *Surviving Hitler's War: Family Life in Germany, 1939–48.* New York: Palgrave Macmillan, 2010.

Vowinckel, Annette. "German (Jewish) Photojournalists in Exile: A Story of Networks and Success." *German History* 31, no. 4 (2013): 473–96.

Wachsmann, Nikolaus. *KL: A History of the Nazi Concentration Camps*. London: Little, Brown Book Group, 2015.

Wegner, Bernd. *The Waffen-SS: Organization, Ideology, and Function*. Oxford: Basil Blackwell, 1990.

Weinberg, Gerhard L. *A World at Arms: A Global History of World War II*. New York: Cambridge University Press, 2010.

Weinke, Wilfried. *Verdrängt, vertrieben, aber nicht vergessen: Die Fotografen Emil Bieber, Max Halberstadt, Erich Kastan und Kurt Schallenberg*. Weingarten: Kunstverlag Weingarten, 2003.

Weise, Niels. *Eicke: Eine SS-Karriere zwischen Nervenklinik, KZ-System und Waffen-SS*. Paderborn: Ferdinand Schöningh, 2013.

Welch, David. *The Third Reich: Politics and Propaganda*. London: Routledge, 2006.

Welzer, Harald. *Das kommunikative Gedächtnis: Eine Theorie der Erinnerung*. Munich: C. H. Beck, 2017.

Welzer, Harald, et al. *"Opa war kein Nazi": Nationalsozialismus und Holocaust im Familiengedächtnis*. Frankfurt: Fischer Taschenbuch Verlag, 2002.

Westermann, Edward B. *Drunk on Genocide: Alcohol and Mass Murder in Nazi Germany*. Ithaca: Cornell University Press, 2021.

Wette, Wolfram. *The Wehrmacht: History, Myth, Reality*. Cambridge: Harvard University Press, 2007.

Wiesen, Jonathan. *Creating the Nazi Marketplace: Commerce and Consumption in the Third Reich*. Cambridge: Cambridge University Press, 2011.

Wildt, Michael. *Hitler's Volksgemeinschaft and the Dynamics of Racial Exclusion: Violence against Jews in Provincial Germany, 1919–1939*. New York: Berghahn, 2011.

Wildt, Michael. *An Uncompromising Generation: The Nazi Leadership of the Reich Security Main Office*. Madison: University of Wisconsin Press, 2009.

Wildt, Michael, and Sybille Steinbacher, eds. *Fotos im Nationalsozialismus: Neue Forschungen zu einer besonderen Quelle*. Göttingen: Wallstein, 2022.

Williams, John A. *Turning to Nature in Germany: Hiking, Nudism, and Conservation, 1900–1940*. Stanford: Stanford University Press, 2007.

Woweries, F. H. *Deutsche Fibel: Worte an Kameraden*. Berlin: Wilhelm Limpert-Verlag, 1940.

Zatlin, Jonathan R. "Repetition and Loss: Jewish Refugees and German Communists after the Holocaust, 1945–1951." *Leo Baeck Institute Year Book* 59, no. 1 (2014): 197–230.

Zatlin, Jonathan R., and Christoph Kreutzmüller, eds. *Dispossession: Plundering German Jewry, 1933–1953*. Ann Arbor: University of Michigan Press, 2020.

Zelizer, Barbie, ed. *Visual Culture and the Holocaust*. London: Athlone Press, 2001.

Zervigón, Andrés Mario. *Photography and Germany*. London: Reaktion Books, 2017.

Ziehe, Irene, and Ulrich Hägele. *Fotografien vom Alltag-Fotografieren als Alltag: Tagung der Kommission Fotografie der Deutschen Gesellschaft für Volkskunde*. Münster: Lit, 2004.

Index